the MAINE
TWO-FOOTERS

Lilliput No. 10 engine doesn't show up too well beside the big Maine Central 10-wheeler No. 284. In the Farmington depot about 1918, the little 10 is ready to highball for Rangeley with a passenger train. The big Class N No. 284 was on the Portland-Farmington run until the middle 1930's, when the bigger Class O engines put the N's on the scrap heap.

the MAINE TWO-FOOTERS

The story of the two-foot gauge railroads of Maine

by LINWOOD W. MOODY

HOWELL-NORTH
Berkeley, California
1959

THE MAINE TWO-FOOTERS

Published by the Howell-North Press
1050 Parker Street, Berkeley 10, California

Printed and bound in the United States of America by the publisher.

This book is dedicated to
NEWELL M. MARTIN
who died May 13, 1938

---

*A true aficionado of the Lilliputs with whom I
made many pleasant sorties into that elfin realm.*

ACKNOWLEDGMENTS

It's impossible to thank everyone for everything all the time. We'd be thanking steady, with scant time to enjoy the favors. To be properly grateful for the help that went into this book I'd have to point a thankful forefinger at everyone who worked on every 2-footer, ever. I'd have to point two forefingers and both thumbs at many of them. They'd think I was crazy. I probably would be. So, I'll simmer down the handshakes to a few who've gone to a lot of effort to keep me out of trouble in the months I worked on this saga of the Midgets.

There's Earl Keef up in Albion, Maine, who worked for the W.W. & F. from 1903 to quitting time, most of it as engineer. He drew the sketches from which the W.W. & F. maps were made. He supplied quantities of interesting data about the engines, the trains, the hard hauls, and the fast runs. Without his help the W.W. & F. story would have run light.

And Gerald Best, railroad fan *superbe* of Beverly Hills, California. He spent precious time while preparing for a railroad picture trip to New Zealand and dominions beyond the seas, to dig out photos and rosters, and to check many builders' numbers and dates with his voluminous records.

H. T. Crittenden, down in Virginia, supplied some early builders' dates and worked hard at reminding me of things we heard and saw and found on our twenty-five-years-ago browsing together.

Then, Roy Linscott, of near-Billerica, Massachusetts, was maybe as much to blame for this book getting written as I was. He pushed on me with his hefty bulk when my steam was down. He kept writing me leading questions, the answers to which amounted to a few more pages of the 2-foot story.

Howard Whitney, former B.&S.R. fireman (as well as the Grand Trunk and the Beebe River), remembered things for the B.&S.R. maps and the lore and legend of this 2-foot road and the Sebago Lake steamboats on which he also ran, as fireman.

My mother deserves lots of credit for listening to the typewriter pounding away three hundred evenings on the kitchen table when she was trying to snooze, and, last but not least, my thanks to our shaggy tiger cat, who wasted one life lying on the box of manuscript and photos and notes, so they wouldn't blow away!

LINWOOD W. MOODY

FOREWORD

If any foreword is in order it's only to say in beginning that I've written *The Maine Two-Footers* because I've wanted to do so for years. And, to simply mention that I've written about them as I knew them.

I've given you the glimpses and long, longing surveys of those fascinating little railroads as I saw them over the years. I've described their midget engines and cars as I measured and observed them. I've spun a few yarns which the railroad boys spun to me, as they came back to my mind, with no attempt to chronicle all of them. In the historical and statistical facets of this book I've either copied from Maine Railroad Commission reports and old newspaper clippings, or from company records (which sometimes have been known to be wrong) and carefully checked accounts from the men who worked on these railroads for years. If you're a hound for perfection you'll find this book lacks much of the all-time, over-all history of the 2-footers. If you've made previous opinions or have found different answers, you'll be skeptical about some of my statements and quotations. All I will say is to repeat—I'm telling you the 2-foot story as I saw it as a railroad-conscious kid, as a railroad man myself these 38 years, and as I've found it in supposedly reliable records and heard it from old-timers who loved these little railroads sincerely.

As a kid I poignantly wanted a backyard Lilliput to play with. In the many years I would holiday by riding on them, I still wanted one to play with. Now, years afterward, I'd still like to have one in my backyard. That's the spirit in which I've told you about 'em in this book, *The Maine Two-Footers*.

L. W. MOODY

Union, Maine
1959

TABLE OF CONTENTS

LIST OF ILLUSTRATIONS

ILLUSTRATIONS—*Continued*

ILLUSTRATIONS—*Continued*

ILLUSTRATIONS—*Continued*

ILLUSTRATIONS — *Continued*

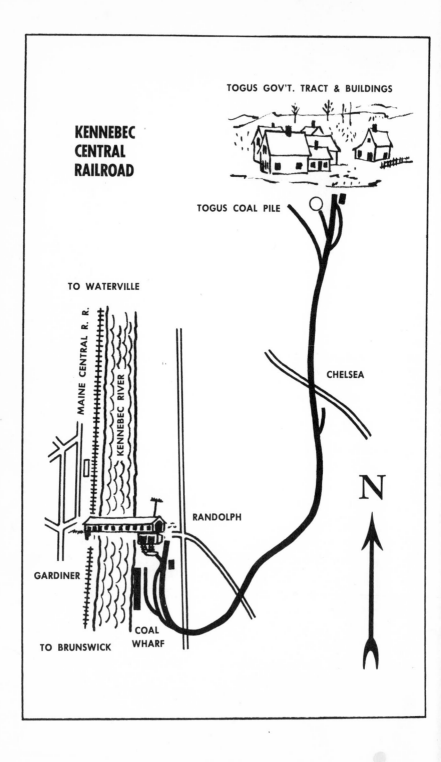

KENNEBEC
CENTRAL
RAILROAD

TOGUS GOV'T. TRACT & BUILDINGS

TOGUS COAL PILE

TO WATERVILLE

MAINE CENTRAL R. R.

KENNEBEC RIVER

CHELSEA

RANDOLPH

N

GARDINER

COAL
WHARF

TO BRUNSWICK

1

KENNEBEC CENTRAL RAILROAD

The first Lilliput I ever saw was the Kennebec Central Railroad.

I was pretty small then, probably ten or a dozen years old. The Kennebec Central wasn't much bigger — only five miles long, and two feet wide. But it seemed to measure up all right in my own half-size estimation. Just the thing for a kid to play railroad on!

We kids were railroad minded. Nowadays you don't see many young ones on hand to greet the trains. They're either making model airships, or tinkering with their hot rod autos. In our day there weren't any flying machines, and the family hot rod was out of bounds to children. The small frame depot in town, where the neighborhood railroad ended, was our hangout. Then, we hustled home and set up reasonable facsimiles of engines in the shed window, and of open platform coaches at the woodshed door.

Evenings and Sundays, when the engine was spotted for the night, and the cars stood invitingly on the siding by the depot, we used them. We became very adept at climbing boxcar ladders, pulling pins, setting retainers, and doing other routine chores of the railroad man. But those big standard gauge cars were too high and wide and cumbersome for half grown boys. We dreamed of smaller ones, nearer our size, whose couplers came to our belts instead of higher than our heads; whose sideladders we could catch without setting an unorthodox cracker box under the stirrup to boost us within reach. We dreamed of such trains, boys' size. But not until I saw the Kennebec Central did I know that such trains existed.

1

The Kennebec Central ran from Randolph, Maine, on the Kennebec River opposite the city of Gardiner, to the National Soldiers' Home at Togus, five miles. The Home was its only reason for being there. Sundays and on certain holidays The Home was open to visitors. It must have been hell for the old Civil War soldiers. Hundreds and hundreds of folks flocked in there. The spacious grounds, speckled with cannon from half a dozen wars, teemed with the crowd which came to hear the band concerts and see the Sunday ballgame.

The Kennebec Central, smallest of all the Lilliput railroads, hauled a good part of the mob. Its four tiny passenger cars billowed and belched with people. Then the midget engine scooted them back for another load.

There was a trolley line, too, running in from Augusta. The competition didn't seem, in those days anyhow, to be making noticeable inroads on the narrow gauge's traffic. Some folks said the electric cars were a serious blow to the Lilliput. However, it would have been a tussle to have packed any more people into the bantam cars, and there weren't any more cars.

More folks came by auto.

That was how we got there. Togus was just under thirty rough, dusty dirt-road miles from home, and after the 90 minute drive my parents sought the clean, cool shade of the comfortable settees where they could listen and look. I beat it for the cookhouse, behind which I was told the dinky little trains came in.

The Kennebec Central had two engines. Both were little boys' size Forney types, numbered 3 and 4. As far as I remember only one ran at a time. The five mile spurt between Randolph and The Home didn't leave much room for another train. And, one of those little Portland engines could easily haul all the road's passenger cars. It was the frequency of the trips, shuttling back and forth with a couple of hundred holidayers jammed aboard, which piled up the passenger-miles.

Soaking up that wonderland atmosphere left me with the indelible impression that those minute engines and cars were the perfect size. Perfect, anyway, for a railroad minded boy for whom the standard gauge equipment was simply too big. That first glimpse of mine was an eye opener. And I didn't miss a thing. I walked around the engine, stopping frequently to make a mental note of just where on me the couplers came, how far I'd have to step to make the one-stirrup climb to the cab. Everything measured up to a T. To have a train like that to play on, where steps were boys' straddles, where couplers came up to the same height on us that standard gauge coup-lings came on a full grown brakeman, and open platforms from which a kid could wave highballs or help dainty passengers to alight, would be a railroad dream come true.

The two-foot railroad was ideal. That's probably why it packed such a wallop in our esteem, and why to this day those pint-size engines and trains are such a nostalgic, haunting memory.

If we chanced to journey to Togus on a weekday we might see the mixed train. Like its passenger patronage, the Kennebec Central's freight business was likewise composed of tonnage going to The Home. It was mostly coal. The Home used quantities of soft coal. It came up the Kennebec River by barge, from Norfolk or Baltimore or somewhere. The narrow gauge hauled it from the riverside dock to the big stockpile out behind The Home's steam plant and cookery.

As I remember, there was a rather high trestle there. With a banshee scream from the full-size whistle, the little train would come rollicking across a field with three or four lowsides and the combina-tion car squealing in its wake. Each lowside carried about ten tons of coal. Usually a squatty boxcar would be cut in ahead of the com-bination, full of small freight for the commissary.

After making a dramatic station stop, with the clanking of link-and-pins and much woooshing of steam from the vacuum brake cylinder atop the cab, the engine would be unpinned and run around the train in order to nose those coal cars up the steep incline onto the trestle.

Those lowsides had swing-out sides. Something like drop bottoms on wide gauge hoppers. Up on the trestle the trainmen would ham-mer the latches loose and coal would pour down into the stockpile. A couple of men with coal scoops helped.

The Home used some ten tons of coal a day and the sizable stock-pile was kept well filled. Two or three times a year a barge would come up the Kennebec with a thousand tons or so aboard. That was when the train assumed the appearance of a coal country drag freight. The rest of the year trains consisted mostly of a boxcar for express and small freight — supplies for the big Government institution — and the combination. Holidays and Sundays the long 4-car strings of varnish ruled.

Along late in the afternoon was the best time for juvenile aspirants to cram on railroad sights and sounds and examinations. The last train to The Home would usually have an hour's wait before beginning its several turnarounds to haul the folks back to Randolph. That was when I did most of my measuring and reaching and poking which warped my personality to narrow gauge devotion.

What a thrill it was to walk around the little engine, peeking under her tiny belly at abbreviated Stephenson gear, at the dinky brake rigging, and to examine the springs and hangers, all less than half the standard size!

Even no bigger than I was then, the center of gravity of the little Portland engine was lower than my own. Her tiny 33-inch drivers scarcely came up to my belt. Her thimble-size cylinders scuffed the ties. A single, easy step lifted you up into her deckless cab. The fire-box of those Forney engines came back into the cab flush with the gangway door. Scant room was left to swing a sawed-off shovel or wrestle with a half-length hook. As you stood there on the deck the top of the little 36-inch boiler was hardly higher than a kid's hips.

But all the smells and hisses and sights of big, wide gauge engines were there in the little engine's cab. The sharp smell of hot oil and coal gas, the vague, familiar sounds which purred inside the boiler and the firebox, and the array of gauges and valves and levers were so identical to those on the big engines that a railroad minded twelve-year-old could identify 'em with keen delight.

The engineer's seat was a mere cushioned shelf built against the side of the cab. He had barely enough room to wedge his rump between the cab and the jacketed boiler butt. The waist-high throttle was at his elbow, and he had to be careful not to bang his crazy-bone when he reached for it, so close it was. The miniature Johnson bar, or reverse lever, was identical in design to those on Maine Central engines, except it was up alongside the boiler crowding the engineer's leg. All the gauges, the lubricator, and the niggerhead were likewise handy to his reach and glance. The whistle chain swayed and slapped an inch beyond his nose.

That whistle! Those Lilliput whistles were one thing which were full sized. I used to stand there by the passenger platform and watch across the long field to where the narrow track ducked over a rise in the ground. Shortly a cloud of steam would billow above the trees while clanking rods and squealing flanges would herald the approach of a train.

Then, halfway across the field, the engineer would haul back on the whistle chain. While her tiny side-rods flashed in a blur, she'd blow for The Home.

I've heard plenty of engines whistle in my time, from depot platforms and from lurching cabs, but never did an engine let out a louder, clearer, bellowing blast than the chime whistle atop the dome of Kennebec Central No. 3 when she clattered into that tiny yard, forty-odd years ago!

Wiscasset, Waterville & Farmington R'y Co.

Arrangement of Train Service

IN EFFECT JANUARY 7, 1924

GOING SOUTH				GOING NORTH		
	Mixed	Mixed			Mixed	Mixed
NOS. OF TRAINS	8	MON. 2* WED. FRI.		NOS. OF TRAINS	MON. I* WED. FRI.	II EX. SUN.
	EX. SUN.					
Stations	A. M.	P. M.		Stations	A. M.	P. M.
Albion lv.	6 00	1 45		Wiscasset lv.	9 50	3 22
So. Albion	† 6 10	† 1 55		Sheepscot	10 10	3 40
China	6 20	2 10		Alna Center	† 10 15	† 3 45
Palermo	6 40	2 35		Head Tide	10 30	3 55
Newell's	† 6 45	† 2 40		Whitefield	10 50	4 10
Week's Mills	7 00	3 00		Preble's	† 10 55	† 4 15
Windsor	7 18	3 15		No. Whitefield	11 10	4 25
Maxcy's	† 7 20	† 3 18		Cooper's Mills	11 30	4 38
Cooper's Mills	7 35	3 30		Maxcy's	† 11 35	† 4 43
No. Whitefield	7 50	3 45		Windsor	11 45	4 50
Preble's	† 7 55	† 3 50		Week's Mills	12 00	5 05
Whitefield	8 05	4 10		Newell's	† 12 05	† 5 10
Head Tide	8 22	4 30		Palermo	12 25	5 20
Alna Center	† 8 32	† 4 38		China	12 40	5 35
Sheepscot	8 40	4 45		So. Albion	† 12 45	† 5 40
Wiscasset ar.	9 00	5 15		Albion ar.	1 00	6 00
	A. M.	P. M.			P. M.	P. M.

REFERENCES. Unavoidable delays excepted and subject to change without notice.   † Stops when signaled or on notice to Conductor

TRAINS 1 AND 2 RUN MONDAY, WEDNESDAY AND FRIDAY ONLY

CONNECTIONS.

At WISCASSET with Maine Central Railroad.   At WISCASSET with Str. Winter Harbor and stage to and from BOOTHBAY HARBOR, A. M. and P. M. excepting train No. 2.   American Railway Express Company transacts business on this line.

Maine Central trains leave WISCASSET for Bath, Portland and Boston at 9.18, A. M. and 2.55 and 7.03 P. M.; for Rockland at 9.40 A. M., 3.18 and 7.52 P. M.

S. J. SEWALL, Gen'l Manager

2

WISCASSET, WATERVILLE & FARMINGTON RAILWAY

Maybe I was lucky. One Lilliput was enough to whet a boy's imagination, but I had a second one over in a nearby valley.

When we jounced to Togus in the family Model T we had the double fortune of crossing the narrow track of the Wiscasset narrow gauge, en route. This second Lilliput was the Wiscasset, Waterville & Farmington Railway, nearly ten times longer than the Kennebec Central, but nary an inch wider. We crossed it at Cooper's Mills, halfway from our home to Togus, and incidentally halfway the length of its own 44 mile line.

Often my father would have to lay back on the Model T's meager brakes to let a Wiscasset train teeter by. So, to a much less extent, the W.W.&F. also figured in my early studies of Lilliput railroads.

It was years, however, before I had a chance to explore and examine the Wiscasset engines and cars. And, I was inclined to consider the W.W.&F. as a railroad a little beyond a possible backyard playground. The Kennebec Central was a small starts-nowhere, goes-nowhere informal little rig, which was easy to imagine as being magically transplanted in the pasture behind our house. It didn't seem important enough to be permanently rooted. But the W.W.&F. was a more stand-back-you-kids kind of railroad—busy, bustling, high-iron.

I'd seen only its passing trains, hauled by what looked in that fleeting glimpse to be bigger engines, and doing business in a more

7

standard-gauge manner, and I stood in some awe of it. It ranked in my mind more with the big, impersonal Maine Central. The Kennebec Central was for years the Lilliput I wished might be relaid out there in the back pasture.

Later on, when I began to get around more, had bought a camera, and knew better (or was it less?) how to appreciate such things, I explored the Wiscasset, Waterville & Farmington Railway. It was just as long as its long-breath name. Instead of the short five miles of the Kennebec Central the W.W.&F. stretched out 44 miles. There were ten stations, not counting Wiscasset and the flag stations. A train came down each weekday morning from Albion, and went back in the afternoon. Another train, a mixed although it was chiefly a freight, left Wiscasset in the forenoon running up to Albion, and back. A third engine was the "transfer engine" in Wiscasset, handling cars back and forth from the main narrow gauge yard, across the long trestle to the transfer yard where freight was swapped from wide gauge to midget cars.

Of its five engines the Wiscasset road had one which was really big. The No. 6. No. 6 was a 25-ton Prairie type with a separate 8-wheel tender, like the Maine Central engines. She was generally hauling the mixed train which, in my younger days, I'd seen at Cooper's Mills. I was to learn later still that another Lilliput existed in the western part of the State, which had engines still bigger than the No. 6. My childhood associations, however, were centered around these two, the Kennebec Central with which I'd taken such liberties as climbing over the engine and furtively trying out its reach, its seat, and the down-to-earth engineer's-eye-view from the right-hand side; and the Wiscasset, Waterville & Farmington.

A splendid view could also be had of the Wiscasset yard and general layout from a Maine Central passenger train passing through Wiscasset. It passed close by the Lilliput's main yard, where the big yellow shop was a landmark. The wide gauge train crossed the midget on a diamond where a ball signal regulated which train had the right of way and which must cool its heels while the other rumbled across. That was the narrow gauge's freight only track, over the trestle to the transfer yard.

hether the venerable old Portland Company, builders of many early engines, kept a supply
stock, or if the W.&Q. ordered engines a year before construction began, is a question. But
.&Q. Nos. 2 and 3 are supposed to have been built in 1893, while the railroad was still in the
ueprint stage. The 18-ton Forney engines rolled up a lot of miles in the 39 years which followed.

1932, a year before abandonment, No. 4 gets an eleven-car mixed train rolling out of
iscasset, bound for Albion, 44 miles away. Engineer Earl Keefe is carefully working her
rottle to keep the little engine's feet from slipping. No. 4 was unique in having her steam dome
side the cab, the whistle and pop protruding through the cab roof. Like the other Forney
gines, she was deckless. This engine originally had a steel cab which, after a few tip-overs and
jammed sliding doors, was replaced with this wooden cab.

Looking north out of Wiscasset yard. The shop is to your right, a car and coal shed in the distant left. The enginehouse was to your extreme left, behind the rough board building—a temporary sawmill. To the far right, behind the shop, you can see the main line grade as it skirts the bay, heading into the north country.

No. 7 engine, a 2-4-4T, was built in the same order with No. 6, having consecutive serial numbers. She was small cylindered, and weighed 28 tons. Many, many times she was clocked running a mile in a minute. Lilliput engines, while wide in overhang, had a low center of gravity and on good track could give you a fast ride—and a scare!

Besides the big yellow repair shop which sat smack in the middle of the yard, there was also a 2-stall enginehouse with track running clear through it, and a long two or three track car shed. The several yard tracks were always dotted with boxcars, snowplows, and spare passenger equipment. Almost anytime you'd see a Lilliput engine, usually either No. 2 or No. 3, scurrying back and forth to the transfer yard, where transferring freight was a busy chore.

The numbers 2 and 3 were typical Portland Company Forney engines, identical to numbers 3 and 4 of the Kennebec Central . . . Except they weren't kept looking so good. No. 4 was likewise a Forney, built by the H. K. Porter Works, so her front number plate declared. But she was rather an ungainly engine lacking the pleasing proportions and lines the other engines had. No. 4 was sometimes pinch-hitting for No. 6 on the forenoon mixed and sometimes she hauled the passenger job.

No. 7 was the regular passenger engine. She was a Baldwin, and would have been a Forney type if she hadn't had a set of pony wheels under her front end. She was cute, a true Lilliput.

No. 7 was fast, too. Her little 33-inch drivers could whisk her over the road at better than a mile a minute. Often, when hauling the Albion passenger train, she would make the five and a half miles from China to Albion in six minutes. If you think that's nothing I wish you might have been wedged up ahead of the fireman some night and watched the narrow track reel under you at a mile a minute clip!

I never rode on the big No. 6. I always wanted to. But she ran out on tubes around 1930, and I hadn't got acquainted over there that early. She was really a big engine. Her gangway was thirty inches above the rail, and her open-deck cab seemed as roomy as many standard gauge engine cabs. You had to step up from the deck to the engineer's or fireman's box, and the cab window sills were higher than your head if you stood on the ground beside her. She had one of those 45-degree throttles; the lever skewed across the boiler butt at a sharp angle, and although the top of the boiler was only breast-high to the engineer, the throttle was tilted so it was shoulder-high as he gripped it. But the fireman had plenty of room to swing a scoop and still didn't have to heave coal a rails-length to put it through the fire-door.

The Wiscasset road had seen its best days before I made its acquaintance. The farmers owned it by my time, and because business was declining fast, not much was being done in the way of maintenance. The few times I rode the train I got the rather unhappy feeling that everything was pretty slipshod. The track was still safe and reasonably smooth, but it was grassgrown and bushes swept the sides of the engine and cars. The vacuum braking system had been allowed to go to pieces, and excepting on the engines it wasn't even coupled up. The conductor and brakeman tied down hand brakes for station stops, and when dropping down the stiffer grades.

The Portland plows—wedge snowplows built by the old Portland Company—were the first Lilliput snowplows I'd seen. This was partly because my sorties to the Kennebec Central were in the summertime only, and partly because the little Togus road didn't boast a real snowplow. Over there the snow equipment consisted of a home-made triangular affair bolted onto a work car. The Wiscasset's Portland plows were identical—and almost as big—as the ones used by the Maine Central. Two of these plows, one kept in Wiscasset and the other on the Albion end, with two 8-wheel flanger cars, took care of the snow problem. All Portland plows had a sort of trap-door leading down into their interior, similar to the hatch opening into a vessel's forecastle. This was handy when the plow was off the track and you had to crawl down in its bowels with rerailing-frogs, jacks, blocking and such. It also was used to carry bags of sand, cast-iron blocks or concrete into the plow to weight it down. Wedge plows had a habit of occasionally climbing a snowdrift instead of breaking it open. The more weight on the car the less often it climbed.

At the last end of the Lilliput's running, conditions were pretty bad. Only one train was left, the Albion job, and even the transfer engine didn't work full time. Many trips the major revenue in the whole train was the U.S. Mail post office car.

The last change of ownership came in late 1930. A lumber dealer bought it, for the proverbial song. He didn't know anything about railroads. The shortline where I was working was getting ready to fold up, so I hit the W.W.&F.'s new owner for a job. He hired me, as superintendent.

For the two weeks I was working my notice it was quite a thrill to think I was about to become superintendent of a real Lilliput— kind of a matured version of the childhood dreams of transplanting the Kennebec Central onto our backyard, where we kids could play train with real, kid-size engines and cars!

But it turned out more like a nightmare. I didn't stay superintendent but one day. It turned out to be a funny kind of official job. In addition to being superintendent I was also to be—as I learned when I reported for work—station agent at Albion during the day, and engine watchman during the night. All for the princely, Lilliput stipend of $18.00 a week.

That was the last I saw of the Wiscasset, Waterville & Farmington, except to watch it being dismantled a few years later.

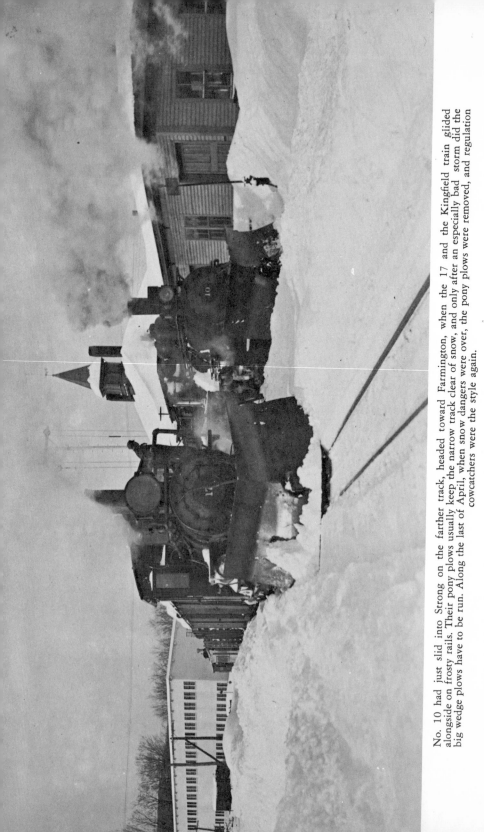

No. 10 had just slid into Strong on the farther track, headed toward Farmington, when the 17 and the Kingfield train glided alongside on frosty rails. Their pony plows usually keep the narrow track clear of snow, and only after an especially bad storm did the big wedge plows have to be run. Along the last of April, when snow dangers were over, the pony plows were removed, and regulation cowcatchers were the style again.

3

SANDY RIVER & RANGELEY LAKES RAILROAD

An Interstate Commerce Commission locomotive inspector, who visited our hometown shortline every month or so, had told me about a bigger and better 2-foot gauge over in the western part of Maine, the Sandy River & Rangeley Lakes. Later, a very appealing feature story about it appeared in *Railroad Magazine.* It was time for me to see what kind of a Lilliput it was which far surpassed my old Kennebec Central pal, and the acquaintance of later years, the W.W.&F.

That first sight of the Sandy River was both a disappointment, and a terrific wallop on the positive side. It was a disappointment because what I saw didn't fit into any childhood notion of using a Lilliput for a playground. It was a positive wallop because the Sandy River was every inch a big railroad except for yardstick and caliper measurements. As far as bustle and noise and efficiency went you might as well have been dropped in the middle of a Santa Fe division point or Mechanicville yard. This was the Lilliputs at their best and biggest. It was a childhood dream grown up.

The Sandy River had scads of engines and ran all kinds of trains. Those engines dwarfed the baby Kennebec Central bantams, and overshadowed the big W.W.&F. No. 6. Its track was laid with big 56 and 60-pound rail, in perfect line and surface. Trains ran at wide gauge speed. Telegraph, train orders, and extra trains there were galore.

I poked my Model T down into the Strong, Maine yard that summer morning in 1932 with only a vague idea of what kind of a railroad I was about to see.

The Strong yard was a triangular affair. The main line from Rangeley through Phillips to Farmington swung through it on a big curve. The old F.&M. line from Carrabsset and Kingfield entered it on another curve. There was a fine chance there to have built an opposite leg to connect it with the other direction, making a wye. For reasons known to Sandy River management this leg was never made.

The stately depot, complete with a towering mast and two sets of ball signals, sat in the crotch of these diverging tracks. The junction was well supplied with yard tracks and side tracks and more tracks. There was a waterplug, and a steel turntable. A lengthy coalshed skirted one side. It was like a big junction point yard, in miniature. I sat in my car and gaped.

Gaping, I heard the distant wail of a chime whistle. It blew again. The faint ripple of exhausts purred on the summer breeze. Whatever was coming was coming fast. I slid out of my car.

The train was coming from the north, down off the F.&M. The station agent, later introduced as Pansy, was pushing mail and express trucks along the cement platform. It seemed like a lot of mail and express for one small train.

But there was a second train coming, too. She blew away to the west. Her exhausts purred louder and faster, it seemed. Pansy began to haul away on the frayed rope which lowered the ball signals. Then, with a miniature roar, the Rangeley train blew in.

In 1932 it had become a mixed train. But it was some train, just the same. An oversize Lilliput engine steamed and clanged on the head end. It was numbered 10. A string of bright red boxcars, in finer condition than any I'd seen before, and a combination car and a coach rolled in behind her. Brakeshoes smoked. There was the familiar wide gauge whistle of releasing air. Conductor and brakemen swung down from the one-step platforms. The big engine buckled to a stop beside the waterplug.

The surprise had burst so suddenly that I'd completely missed the back-handed arrival of the other train, the one from the F.&M.

She had sneaked down the big curve from the north while the Rangeley job was fixing my attention. The F.&M. trains had to back into the station at Strong. When they nosed down the big curve into the yard, they were heading toward Phillips. When the tail end had cleared the switch they had to back up down the main line— or a track paralleling the main—to the depot. When the two trains were abreast one was heading toward Farmington, and the other toward Rangeley, or Phillips.

Hustle and bustle followed. Passengers got on, and passengers got off. Other passengers got in the way. Trainmen joined in the melee as mailbags flew and pieces of express skidded from one train to the other. The register book was signed. Then, while I still gaped, undecided whether to laugh or cry, the Number 10's bell began to clang again. Steam shot from her cylinder cocks. With quick, staccato exhausts the main line train was off down the yard, dust sucking in little clouds in her wake.

The F.&M. engine, a neat Prairie type with the number 16 and a headlight the size of her 33-inch driving wheels, cut off, ran down by her train onto the table.

That was my introduction to a too-short friendship with the biggest and finest of the Lilliputs—the Sandy River. It developed into such a friendship that comes only once in a lifetime. One which, when it was ended by the Lilliput's death, has stayed with me poignantly through the years.

An impressive side of the Sandy River's personality was the fondness and devotion for it which was shared by the communities through which its narrow track curved and climbed. Community devotion was conspicuous by its absence with the other midget railroads. But the folks along the hundred-odd miles of the Sandy River's line loved it.

One manifestation of their love was the boodles of photographs which everyone and his sister had taken. From its first engine, the arrival of new ones, and the misfortunes of its childhood—a wreck here and a spill there—to replacing trestles with fills, and the advent of bigger rail, the Sandy River's span of years were chronicled on plates and film. The neighborhood kids didn't get such attention from the old rapid-rectilinear lenses as did the Lilliput trains.

To find photographs of the brother and sister two-footers you have to dig with vigor and persistence. But the good people in Franklin County, Maine, ran their shutters hot photographing the Sandy River.

In that Lilliput's sad, final days railroad fans from far and near came to see the vaunted 2-footer they'd read so much about, and to scour the countryside for oldtime pictures. Plenty were found. In some instances the more fortunate of the fraternity paid as high as a dollar apiece (1935 dollars, too!) for originals. Franklin County folks enjoyed a brief bonanza of picture dollars—their reward for loving the little railroad in its yesterdays.

That first day I visited the Sandy River, after seeing the two trains connect at Strong, I drove on to Phillips.

Phillips was where the main offices, the engine and car shops, and the spare equipment was. What a sight that was. The yard was sizable, with plenty of tracks for even the peak year's traffic. There was a neat brick roundhouse, ten stalls. Hitched to it was the brick locomotive shop, with drop-pit, hoisting gear, lathes, and all. Likewise connected was the brick car shop, where they built freight cars from scratch. Even in the dark days of decline two, three and four men were kept busy in the shops. Sometimes, to be sure, they would pinch-hit as Bridge & Building force, fence crew, and even cover for a fireman or brakeman who happened to be off. Most of the Sandy River boys had at sometime been a fireman or engineer, a brakeman or a conductor.

I enjoyed that first look at Phillips. I enjoyed, too, seeing the spic-and-span No. 24 come breezing in with a short freight from Rangeley. It happened quickly; she sneaked into the yard without my hearing her blow. Someone threw a switch onto the run-around track in front of the depot and she teetered in, dropped her short train—which I remember was tailed by the equally spic-and-span caboose No. 556—and scampered onto the table. Like the No. 16 on the F.&M. train, the 24 engine sported an oversize headlight half as big as her 44-inch diameter front end.

I met the superintendent that day, Orris Vose. He'd once been a fireman and a brakeman on the F.&M., where his father had been

wenty-six people—by paying an extra dollar—could ride in the *Rangeley*. Steam heat, hot water,
d a spacious toilet were among the comforts offered by this Lilliput palace car. This car, renamed
e *Ellis Atwood,* still runs on the Edaville Railroad today, when some guest of ultra importance
justifies the signal honor.

Just up from Farmington, with two extra cars for some Flagstaff-bound C.C.C. boys, the train about to turn its engine, back out of the Strong yard, and head to your left onto the F.&M. It the daily mixed run to Carrabasset, and the photo was made just three days before the Lilliput ra for the last time, in 1935.

The last few summers of operation the S.R.&R.L. covered passenger jobs with the rail buses, whil a freight train ran from Phillips to Farmington and back, and also over the F.&M. to Kingfield an Carrabasset. This train is it. Engine 24, shining like a new bottle, a boxcar for wayfreight, and baby caboose. Before she reaches Farmington, however, she'll have a 10-car train tied to her tai

Here Dana Aldrich has his beautiful No 10. on the Phillips table, turning for the run back to Farmington. The 10's 38 tons made her steady and her 36-inch drivers made her fast. Dana covered many a mile on his pet engine in 60 and 70 seconds, to the consternation of the train crew and "oscillating" passengers. But while the coaches lurched around, the big 10 was riding like a Pullman car!

Steam up and ready to go, the 16, *Old Star* of other days, waits in front of the Phillips roundhouse. This was in 1932, the year her tubes ran out and she went into dead storage. She little resembles the small-girthed mogul in another photo, carrying the Laurel River and Hot Springs name on her tank. The Maine Central did a beautiful job of rebuilding these engines to big boilered Prairie types.

Supt. Orris Vose and his Model T track-auto. The Sandy River built a number of these motor cars in its Phillips Shops, and handy rigs they were. This one today reposes in the railroad Museum at Edaville, Massachusetts. Another is still in use on the Edaville, along with the old Sandy River No. 4 railbus. Supt. Vose found the Model T's excellent in snow, too.

S.R.&R.L. 15, 2-6-2 in front of the Phillips depot, about 1916. Second from left is Conductor Clarence Fairbanks, and standing by the cab is Engineer Dana Aldrich, ready for a run into the woods after a pulpwood train. The 15 was originally P.&R. No. 3, the *George M. Goodwin,* a Baldwin mogul. With the other moguls she was rebuilt as a 2-6-2 after the Maine Central took over control of the Lilliput.

Engine No 22, a long-gaited Forney which once sported the Eustis Railroad name on her tank and the number 9 on her cab. When these engines were new they "oscillated" so vigorously that crews insisted on running them tail-end first, making them in effect a 4-4-0. Later, however, the hard riding qualities were taken for granted, and these engines piled up thousands of trouble-free miles.

Biggest of all Lilliput engines was the mighty 23, 32 tons of power and puff turned out by Baldwin in 1913. Her cab and tank were 7 feet, 8 inches wide, yet she was as free of oscillations as any standard gauge engine. Her 48-inch boiler and 13x16-inch cylinders gave her the wallop and stamina needed for hauling heavy trains over the sharp grades and tortuous curves between Phillips and Farmington.

Stored opposite Phillips station in 1934 are spare cabooses and passenger cars. The end-cupola cabooses were built for the S.R.&R.L., number 556 to 558. The center-cupolas were former Sandy River cabooses, carrying S.R.&R.L. numbers 551 to 554. The odd one, 555, was the old P.&R. caboose, bigger than the others, built up from trucks and running-gear of a P.&R. combination which burned at Green's Farm, on the Eustis road, years ago.

S.R.&R.L. No. 8 and caboose 557 (now at Edaville) posed on the main line at Madrid Station, about 1910. She hadn't yet been equipped with air, the old vacuum dingus still atop her cab. Next to the nose of the engine stands Dana Aldrich, engineer, who was the last man to run an engine on the S.R.&R.L. Next to him is Conductor Elmer Voter, who retired in 1934 with some 50 years on the Sandy River.

superintendent. Orris was a quiet kind of man, said little but was generally good natured and cooperative. Because of a nod from him I enjoyed many rides on the little engines and trains, and came to feel almost like a Sandy River man myself. I soaked up quantities of Lilliput atmosphere, and learned a lot about railroading that the wide gauge roads hadn't taught me.

At first it was rather a scary experience, riding the head end of a Sandy River train. For a wide gauge man to perch up ahead of the fireman on an engine running 45 miles an hour, the razor-edge track streaming under the cowcatcher like a doctored movie stunt, was something new. Your hair rose. You knew she couldn't make it, she'd roll over halfway around that sharp curve. . . . Such a sizable engine simply couldn't keep her equilibrium on that narrowest of narrow track—which looked still slimmer because of the big, heavy rail—Plunging down tangents, reeling 'round sharp, reverse curves working steam at wide gauge speed, was suicide, you screamed to yourself.

But, she did make it, every time. Sure, she rocked and reeled, and you slammed your head against the side of the slatting cab. Sweat ran down your pantleg like water out the overflow pipe. Before you knew it, however, the engineer was spilling air and brakes were grinding the pint-size train to a stop at one of the neat stations.

So, gradually I adjusted to the skimpiness of gauge and wasn't scared any more. Not much, anyway.

Those early visits to the Sandy River were exciting. Usually the big, beautiful 10 was hauling the Rangeley job. She was one of the modified Forney types with a solid frame clear back to her tail. Boiler, cab, short tank and all was on that single frame. A set of pony trucks kept her from dodging and nosing, as the true Forney engine tended to do. Her two sets of drivers were set inside the frames, with counterbalances, cranks and rods on the outside. Her square little firebox was behind the drivers, overhanging the rails a foot on either side. Behind that came the trailing or tank trucks, carrying about two-fifths the total weight of the engine. The 8, 9 and 10 were built this way. All the other solid-frame or *tank* engines, were Forneys, with no pony wheels.

I don't know anything about Forney engines on standard gauge or three-foot roads, but I've had the daylights shaken out of me on about every Forney the Lilliputs owned in their latter years. They all rode hard. Those naked head drivers, with no guiding truck to keep them straight, were perpetually nudging from one rail to the other, seemingly hunting for a place to climb off. The Lilliput engineers didn't seem to mind. They were used to it. But I minded, fresh off conventional types of wide gauge engines. As much as I loved an engine, I usually rode the rear when a Forney was hauling the train.

As a matter of explanation, I keep using the word *wide* gauge when referring to standard. That's the terminology the Lilliput boys always used, so I picked it up as part of the bantam railroading I was absorbing. Naturally there were no truly wider-than-standard gauge roads in Maine in the last forty years.

As I started to say, the big No. 10 was usually on the Rangeley mixed train. When she was tied up either the smaller No. 9 or one of the Eustis engines—mostly the 21—hauled her job. The 20, 21 and 22, identical long-legged Forney types, once belonged to the Eustis Railroad, and were referred to until the junkmen destroyed them as "the Eustis engines".

The 18 or 24 would be up on the Rangeley road hauling an extra or a pulpwood train, and some days working the branches. The Forney 17 was usually the spare engine for the F.&M., although no set rule governed what engine went where. Another engine would handle the morning train from Phillips to Farmington, and lay over back in Phillips the rest of the day, as a spare.

The rest of the midgets were stored dead in the Phillips round-house. In fact, the trim 19 and 22 never ran again, in my time. Their tubes had run out and they weren't needed after business began to slump. They just snoozed there in their stalls year after year.

Yes, the Sandy River was a fairyland.

How I liked to browse in the silent, ghostly roundhouse, along the sidings where many well-kept passenger cars waited for passengers who never came, and through the eight saucy cabooses which slumbered on a rusty track.

Those cabooses were jewels in the rough. Except for their full headroom the tiny cars were true boys' size. They were only six feet wide. Their end platforms were a couple of feet above the rails. They were such easy cars to swing onto with the single, easy step and their ample, handy grab-irons. Inside there were the usual cushioned seats, with stowage space underneath for replacers, tackles, extra air hoses, and the like. The typical caboose stove. The ice-box. The hanging lockers at one end, where not only the trainmen's raincoats could hang, but hooksful of lanterns and other trappings of the trade were kept.

I liked the abbreviated cupola. Different from the *wide* gauge buggies these Lilliputs had lookout seats on only one side, because of the narrowness of the little car. That one seat was spacious, but it left just room for a man to pass by it through the car. Unlike the wide gauge trains, with boxcars of heights exceeding the top of the caboose, the Lilliput freight cars were of fairly uniform height, and thus the cupola was always riding high enough so you could watch over the cartops and see the bantam engine working up ahead.

Then, there was the Old Stone Fort to explore. That place was hard on your pants. The brambles grew in profusion. The Old Stone Fort was the long abandoned granite engine house of the onetime Phillips & Rangeley Railroad, which tied up in Phillips. It was across the river from town, to one side of the ruins of the old P.&R. yard. The main line to Rangeley crossed the white water Sandy River through one of the famous covered wooden bridges. The Fort was just beyond the west end of the bridge. Inside the roofless granite walls were the remains of four Lilliput engines which had finished their run. The ancient No. 7, a Portland Company Forney; the battered No. 20, which had jumped the track by Madrid Tank years before, and banged her nose into a ledge; the deboilered carcass of the big No. 15, which had busted a driver axle below South Strong one winter morning, and was retired forthwith; and the chassis of the old No. 8, which had been the last of the Sandy River's inside-frame engines. I used to wade through the thorns and puckerbrush from one deserted stall to another, trying to talk to those dead old engines of days gone by.

As those engines had been retired they had been poked off into the Old Fort and forgotten. But in my book they were still a part of the Lilliput railroad, and deserved respectable attention.

The old coaches and combinations and express-RPO cars came in for inspection, too. The time was far off, then, when these venerable wagons had been snaking over Sluice Hill and down the Eustis road on the famous *Rangeley Express*. Besides, the thought persisted "What a place this would have been, twenty-odd years ago, for us kids to play!"

Some of the passenger cars vied with 3-foot gaugers for size, too. Many of them were a full 7-foot-and-a-half wide. Their open end platforms were two feet above the rails, and the step up into the cars themselves made the floors 30-inches high. Most of them were just short of 40 feet long, less the platform at each end. They all had single seats, identical to wide gauge seats except for being singles instead of doubles, with a spacious aisle between. Most of them had the conventional clerestory roofs, although two or three had roofs more like the old Kennebec Central passenger cars—kind of an arched affair. They were all built back in the days when mahogany and filigree were the vogue, and elaborate kerosene lamps hung in ornate brass chandeliers from the clerestory roof.

Of course, the parlor-car was the Hope Diamond of the lot. I didn't see her until just before the end. She was the prized possession of the Sandy River, and had been kept housed at Kingfield for years. They hauled her to Phillips for final disposal a few days before the Sandy River was abandoned.

That parlor-car was a gem. She had been built, many years before, for the hotsy-totsy summer trade. The Rangeley Lakes region was, and still is more or less, a swanky summer resort. Before the Maine Central went north into that country the Sandy River hauled most of the ladies and gentlemen from New York and Pennsylvania. The parlor-car was primarily for them. She was finished in mahogany, beset with plate-glass mirrors and green plush swinging chairs. Like most of the passenger cars she had hot water heaters for heat. A smoking compartment graced one end and a huge, hoopskirt toilet room offered all the comforts of home at the other. No wide gauge road had anything finer, in the day the *Rangeley No. 9* came out of Jackson & Sharp's Wilmington, Delaware shops. The *Rangeley* was not only a super eyeful, but she was the only parlor-car any of the Lilliputs ever had.

Another gala event in my acquaintance with the Sandy River was the day that Traffic Manager Clarence Roy let me go up overhead in the Phillips station and help myself to whatever I wanted up there. After a few minutes poking around under the dust of years, I wanted plenty.

There were stacks of old timetables, both public and employees'. Excursion posters telling about the special trains to the Farmington Fair, and picnic trains to Rangeley. There were nickel and brass buttons for trainmen's uniforms. Some said *"Conductor"* on them, others had the initials *"S.R.&R.L.", "P.&R."* and some were dated by fancy lettered *"Sandy River R.R."* Too, there were cap badges for conductors and brakemen from the different companies which later became the Sandy River & Rangeley Lakes Railroad. Ticket punches, ticket daters from long forgotten stations, and cords of unused tickets tied in stacks, in numerical order. I was fascinated by old card tickets, multicolored and printed in gingerbread type, reading between such stations as Redington and Camp Eight, Gull Pond and Quill Hill, and Bigelow and Maplewood. Then, there were long, coupon tickets on which you could have ridden from Rangeley to Key West. Those tickets were as long as a side rod. These mementos of the Lilliput's grandiose yesterdays told many a story of the big little railroad, stories which the boys themselves couldn't have told. I spent the rest of the day lugging boxes downstairs, into my car.

Those Sandy River boys, many of 'em 50 year men, weren't loquacious story tellers. None of them would talk your arm off with tales of long ago. No finer bunch of fellows ever lived than the Sandy River enginemen, trainmen, shopmen, and "officers". But they just weren't talkers. They were railroaders!

Each one of them loved the Sandy River. When he got acquainted with you he would reminisce. It was then that I really began to know the Sandy River and its colorful history. I knew, as well as old Dana Aldrich knew, what kind of a steaming engine the old *Bo-peep* was. I knew just how hard the Sandy River's first No. 3 rode—my innards ached hearing the old timers cuss her. I knew, too, such mundane matters as the 19's copper tubes and flue-sheets made her a much more economical engine on coal than her sisters. For some reason, which I never did learn, the 19 was slippery on her feet. You had to handle her throttle about right or she'd throw a tantrum and spin her drivers 'til your sand was gone. Master Mechanic Lee Stinchfield mentioned a dramatic bit of information one day; he told me that only one-eighth of an inch of play could be set between the tank friction blocks of the Forney and 2-4-4 engines. That was really a jolt when I remembered that wide gaugers carry two or three inches of slack!

A number of times, when he was going out somewhere in his Model T trackauto, Superintendent Vose asked me to climb aboard. I always did. In today's jargon Orris might have qualified as a hot-rodder. He liked to haul the Ford's hand throttle down, and sit back to enjoy the ride. I didn't enjoy it so much, sometimes. Those Model T converted trackautos rode about the same as their nonconverted mates. They leaped and dived and slapped around in the manner traditional to Model T Fords. When Vose's private inspection auto was larruping down the line at 40 or 45 miles an hour, the narrow track pouring under her front end like a roller-coaster, you were too sharply aware that the track was only 24-inches wide.

But Orris had ridden a good many miles in those cars, and never had broken his neck yet. I consoled myself with that thought, and enjoyed the rest of the ride.

I saw that Model T one time hauling a standard passenger car into Phillips. One of the big coaches had broken an axle up near Kingfield. They took her out of the train, and wired Phillips. The spare engine was out on one of the branches, and Master Mechanic Stinchfield wanted the crippled coach as soon as he could get it. They went up on the F.&M. after it, with Orris' Model T. No one recommended laying up the engines and using the trackautos for motive power, but everyone was calmly surprised how easily the Ford hauled the heavy passenger car the 20-odd miles into Phillips.

Those years of riding the Sandy River and browsing around its spacious plant were keenly pleasant. But they were experiences shadowed with sadness. Already the proverbial handwriting was standing out on the legendary wall in three dimensions. The two-footer even now was only a shadow of its onetime dash and grandeur. Instead of seventeen crews keeping the iron hot, it had dwindled to four, each train hauling a fraction of its potential tonnage. The Depression was on. So were the trucks. I never subscribed bombastically to the "Damn-the-trucks!" attitude, because trucks have their place in our economy, and today many railroads operate their own trucklines the while they damn other trucks as competitors. And, maybe there's no reason why business men should haul their products as far as the first railroad siding, and pay freight charges to hire the goods carried the rest of the way. A good part of truck freight is some product, like pulpwood and lumber, which the owner trucks himself. That was where much of the Sandy River's tonnage had gone. The pulpwood dealers and lumber men, who had to haul their logs out of the woods, simply kept the loads on those trucks all the way. Be that as it may, the narrow gauge railroad was pegging out.

Then, it was gone.

During that last sickness of the moribund little two-footer I sat up with her nights, so to speak. I was there when she died. I stood back and watched while they buried her.

It would break your heart to have seen them ripping the rails off the stout cedar ties; to watch them haul a baby Baldwin out of her warm stall, and attack her savagely with an acetylene torch; to see hundreds of trim, husky boxcars being trundled down the line to Howland's Pit, where they were tipped over and burned for the metal.

At first, while the "wrecking trains" still had many miles to run hauling the scrap down to Farmington for reloading onto the Maine Central cars, I used to ride in the cab of the No. 18 engine with Dana Aldrich. On those long runs it was easy to imagine that this was just another revenue freight train, that nothing terrible had happened, that we were merely scurrying over the road as other thousands of trains had done. The same jolts and squeals and oily-steamy smells came from the little Prairie type. The shrill wail of her chime whistle, hollering for crossings mile after mile, was as sweet to hear as when it cleared the road for the fast-running Rangeley Express. The lurch and slue as the little engine swung back and forth through the tortuous curves, the same hollow drone of exhausts as heard from the firebox end, and the sharp bark from the stack when Dana dropped the lever down on some three-percent, were no different than a few weeks before, when the Sandy River was a going concern. Now, it was gone.

But its passing, so I felt, was as much a part of the Lilliput as were its better, happier, promising years. That's why I stuck with her 'till the end.

When the grisly job was done, and only the empty, lonesome grade was left of the biggest and grandest Lilliput of all, many of us railroad fans felt that the most colorful chapter in the florid history of railroading had closed forever. Big railroading with little trains on the narrowest of small-boy track had ended. Plenty of big boys felt, as I did, that something essential and expedient had gone out of our lives. Symbolically, we were losing the real McCoy and must revert again to woodshed windows and tinplate models, to abandon a delightful reality and retreat to the half-world of vicarious railroading again.

Ever since, I've lamented that not one of those Lilliput engines survived. Unlike the engines of the Bridgton road, and the Monson, which were preserved to run again on the last 2-footer—the Edaville —not one of the Sandy River's splendid Baldwins escaped the torch. One, to be sure, the shapely 24, was bought by a railroad fan for $250.00. But the following year he sold her, too, for scrap.

Most of the passenger train cars were sold—the bodies—for camps, for workshops, for hencoops, to farmers along the road. Even the old, old coach which had been built in 1877 for the Billerica & Bedford Railroad, and named the *Sylvan,* with her mate the combination *Fawn,* were relegated to backyards, to sit truckless on earthy foundations, until time and weather should reduce them too to earth.

Ten years later two of the newest coaches, the 21 and 22, were found to be still solid enough to move, and went down to Massachusetts to join the Edaville ghosts. A couple of cabooses, too, had survived the years well enough to be taken down there. Boxcar trucks at least gave them motion again.

Turning the 18 on the Strong table one winter day in 1934. Strong depot and the mixed train are behind her tank, half obscured by drifting steam from the inspirator overflow pipe. Trains coming down the F.&M. for Farmington had to turn their engines at Strong, because the F.&M. entered the yard heading towards Phillips. The white smokestack over the 18's bell is the toothpick mill.

Pulling up the last F.&M. rail, in Strong Yard, on August 13, 1936. It was up around this curve that F.&M. engines, and borrowed Sandy River power, had blasted with trumpeting exhausts, as they headed out of Strong for Kingfield, Bigelow, and the oldtime logging branches. Today not a sign of the railroad can you find here in Strong yard. New building has covered the grades.

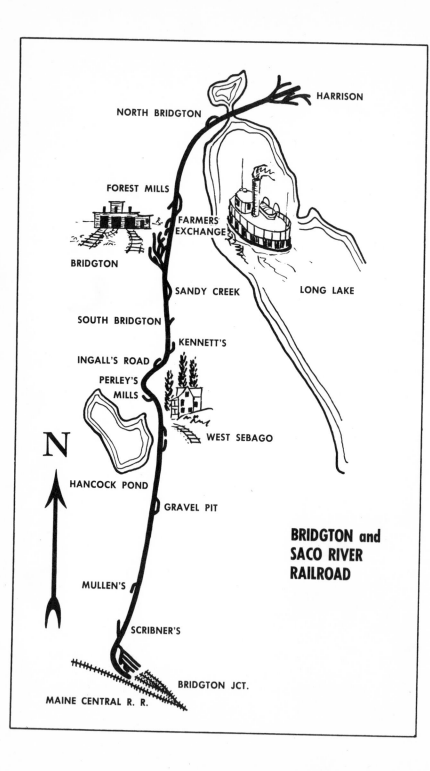

HARRISON

NORTH BRIDGTON

FOREST MILLS

FARMERS EXCHANGE

BRIDGTON

SANDY CREEK

LONG LAKE

SOUTH BRIDGTON

KENNETT'S

INGALL'S ROAD

PERLEY'S MILLS

WEST SEBAGO

N

HANCOCK POND

GRAVEL PIT

BRIDGTON and
SACO RIVER
RAILROAD

MULLEN'S

SCRIBNER'S

BRIDGTON JCT.

MAINE CENTRAL R. R.

4

BRIDGTON & HARRISON RAILWAY

My association, both physical and spiritual, with the Kennebec Central had come early in life. Likewise, the first impressions of the Wiscasset narrow gauge were youthful ones. Those experiences and observations had given me a pretty solid Lilliput background. While the first sight of the Sandy River had been something of a jolt, I'd absorbed it well and adjusted to the big, busy midget quickly. These facts might explain why, when I belatedly encountered my fourth Lilliput, the Bridgton & Harrison Railway, it was sort of an anti-climax.

It was a July day in 1933 that I first visited Bridgton, Maine. The B.&H. was a fine little railroad. It was a true Lilliput. It had piled up half a century of he-man railroading. But it was a let-down.

When I drove up to the sizable wooden depot on the edge of the village, I felt the let-down coming. There was Bridgton yard, all in sight from the station. It wasn't the imposing array of tracks that the Sandy River sported. Besides the main line, which stopped just beyond, at a bumper-post, there was the runaround, a long siding by the freight house, and a few storage tracks. Another track ran across the turntable into the enginehouse. Another went into the small car shop. The tracks weren't in too good shape. Rails were inclined to wobble a bit, and there was a general seedy appearance everywhere. The B.&H. had been in evil days for some time, and money for standard maintenance wasn't forthcoming.

The machine shop, across the yard from the station, was a small wooden building and no tracks entered it. Any parts which needed repairs had to be removed and taken into the shop.

As compared to the Sandy River's 500 freight cars the B.&H. had only sixty-odd. That explained why the lengthy Bridgton yard looked rather empty that day. Off on a way-out-back side track were the passenger and baggage cars. The car in use at the time was Combination No. 25, a pretty little baggage-passenger car.

They were running old No. 6. She was a 1907 Baldwin 2-4-4 rear tank engine, with frames inside the drivers. She teetered and rocked when she scooted along the wobbly, out-of-line yard tracks. The boys confided, later on, that she teetered and rocked wherever she was scooting.

One of my first-day impressions of Bridgton was the volume of express the little train handled, and the paucity of passengers. The Sandy River trains had been the other way; there were numerous passengers but only a small pile of express in one corner of the combination car. It seemed, from the looks of the Bridgton's car, that the townsmen ate fairly well, but didn't get around much.

A couple of years earlier, the trains had been running on through Bridgton to Harrison, five miles north. But for some reason or another—maybe declining business—the Harrison end had been lopped off. The track was still there, but nothing ran over it.

The 16 miles from Bridgton down to the Junction was laid with big rail, 56-pound stuff, I believe it was. It looked big, anyway, spiked so close together. The rusty track north to Harrison was 35-pound.

I used a lot of film that day. Besides shooting the No. 6 as she scampered around with her switching duties, the boys took time to haul the 7 and 8 out of the house for me to shoot. Those three Baldwins, the 6, 7 and 8, were all the serviceable power the B.&H. had then. Out near the stored passenger cars, on a really weed-grown siding, sat the old No. 5, intact but out of service. She was much like the 6 in general appearance, except that she was a Portland engine—the very last engine the Portland Company ever built, I was told. She'd been out of service for two or three years.

Near her were the bones of old, old No. 4. There wasn't too much left of No. 4 when I saw her. Just the carcass, minus the cab and fittings. What the old timers offered in the way of comments about No. 4 weren't flattering. I gathered that she was hell-on-wheels to work on. It was strange, too, because the Wiscasset's No. 4 was a mate to her, both being built by the H. K. Porter Works in the same order. The Wiscasset fellows thought their No. 4 was quite an engine, right up to the time the W.W.&F. bit the dust. But these Bridgton boys liked the 7 and 8 best.

A steam mixed train was running on the morning trip, and in the afternoon the *railbus* made the run to the Junction and back. That railbus was something to see. It resembled the Sandy River's neat, gliding railcars about as much as a McKeen motorcar of forty years ago resembled a Budd train of today. I don't know why the boys hadn't sweated just a little more when they built it. Half its ugly appearance could have been covered up by another day's work. She was, or had been, a 1930 Chevrolet Sedan. They'd unwheeled it, and put a set of light sheet-iron wheels under the front end. Under the rear there were other wheels of unattractive appearance, and behind this power unit a crate-like trailer towered, moving on a single set of old boxcar wheels. If Walt Disney had the wagon today it might excite a lot of interest and delighted yelps. But nothing short of Walt Disney and his staff could have made it seem dignified and efficient in 1933!

However, in writing about B.&H.'s self-propelled car I'm not making any dirty cracks. I'm just "remembering". The boys in the shop probably did the best possible with the limited material and parts, and the dearth of money they had to work with. Maybe with the excellent shop and machinery the Sandy River boasted at Phillips, plus the unquestionable genius of Master Mechanic Stinchfield, the B.&H. might have startled the world.

I never rode in the railbus. I did my riding forenoons on the mixed train, and devoted the remainder of those days to seeing what I could see afoot.

The town of Bridgton owned the railroad. They'd recently bought it from the local company which had been formed to take it over from the Maine Central. A Bridgton oil dealer, Howard Burnham, was president then, and his oil business accounted for the two only-two-foot-gauge-tankcars north of Mexico. Maybe there weren't any in Mexico either, but to play safe I always told people that. There were two or three Lilliputs deep in the heart of Mexico at one time, and I never knew for sure whether one of 'em might have had a tankcar and a parlor car, or not.

Up until the first of the 1930s the Maine Central had been running two passenger trains every week day on the Mountain Division. One left Bartlett, up in the White Mountains, in the morning and ran to Portland and back. The other left Portland in the morning and ran through Bartlett to St. Johnsbury, Vermont, and back. The Lilliput connected with all of them. This setup gave excellent passenger service from Harrison and Bridgton into Portland, and back the same day. Then the Maine Central abolished the Bartlett-to-Portland-and-return train. What little passenger travel was using the rails, left it then. You couldn't leave Bridgton and go anywhere to get back the same day. The few people who still rode were either folks coming up from Boston, who had left on a midnight train which connected with the Maine Central's Portland-St. Johnsbury job, or they were local travelers—going from Bridgton down the line to spend the day with Aunt Sarah at Rankin's Mill.

During the next six or eight years I got pretty chummy with the B.&H. It was about all there was left to be chummy with. Besides, being handy to the Boston area, and being about the only Lilliput left, the railroad fans were beginning to show an interest. Eastern Massachusetts packs a lot of fans. They began to come up, either in pairs, or in organized groups. These fan excursions probably kept the B.&H. in loose change for its last two or three years.

Like anything else which is owned by a town, the folks got to fighting over it. The town of Bridgton didn't have much money invested in it, around $30,000 if I remember right. But to hear opposing factions scrap at town meetings you'd have thought the whole future of Bridgton rested in whether they kept the railroad, or if they scrapped it within the next two weeks.

By this time Lester Ames was president. He sort of inherited the office because of being First Selectman of Bridgton. Lester was pro-

This 4-stall house was one of the three enginehouses the B.&S.R. owned. The others were at the Junction, and at Harrison, the north end of the 21-mile line. When this photo was taken in 1933 the 5 miles to Harrison had been abandoned. Nos. 7, 8, and 6 respectively, poke their noses from the big doors. The retired 4 and 5 were out behind on a storage track.

This contraption was the B.&S.R.'s first attempt at motorized equipment. It worked, but wasn't popular. In the early 1930's the Bridgton line began to feel the sharp pains of hunger, as business fell off sharply. This railcar substituted for steam trains when there was no freight to be moved, and was later replaced by a rail bus of better appearance from the Sandy River.

No. 6 engine was a mate to the S.R.&R.L. No. 8, built by Baldwin in 1907. These, and two of the Monson Railroad engines, were the last inside-frame engines built for the Lilliput roads. Being much larger and heavier than the early inside-framers these engines teetered and "oscillated" more than their predecessors, being not nearly as steady riders as the outside-frame engines.

No. 7, a big 35-ton Baldwin of 1913 vintage, was the first of the B.&S.R.'s outside framers. She was always a nice engine to work on, was economical, and reasonably easy on track. She served the road well, for twenty-eight years, and is still going strong hauling passenger trains on Massachusetts' Edaville Railroad. This photo shows her at Bridgton Jct., loading for the run to Bridgton, in 1933.

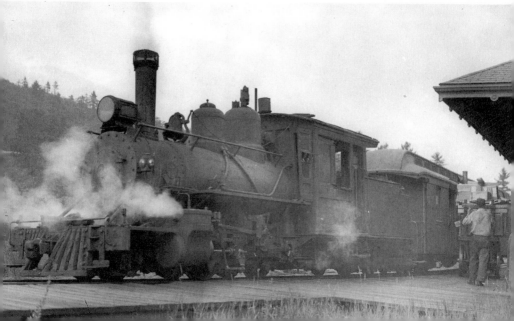

railroad. He rooted for it. He worked hard for it. He was a staunch friend of the railroad fans, and there's no doubt but what between him and the fan groups, they kept the Lilliput alive two or three years longer than if the Progressives in Bridgton had had their own way.

One thing which made President Ames hopping mad was when those Progressives inferred that the town had to help pay the railroad's bills. It didn't. The railroad paid its own. To the end of its days it was self-supporting, although the virtue was possible only by not spending money. Property wasn't maintained in its pristine elegance. But not one penny of taxpayers' money did President Ames spend on the little railroad.

My pilgrimages to the Bridgton road began after the Lilliput had seen its best days. All that was left of the fast runs, the gleaming engines freshly wiped, and the palmy days of big little railroading were the old timers' reminiscences and yellowed records. This misfortune—mine and the Lilliput's—probably accounted for the let-down I felt when first viewing the narrow gauge.

Except for two or three sorties in 1933 and '34 the rest of my visits were on the occasions of railroad fan excursions. These usually came on a Sunday. Two or three flatcars would be fitted with lateral benches, while a baggage car and a coach would be hauled, partly in case of rain, and partly for nostalgic atmosphere. Usually the open cars were pushed ahead, on the engine's nose.

Too often lots of people climbed aboard for those excursion rides who weren't railroad fans. They went along to see what railroad fans were and what they did for excitement. Sometimes one of these hangers-on, usually one of the "summer" people staying in Bridgton, would kick up a stink and nearly spoil the party. They soon tired of the browsing method so pleasant to the fans. Before the trip was half finished the "summer complaint" would begin to howl; he wanted to be taken back to Bridgton at once. One such specimen, who shouted that he was a famous Washington lawyer, demanded to be returned to Bridgton or he'd sue the company. (He finished the leisurely trip, with the rest of us!)

I remember another summer Sunday fan trip. Coming back up from the Junction that hot, sweaty afternoon, the train stopped at the watertank on the shore of Hancock Pond. Someone in the crowd suggested a swim. The majority yelled in agreement. So, more than half the crowd pulled swimming trunks out from their hip pockets and in the privacy of the baggage car, piled into them. One of our group, a gentleman of some dignity and position, didn't have any. He suggested, however, that he'd take a plunge without any if Engineer Everett Brown would be kind enough to haul the baggage car up to that clump of pondshore bushes, where he could scuttle into the water without his nakedness being seen.

Everett obliged. Everyone, including the naked one, splashed and yelled and thoroughly enjoyed themselves. Even No. 7 engine took the cue, and Engineer Brown backed her to the tank, and filled her up. That put the cars, including the baggage car, a hundred yards away from the pondshore and that clump of protecting bushes.

Shortly the swim was finished. The boys raced down to the train and swarmed aboard to change back into their clothes. Someone gave a highball. We were off. No one thought of the gentleman whose nudeness had demanded the cover of the bushes. We were half a mile away when the alarm was sounded, and the brakes applied. The train backed to Hancock Pond. There he was, up to his neck in the water, waving frantically, with a distressed expression. The baggage car was carefully spotted beside the merciful verdure, he slithered aboard, and the trip continued. That was a realistic example of the Lilliput cars being just a boy's size. Had he been forced to climb up the side of a wide gauge baggage car no clump of bushes would have sufficed. A two-acre woodlot would have been in demand.

Came the Spring of 1941, and President Ames' opponents were getting tough. They demanded action, and action meant ridding the town of Bridgton of the ownership of what they called an anachronism—the narrow gauge railroad. The majority vote was to sell the Bridgton & Harrison Railway at public auction. The only bidder with money in his pocket was a junkman. He bought it, or at least got an option on it, for $20,000.01.

I wasn't over there during the haggling, but it wasn't long before the I.C.C. gave its usual permission to abandon operations, and the scrappable property was turned over to the Massachusetts junkman. He lost no time in doing the job.

My last leave of the little B.&H. was at the last end of the junking process when I journeyed over one day to see how the work was progressing. Two or three railroad fans had bought, for a usurious price, No. 8 engine and two or three of the passenger cars. He, the junkman, was holding off scrapping the other engine and the cars— all of which had been brought to Bridgton Junction for storage— until he was sure a few more fans wouldn't show up to buy them.

That ended my acquaintance with the Bridgton & Harrison, another Lilliput which had once been a money-maker, and was now in the undertaker's hands. That is, it ended my acquaintance with it for a number of years. When I met this Lilliput again it was under quite different circumstances. We'll come back to that later.

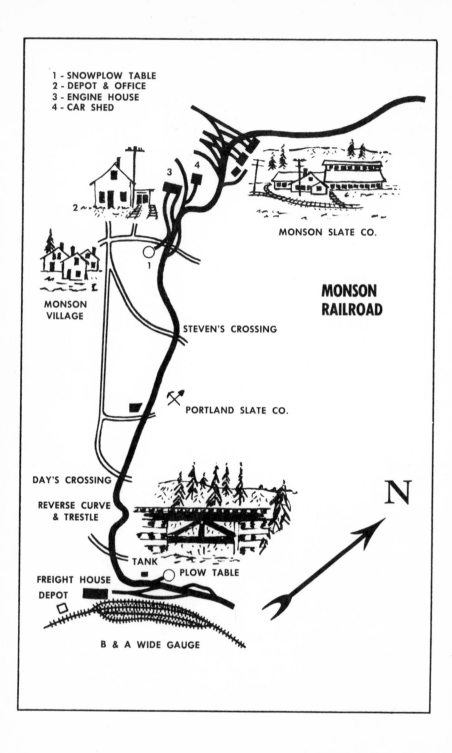

1 - SNOWPLOW TABLE
2 - DEPOT & OFFICE
3 - ENGINE HOUSE
4 - CAR SHED

MONSON SLATE CO.

MONSON
VILLAGE

**MONSON
RAILROAD**

STEVEN'S CROSSING

PORTLAND SLATE CO.

DAY'S CROSSING

REVERSE CURVE
& TRESTLE

N

TANK

PLOW TABLE

FREIGHT HOUSE

DEPOT

B & A WIDE GAUGE

5

THE MONSON RAILROAD

Periodically, when the Government engine inspectors visited the road on which I worked I pumped them dry of information about two-footers as well as the wider gauge shortlines in northern New England. So, I knew there was another pygmy railroad a hundred miles to the north, on the edge of the Big Woods. The Monson Railroad.

I'd never seen the Monson, or the *Two-by-six* as they called it up there. The engine inspector had told me about it. It was the only railroad in Maine which boasted rock ballast on its entire system. It was also the only common carrier railroad left which hadn't equipped its engines and cars with automatic couplers and air brakes. It also still used the original stub switches, he added.

I should see the Monson. Not only its antediluvian link-and-pin couplers, its patriarchal hand-brakes and archaic stub switches, but I should see the Monson, *period.*

One hellishly hot July day I set a course toward where the North Star blinked in the pre-dawn sky. Monson, Maine.

If Maine climate can drive an Eskimo to cover in winter, can pile up snow deeper than the eaves of a wide gauge boxcar, and freeze the whiskers off a brass monkey, it can likewise put equatorial Africa to shame on a hot, muggy summer's day. This was one of them. When I jounced into Monson Junction yard that forenoon the heat waves were making the Lilliput track seem to writhe like a full-blooded python. I felt that rock ballast before I saw it. Some

33

places in the yard were hotter than others. The hot spots were between the rails where that rock ballast laid.

The Monson Railroad's chief excuse for being on earth was—by this time, anyway—to haul slate products from the slate mill in Monson, to the wide gauge at Monson Junction. Where there is quarrying or mining there is always a plentiful supply of waste. The waste slate was the Monson's system-wide rock ballast—on the whole six miles of it.

The steam train was running that day. As long ago as that, in the early 1930's, it ran most every day. It even hauled the venerable 1883 model combination car. Most of the *Two-by-six's* (two feet wide by six miles long) equipment was either original or pretty close to it. The 1883 passenger car was built when the railroad was built; most of the box- and flat-cars were, too. The two engines were newer. They had been built thirty years or so afterward, to replace the originals. They were practically identical, the No. 3 and the No. 4. Both were built by the Vulcan Iron Works and both were conspicuous by the absence of any number painted on their sides. The easiest way, I soon found, of telling which was which—without walking around to squint at the front numberplate—was that the 3 had a single stirrup to lift you up into the cab. The 4 had a double step. The middle step on the No. 4 wasn't necessary, either, because the deck was only 30 inches above the rail.

That sizzling July day was the first time I'd ever seen a railroad train with no power brakes. A few times in my younger days I'd forgotten to cut in the air behind the engine and we'd made the trip with no train brakes. But that wasn't due to antiquated equipment. The Monson's absolute absence of any stoppage other than the hand brake with a husky brakeman twisting it, was a realistic glimpse into Yesterday. The rear end boys were doing the braking that morning, using a pick-handle for emphasis. The engine's steam brakes may have helped, but I noticed the two fellows on the cartops were sweating as they eased the train down the hill into Monson Junction.

Years and years before, I'd seen link-and-pin couplers on the Kennebec Central. The stub switches weren't unknown to me, because at home we had one at the stem of both our wyes. But to have stub stwitches everywhere, main line and all, was interesting. I never

In summertime the Junction yards look different. The ante-bellum stub switches show up better, as does the tiny turntable for snowplows, at the far right. At the far left is the main line of the B.&A.'s branch from Milo to Greenville, the one-time Bangor & Piscataquis Railroad. Today even that is freight-only. (To be exact, you may still ride in the baggage car.)

One of the disadvantages of any narrow gauge was the transferring of freight from wide gauge to narrow gauge cars. Here the Monson Railroad boys shovel polishing sand (for the slate mill) from a wide gauge gondola to their own Lilliput car. When this photo was made in 1940 the Monson road was about washed up, and the train crew did the transferring.

This is Monson Railroad No. 3, although you'd never suspect it. Nary a number or a letter is in sight. Vulcan built her in 1913, and her five-year-younger mate, the No. 4, is identical to her except the 4 has a 2-stirrup cab step, and the 3 has only one. No. 3 now runs on the Edaville, along with her mate and the two Bridgton engines. In later years the Monson engines had no headlight, because, as they explained, trains didn't run after dark.

A very mixed train coming down from Monson, entering the junction yard, crossing State Highway 15. Flatcars of crated slate products pretty well surround little No. 5. The ancient Laconia combination car, of 1883 vintage, tails-up at the rear. August 18, 1937.

Photo by Hugh G. Boutell

knew how the Two-by-six got away with it. If we, at home, had deviated from the I.C.C. safety regulations, as we sometimes did, we would have heard about it in no time. The Government had only lately climbed up one side and down the other of the W.W.&F.'s new owner for certain failures in regulation requirements. Here was a common carrier hauling freight and passengers destined for lands beyond the seas, which could be photographed from all angles, and the picture labelled *Circa 1865,* and no one could dispute it.

Neither did these Lilliput engines wear headlights. An old builder's photo which I begged from a Monson photographer showed an oil headlight, as when the little pot was new. But somewhere along the years she'd lost it off. Someone up there told me the Government men had raised this question one time, and the Monson brass had replied that they didn't need headlights because they didn't run after dark. However, later on they had bolted an old automobile headlamp on the engines' nose, and wired it to an ordinary storage battery.

The train, that July morning, clattered down into Monson Junction yard, set off its freight cars with the brakeman wielding his pick-handle and the fireman literally pulling pins, then backed the combination car up to the depot. The superintendent was also the conductor. The depot was an undepotlike frame building owned by the Bangor & Aroostook Railroad, and served jointly that wide gauge system and the two-foot Monson Railroad.

The little, half-long combination car had the name, Laconia Car Works, Laconia, New Hampshire, emblazoned in an end panel inside the car. Its seats ran lengthwise of the car, settee fashion, like the Kennebec Central's. I never rode in it, but the midget car had a romantic aura. I mused that it would have been a pleasing experience riding up to Monson on a dark winter's night, the tiny coal-stove roaring, the single oil lamp flickering yellowishly, and passengers relaxing as the bantam car lurched and rumbled through the snowy woods. Kind of a coming-home-by-train feeling.

After the Bangor & Aroostook train for Bangor had left Monson Junction, and the Lilliput was preparing to chug back to Monson, I took off in my car to be in Monson to witness its arrival.

Monson, Maine, is a relatively small village. The railroad yard and depot were a short distance off the main street, so often the location of railroad premises. There was only a token yard at Monson, a runaround, a team track, and a couple of short sidings for storing cars. The simple frame depot also served as the general office for the railroad company, which didn't require too much space. The two-stall enginehouse and a narrow shed nearby which apparently had once been the housing facility for the Laconia combination car, about completed·Monson's meager yard. The short, floppity turntable was for snowplows only. The *Two-by-six* never turned its engines. They ran down, and backed back. If we wanted to be funny we could make the wisecrack that Monson engines were 0-4-4's southbound, and 4-4-0's going north. While there wasn't much choice in the matter, Monsonwise, the engine boys got a little easier ride going home as a 4-4-0. The Forney engines rode a little better that way.

After watching the train come in and do its mite of work, I walked down the extension which went to the big Monson Slate Company plant. This track switched off in front of the depot and dropped down a hill that looked like about a 10 per cent grade. It probably wasn't. But later I took especial note that when a Lilliput engine hauled one carload of slate up the hill there was some mighty puffing. He didn't exactly have her hooked up to center.

I got quite a kick out of prowling around down there at the slate plant. Tracks went in all directions. They ducked into long, squatty stonecutting sheds. Others ducked out again. They crossed the main line and each other. There was enough diamond crossing down there to build a mile of track from. And the stub-switches: there were stub-switches enough to have rebuilt the Georgia railroads after Sherman's nefarious orgy. Either at one day-and-time there was some booming railroading down there under the hill, or someone goofed and built more yard track than was ever used.

The quarries weren't in sight. I looked for them. I was accustomed to quarries as being holes in the ground. But at Monson they consist of a maze of subterranean tunnels, some being as much as 900 feet deep. Down there, so they told me, more Lilliput tracks and trains rumbled hollowly through the maze. Electric locomotives hauled them.

I was invited to go down and see what an electric Lilliput engine looked like and to get an eyeful of railroading two-tenths of a mile below. But with one foot reaching for the elevator, I suddenly changed my mind. You should see that elevator! It's hardly more than a flat steel platform hooked to a long cable which reels it down the well-like shaft to the depths where the landing is. You stand on that swinging platform, trusting the cable to hold, and the windlass to hold, and your breath to hold that long! I didn't go down. I looked down the shaft instead. At the bottom there was ice, which the boys told me stayed there the year 'round.

Wandering through the sprawling, dusty finishing shed, where hunks of slate were brought to be made into tabletops, bathtubs, switchboards and shingles, was like thumbing through a geography. There were crates to be loaded into Lilliput cars, ready to leave for every country in the Americas. Each crate must start its journey over the *Two-by-six*.

Getting back out into the broiling sun again, to where the main line track clunked through all those cross-overs, I spotted what looked like the nose of a little engine, 'way off to the further end. I walked over it. It was. Nothing less than the remains of old Hinckley No. 2, a Forney engine of 1883 vintage. She was rusty. Her cab was gone. So was her tank. Just the boiler and driving wheels. I couldn't figure out why she was in such a state of dismemberment and yet apparently used for something. So, I asked questions the next chance I got.

It seems the Monson Railroad had snowplow troubles. Most railroads in snow climes do have. The small wooden wedge-plows are light. They have a habit, even on regular wide gauge roads, of climbing up onto snowdrifts instead of busting into them. The result is a snowplow out over one fence and the engine sometimes out over the other. The Monson men had dreamed up the possibility of taking old derelict No. 2, sheathing her in a snowplow body, and maybe she'd be so heavy she would break the drifts open instead of skidding out over the tops of them. That was why the fifty-year-old engine was sitting out there in the weeds rusting.

The scheme hadn't worked. I didn't learn why, but it hadn't, so the corpse of No. 2 had simply stayed there on the side track, simmering in the summer sun and crystalizing in the winter cold.

The main track meandered over its last cross-over and disappeared around the end of a storage shed. I wondered where it went. A few steps took me around the shed.

The track, now just two rusty, kinky rails laying on sun-bleached ties, struck out across the woods as if it knew where it was going. I took the scent, and the chase was on.

Half a mile away, the bushes hedging in closer and closer as I walked, was the ruins of another old quarry and shed. Sometime the *Two-by-six* had switched that operation and hauled another car or two of slate back to Monson yard.

The track went on. I turned back. That scorching summer sun was too much for me.

The track went, they told me later, to still another, and bigger operation abandoned for many years. That final quarry and shed were two miles beyond Monson yard. That explained why some railroad reference lists showed the Monson Railroad as being 8.16 miles long when Monson was only 6.16 miles from the Junction. They added those two miles out through the woods.

During the next few years I visited Monson a number of times. Once was in mid-January. That was a lulu of a trip. It was 30 degrees below zero when I landed at the Junction that morning. Snow was four feet deep.

At home, a hundred miles to the south, we have more snow than we need. But up there in Maine's snow-belt there is three or four times as much. You can't see out your automobile window because of the high banks the highway snowplows roll back. Until a few years ago they didn't plow the highways up there. They *rolled* them. Huge wooden cylinder-like rollers, weighted with rocks and hauled by innumerable horses, rolled the snow down after each storm. The roads were shortly solid ice, two or three feet thick. But now big plow-nosed trucks and tractors keep the highways

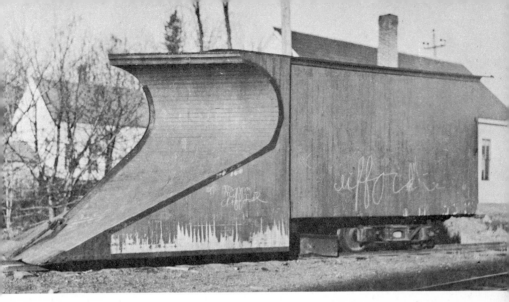

A slightly abbreviated version of the big airplows the standard gauge roads use, was this diminutive Monson snow fighter. Like its wider cousins, it had a flanger built in. You can see the flange rigger just ahead of the rear trucks. This device, lowered to ride on the rail, dug snow out from between the rails.

All the Lilliput railroads were in snow country, and the Monson's latitude was the most northern of them all. The big snowplow had kept the tracks open and the spreader had winged it back during the long months of winter. Yet the midget boxcar is halfway out of sight sitting on the B.&A. transfer track.

Monson trainmen seemed to be content, no matter how their train was made up. Sometimes car were ahead of the engine, sometimes behind it. Sometimes some were on both ends. This mai line freight train, made up mostly of crates of slate goods, is crossing one of the few bridges o the road. There are some more cars trailing the engine, and speed is a nice 8 miles an hour!

Half a mile beyond the Monson depot are the big slate quarries and finishing mill, which ships slat products to half the world. The track to your left, curving to the right, is the main line to th quarry. Years ago it continued on for a mile and a half through the woods to another big quarr and slate operation. The underground slate mines had a railroad network of their own.

clear. That may have contributed to the decline of the Lilliput, although its earnings appear to have slumped while the big rollers were still on the job.

That winter morning the *Two-by-six* was plowed out, and men had the yard at the Junction clean. Stub switches and banjo switch-stands were shoveled out. Tops of baby boxcars stuck up two or three feet above the snow.

A lusty plume of coal smoke was spewing from the depot chimney, and I went in.

I was still in there, gabbing with Agent Fogg about his forty-odd years agenting at Monson Junction, when a piercing whistle opened the Piscataquis County sky wide open. It was No. 3 and the mixed train coming in. That Lilliput whistle, like the years-ago chime on Kennebec Central No. 3, was just as loud as the goliath engines' were. In fact, a few minutes later when the B. & A.'s Greenville-bound train came booming in, the whistle on the Pacific didn't seem nearly so loud.

I rode up to Monson that day on the train. Snow was deep. The Monson Railroad had the biggest snowplow on any of the Lilliputs. It was designed and looked like the big air operated wing-plows such as the B. & A. and the C. P. use to keep their snow belt roads open. Only this one had no wings and no air. There was also a snow spreader. It resembled, by letting your imagination slip a little, a Jordon Spreader which big roads use to ditch with, and to widen cuts. It was basically one of the Monson's flatcars fitted with side swinging wings which pushed snow back six or eight feet. It made room to put the next blizzard.

About midway between The Junction and Monson Village the *Two-by-six* passed still another slate operation, the Portland Monson Slate Company. There were several sidings and yard tracks there, but the boys told me it had been years since the railroad had hauled any freight from there.

In those few years I had several rides on the train and the engines. Sometimes, in season, I rode perched on top of a swaying boxcar. There was more room up there. Being a boating enthusiast the billowing motion didn't make me seasick.

Monsonwise, I kept pretty much off the engines. They didn't ride well. It was easy to imagine them leaping over the fence or off the bridge. Besides, their cabs were six inches too soon. I gave my old head many a resounding crack on those low roofs. The two Monson engines were the only Lilliput engines which didn't have plenty of headroom in the cab.

The Monson Railroad men were nice fellows, all of them. Superintendent-Conductor Morrill looked stern and "official", but either he didn't realize it, or perhaps affected the manner for reasons of his own. He was an agreeable man and not only gave me rides but gave me a lot of information about the little train which he'd grown up with and worked on those fifty-odd years. The engineer and fireman-brakeman, too, were friendly, and I thoroughly enjoyed my several sojourns to the *Two-by-six*.

The last time I saw the Monson Railroad was in 1941, I believe. Things weren't looking too good then. No more regular trains were being run. In fact, only one or two steam trains were out in a week. The slate company's business was all that was left, and after ten years of Depression that was down. Maintenance of track and of equipment had been cut close for a number of years. That day the down train was off the iron three times in the six miles. If the track hadn't been in pretty good condition in its better years, the tiny, original 30-pound rail wouldn't have stood neglect as long as it did.

The macabre script was scrawled all over the Lilliput. I'd seen the death-cipher before, I'd watched too many two-footers check out not to know that this trip might be my last visit to a Lilliput railroad—the last of those boys'-sized midgets, which had so captured my fancy so many years ago.

After that 1941 visit I never saw the Monson Railroad again. When it pegged out I was working in Portland for the Grand Trunk, and heard about the dinky little bantam being abandoned. I was surprised it had lasted as long as it did. Although I didn't suspect it at the time, Fate had it up her sleeve that I was to meet up with the Lilliputs again.

6

THE EDAVILLE RAILROAD

It happened right after the war. As I said a minute ago, I was working on the Grand Trunk. One day, out of a clear sky, I got a letter from a man who had quietly bought much of the Bridgton equipment—an engine, some cars, and some rail—four years before, when the Bridgton & Harrison was being scrapped. He was Ellis Atwood.

Mr. Atwood was something like myself: he'd wished he had midget engines and cars to play with when he was a kid. So, many years afterward, when he first heard about the little railroads up in Maine, he got the same idea I had when I first saw the Kennebec Central. The difference was that Ellis Atwood had money enough to do something about it.

Mr. Atwood had a few other material things inducive to genuine Lilliput railroading which I had lacked. One was an 1,800-acre farm. A cranberry farm. It was, and still is, located in southeastern Massachusetts, not far from famed Plymouth Rock and the almost-as-famous Cape Cod Canal. That's the place where most of the world's cranberries come from. Atwood's home town, South Carver, is the biggest cranberry producing town of this biggest cranberry producing area. His 1,800 acres was a perfect place to build that backyard railroad.

He quizzed me to see how I'd react to coming along. I reacted the way he thought I would. I went.

41

That fall, 1945, we made lots of plans. Up in Bridgton Junction, Maine, Atwood owned an engine, several cars, and enough 35-pound yard rail to make a start. He hoped to buy the other Bridgton engine, which had been bought by a couple of other Lilliput fans who were already becoming a little concerned about the expenses involved with establishing their own railroad.

Still another fan owned some more of the cars. This connoisseur also owned the Sandy River's elegant parlor car, a passenger car, a couple of cabooses, and two of the Sandy River's matchless Model-T trackautos. As far as we knew then these items were all that survived and Mr. Atwood entertained ideas of adding them to his own meager stock.

Ellis Atwood was the logical man to build such a railroad. Massachusetts was the logical locale. The father of Lilliput railroads, in the Western Hemisphere anyway, had been a Massachusetts man. The very first American Lilliput had been built and operated in Massachusetts seventy years before. Now, with the last one gone, we thought it was not only appropriate that the surviving equipment should return to the Mother State, but also that a Massachusetts boy should, by a kind of reversal process, achieve that wonderland dream of many boys—his own Lilliput railroad. We proceeded to set up Ellis in Wonderland.

Ellis was apt with a surveyor's level. He laid out the lines and branches and yards. It was late fall, and the cranberries were harvested. The farm crew became frontiersmen, building the first railroad to span Atwood's bogs, pioneering in establishing a half-sized, miniature railroad for boys to play with.

Before freeze-up we had a few yard tracks laid. We also had the engine and cars from Bridgton at their last home—South Carver.

I spent two weeks at Bridgton Junction that fall, with a few of the cranberry boys. A trucking company in Boston supplied the transportation. One boxcar or one passenger car could be hauled on a trailer-truck, but the flatcars we stacked three high. We had thought the engine, No. 7, might present difficulties because of her 35 tons. But she didn't. She trundled aboard the low trailer as if she were

This meet was staged for picture-taking purposes. Bridgton No. 7 with a passenger train streaks by the gravelpit switch, where Monson 3 and a trumped-up freight is in to clear. Makes a nice picture, anyway.

Ellis D. and Mrs. Atwood beside the former B.&S.R. luxury coach, which he named for Mrs. Atwood—*Elthea*. Mr. Atwood died in November 1950, and Mrs. Atwood sold the railroad property a few years later to F. Nelson Blount, with right-of-way privileges around the Atwood's 1200-acre property.

Linscott Rail Photos

An Edaville train scooting across the cranberry bogs in 1958. Monson engine No. 3, dressed up in capped stack, big headlight, and brass bands is hauling an old Bridgton & Saco River coach. Edaville equipment is painted in bright colors to attract the crowd, with big stacks and red paint added, but it's still the real McCoy.

Monson engine No. 4 and a string of B.&S.R.-S.R.&R.L. cars, picks up sightseers at the new station at the north end of the 5½-mile loop. They ride down to Edaville proper, see the sights, and ride back to the parking lot—the very last ride you can have on a 2-foot gauge train!

Linscott Rail Photos

chuffing into her stall in the Bridgton enginehouse. And she rode down the Turnpike as smoothly as she'd ever wheeled along the B.&S.R.'s winding track.

In the course of the winter Atwood negotiated with the other fan-owners and emerged with a clear title to the connoisseur's cars and the boys' No. 8 engine. I'd also dug him up a few more Sandy River cars, which had reposed on blocking behind people's houses the ten years since the Sandy River's demise. They were trailered to South Carver and with freight car trucks from old B.&S.R. boxcars they made quite an array of equipment.

The Kennebec Central's cars were too far gone to rehabilitate. In fact, when the Kennebec River went on a rampage in 1936 it had swashed the cars around so badly that they were wrecks. One combination had floated down river and was never seen again.

There was nothing left of the Wiscasset's equipment worth salvaging. The trucks had been scrapped and the car bodies had rotted beyond repair. What nature hadn't done by rot, vandals had done. The Wiscasset & Quebec had nothing to offer.

The Monson Railroad had gone, of course, a couple of years before. The junk man hadn't missed anything. Nothing was left up in Piscataquis County to haul to South Carver. It looked, in the Spring of 1946, as if we had cornered the entire Lilliput market. The single exception was one of the old Portland Company Forney engines, W.W.&F. No. 9, ex-Kennebec Central No. 4, and originally an old Sandy River engine. This engine, some 35-pound rail, and two flatcars were bought by a railroad fan at the time the Wiscasset Road was being junked. It was trailered to the Connecticut farm of a friend of his, where it still reposes—in 1959. Mr. Atwood made no strenuous efforts to get this engine, as its owners had a strong sentimental feeling for it themselves.

1946 was the year most of Atwood's Lilliput railroad was built and the badly deteriorated equipment more or less rehabilitated.

Rehabilitation ran all the way from face-lifting badly rotted sills and sheathing with plain wood-putty, to practically rebuilding some of the freight cars, with stout, solid timber.

Sometime in the Spring of that year, 1946, I blundered onto the startling news that two more Lilliput locomotives were still in existence, and for sale. The two Monson engines.

Try as I have, I can't remember how that information reached me. Of course, in that period part of my job was to discover and muckle onto all the 2-foot gauge equipment I could find. I perpetually had two long, flapping ears spread out to catch any whisper which might be wafted on the gentle breeze. One of those ears caught the Monson whisper, it would seem.

Anyway, the story developed that when the junk people salvaged (a nice word for *to scrap*) the Monson Railroad they reversed their usual procedure, and spared the two engines. Numbers 3 and 4 were inched onto standard-gauge flatcars (excuse it; *wide*-gauge flatcars!) at Monson Junction, and tagged to the junkman's used equipment yard in Rochester, New York. They were there, intact, and for sale.

I grabbed my hat, a toothbrush, and a Boston & Albany train for Rochester.

There they were. Both of them. Midget No. 3 and Bantam No. 4, sitting there amid acres of other junk. I say *other* junk, because the poor little Forney *Two-by-Sixers* weren't far from being junk themselves. In the last days at Monson they had got some pretty rough treatment. For one thing, as an example, the brasses in the tank trucks of one of the engines had been run without "dope", and the brasses had worn completely through, letting the little axle grind away on the journal box itself. The whole shebang was worn to a frazzle. There were other comparable signs of neglect.

In spite of a lifetime spent on steam engines, there was so much I didn't know about them that, before giving the junkman Mr. Atwood's check I arranged for a New York Central boilermaker and an engine inspector to give the engines the best going over possible. These craftsmen emerged from the bowels of the Forneys with several typewritten sheets of reports. It was bad enough so the owner agreed to accept $1,500 for them instead of the asking price of $2,000. They headed for Massachusetts over the B.&O. The used equipment yard at the corner of Read Street and Lyell Boulevard was cheated out of 36 tons of assorted junk!

Boxcar No. 1. It was numbered "1" only to create a boxcar No. 1 for people to look at. The Moody-designed herald, *The Cranberry Belt,* still appears on many Edaville freight cars, advertising brochures, etc.

B.&S.R. No. 7 with a string of Bridgton, Wiscasset and Sandy River cars, clatters along the big dike which separates the Atwood 300-acre reservoir from the cranberry bogs. The famous parlor car *Rangeley* brings up on the rear.

As the last survivor of the fascinating Lilliputs the Edaville Railroad gives us a glimpse into Yesterday. We may still see a flash of Lilliput railroading from the cab window of a genuine 2-foot steam engine.

When they had been trucked down from the New Haven railroad in Plymouth, Massachusetts to the new railroad in South Carver, I settled down to renewing old acquaintances—and cracking my skull on their low-posted cabs again.

During the first months of reviving these acquirements, Mr. Atwood and I spent hours trying to conjure up a good name. We considered many cognomens and appellations; the Carver Central, the Cranberry Valley, and the Plymouth County Railroad. Atwood clicked onto it first—the *Edaville* Railroad. It seemed just the thing.

In pre-railroad days his little village had been affectionately called Edaville. That was from his own initials, E.D.A., Ellis D. Atwood. Today, the Edaville Railroad is known all over the country, not only by railroad fans, but by the three million people who have visited it in the last ten years.

I designed what I thought was an appropriate herald, copied pretty much from some of those seen on freight cars of several different roads. It was a big circle inside of which were the words, *The Cranberry Route,* with the initials EDA in the center. We painted that on all the boxcars. *I* thought it looked pretty good.

Building the Edaville Railroad was fun, along with the growing pains and frustrations. Maybe it was more or less the materialization of boyhood dreams—the Kennebec Central impressions and the daydream of its being transplanted to my own backyard for us kids to play with. From all appearance Ellis felt the same way, although he had dignity enough not to spill the beans.

I never could guess exactly what Mrs. Atwood thought of the whole thing. She was the most diplomatic of people. She just smiled through it, and might as well have said, "Have a good time, boys. It could be worse."

Mr. Atwood's mother, a venerable matron of some 90 summers, had different reactions, and voiced them. But Ellis didn't seem to mind, and I kept out of her way. The Edaville Railroad pushed its rails in a circle.

As miniature track crept farther and farther around the 1,800 acres the four pigmy engines got plenty of workouts. Ellis didn't care so much about actually riding on the engines and trains (he'd cracked his own head on the Monson cabs, too), as he enjoyed driving out among the bogs in his Packard, and sitting there watching the smoke and cinders fly. We belched plenty of it out the high stacks so he'd get his money's worth.

Shortly the big cranberry farm developed into a mecca for people. At first, many were railroad fans. Many more were Plymouth County people who had heard, perhaps to their horror, that another attraction was competing with their Plymouth Rock. And people came from Boston, hundreds of 'em. Sundays and holidays were the worst. Mr. Atwood toyed with various schemes to discourage them, at first. Shortly, however, it dawned on him that he and I weren't the only ones who might like to play on boys'-sized trains. Thereafter, everybody and his neighbors were on a permanent invitation.

The throngs of people riding among the cranberry bogs, especially at harvest time, wasn't bad publicity for the cranberry industry, too. It always seemed to me the industry passed up a good thing in not doing more to further that end.

Along with laying yard tracks and the 5½-mile circle around the big farm, there appeared new buildings. A big frame building sprang up, in which was a typical ticket office. A lunch counter, gift shoppe, and cranberry products dispensary flourished in the big waiting room. A water tank for thirsty locomotives was built. One end of the immense screenhouse was altered to accommodate passenger cars up for repairs. The precious treasure-piece the parlor car *Rangeley,* was housed in there.

Mr. Atwood went in for little railroading in a big way. It cost him a fortune, but I think it was worth it to him. He ran trains one after another on holidays and Sundays, all of them well patronized by visitors from every State in the Union. During the Christmas-New Year week he staged a grand pageant in which there was a miniature village, called Peacedale, with Santa Clauses and reindeer and other legendary figures, all illuminated by floodlights and colored lights. Crowded trains ran daily during this fiesta, until late into the evening.

At first, no charge or fee was collected. Everyone rode free, as the guests of Ellis and Elthea Atwood. Later, after my time, a small charge was made, to help defray the mounting expenses.

I left the Edaville Railroad on Labor Day, 1947. In years which followed there were further additions to the diversions at Edaville. The garage section of the screenhouse—a sizeable space in itself—was converted into a museum of railroad antiques and items and models and photographs. New "excursion cars" were built from scratch, to accommodate the increasing crowds which flocked into the new playground from all over the northeastern States. Edaville now even apears on most highway roadmaps. People know how to get to Edaville who never heard of the town of Carver!

In November, 1950, Mr. Atwood was adjusting the big heating unit in the screenhouse. It exploded. He died a few days later without regaining consciousness. Buried in his family lot in the cemetery near the Edaville Railroad, today every train making the loop toots its whistle in salute to the man who brought the Lilliputs back home to Massachusetts, and saved them from eternal extinction—Ellis Atwood.

BILLERICA & BEDFORD RAILROAD.

ENGINES "PUCK" & "ARIEL"

Henry D. Crittenden

7

GEORGE MANSFIELD
BILLERICA & BEDFORD RAILROAD

Probably two men were responsible for giving the Lilliputs to the world. Ellis D. Atwood's contribution was in preserving the species—an act of absolute importance to the generations of today and tomorrow. The other man, likewise a son of the Bay State, was responsible for the first Lilliput being planted in the New World. This man was George E. Mansfield.

I don't know much about George Mansfield. Neither does anyone else, apparently. Whether he was a railroad man previous to the early 1870's, or whether he was the Victorian equivalent of today's railroad fan, is anyone's guess. Whatever his background was, he introduced the Lilliput railroads to the United States.

There had been two or three alleged two-footers in the early 70's. They hadn't amounted to much. They seemed to have been pure and simple industrial tramways. One was listed for two or three years in old Poor's Manuals and The Official Guide—The Peekskill Valley Railroad. It connected a mine with vessels on the Hudson River, near Peekskill, New York. It was for freight only, and owned, so an old, old Poor's says, one engine which weighed 4½-tons! It shortly disappeared from published lists.

Wales seems to have been the birthplace of the original Lilliputs. The most widely known was the Festiniog Railway, built in the middle 1800's, like our own Monson Railroad, to haul slate from quarries in the hills to tidewater. It was 23½-inches wide. It's miserly

49

width was neither two feet nor the subsequently popular 60-centimeter (23⅝-inches), which toddles around Metric System countries even to the present time.

Sometime in the middle 1870's George Mansfield, went to Wales, saw the Festiniog Railway, and called it good. Back to the States he came, his vintage carpetbag sagging dangerously with the weight, so to sepak, of the Lilliput idea.

In those days of many gauges, some as wide and gaumy as the six-foot Erie and the seven footers in England, the flexible, dinky Festiniog Railway must have impressed Yankee Mansfield as something which, properly promoted, could revolutionize the cumbersome, floundering railroad expansion in America. He was just the boy who could promote it.

Skimpy track widths were uncommon then. The Old World had a few, as is attested by the Festiniog's existence. There may have been brother and sister roads.

When George Mansfield excitedly hopped around this little slate carrier it hadn't developed any big capacity cars, powerful engines, or even gallon-sized earnings at pint-sized costs. In the New World the Lilliput idea needed introduction, and a man of vision to promote it. I don't mean to infer that George was swelledheaded, but in the light of events which followed, he was pretty sure he could sell it.

In the months following his return from Wales, he busied himself arranging and studying his carpetbag full of tricks. He naturally reviewed the design and structure of the Cymric midget. The fact that the Festiniog was only 23½ inches wide either escaped his attention or he was too engrossed in his dream to deal with petty fractions. George settled for an even two feet.

Whether Mansfield's hassles with the Lilliput idea took months or years is lost in history. Sometime after recuperating from the rigors of his trip abroad he went to work. Why he thought it necessary, after riding and teetering and studying the Festiniog's cars and track, to build his own experimental backyard Lilliput is another puzzle. But he did. On his Massachusetts farm he built the *Sumner Heights & Hazelwood Valley Railroad,* all wood and scant inches wide.

Heliotype Printing Co.　　　　　　　　　　　　220 Devonshire St., Boston.

LOCOMOTIVE,

FOR THE

BILLERICA & BEDFORD R. R.

Gauge, Two Feet.

GEO. E. MANSFIELD, Projector and Manager.

Built by the HINKLEY LOCOMOTIVE WORKS, Boston, Mass.

Weight of Engine { 23,750 lbs.
in working order }

Cylinders, { 8 in. dia. x 12 in.
stroke }

Driving Wheels, 30 in. dia.

Total Wheel Base, 13 feet.

Driving " " 3 ft. 6 in.

Grate, { 30 in. long x 27¾ in.
wide. }

Ellis Walker

Heliotype Printing Co.　　　　　　　　　　　　220 Devonshire St., Boston.

LOCOMOTIVE,

FOR THE

BILLERICA & BEDFORD R. R.

Gauge, Two Feet.

GEO. E. MANSFIELD, Projector and Manager.

Built by the HINKLEY LOCOMOTIVE WORKS, Boston, Mass.

Weight of Engine { 23,750 lbs.
in working order }

Cylinders, { 8 in. dia. x 12 in.
stroke }

Driving Wheels, 30 in. dia.

Total Wheel Base, 13 feet.

Driving " " 3 ft. 6 in.

Grate, { 30 in. long x 27¾ in.
wide. }

Heliotype Printing Co.   220 Devonshire St., Boston.

PASSENGER CAR,

FOR THE

BILLERICA & BEDFORD R. R.

Gauge, Two Feet.

GEO. E. MANSFIELD, Projector and Manager.

Built by the RANLET MAN'F'G CO., Laconia, N. H.

Weight, 9,000 lbs.
Capacity, 30 Passengers.
Journals, 2⅝ x 5.
Miller Platform.

Length, 40 ft.
Width, 6 ft, 2 in.
Diameter of Wheel, 18 in.
Empire Vacuum Brake.

Ellis Walker

Heliotype Printing Co.   220 Devonshire St., Boston.

EXCURSION CAR,

FOR THE

BILLERICA & BEDFORD R. R.

Gauge, Two Feet.

GEO. E. MANSFIELD, Projector and Manager.

BUILT BY THE RANLET MAN'F'G CO., LACONIA, N. H.

Weight, 5,500 lbs.
Capacity, 60 Passengers.
Journals, 2⅝ x 5.
Miller Platform.

Length, 25 ft.
Width, 6 ft. 2 in.
Diameter of Wheel, 18 in.
Empire Vacuum Brake.

We can imagine the old codger experimenting with cars of American style to see if six-foot-widers would stay right side up on two-foot track. In those days, you must remember, even the *wide gauge* cars weren't much wider than that. In the mid-70's Mansfield was pretty much using standard equipment to try out on the Lilliput gauge.

We may imagine, too, that he studied engine designs and performance to find something better than the two-faced Fairlies which had lately replaced steaming mule power in Wales. I like to think that George's objective was to perfect the then conventional American equipment to this narrowest of narrow track.

Anyway, from Mansfield's genius and his backyard railroading there emerged a pint-sized railroad, Yankee as hard cider and stout as a yoke of Bay State oxen.

With such technicalities ironed out, let's assume he was ready to charge into the brawly railroad frays. He either had faith in the ideas he'd brought from Wales, or had faith in his own line of barnyard public relations. Whether his enthusiasm sparked from a patriotic obsession to serve his country, or he was wise to the ten per cent plus cost racket, I couldn't seem to dig out. All he needed were prospects with money and with intentions of building a railroad. He could do the rest.

Fate mustered an audience—or Mansfield was shrewd. The Massachusetts towns of Bedford and Billerica, eight miles apart, needed a railroad. One was served by one road and the other by another, but the folks were tired of changing cars. They wanted one all their own. The townspeople were conveniently in a fevered lather. Mansfield sniffed the smell. He was off—to Billerica, figuratively baying with joy.

That was in 1875.

You may read old records of meetings, speeches, back-whacking and other tricks of the promoters' trade. Mansfield was an artist, it would seem. He had a civil engineer tagging along. This lackey barked in unison that because of the rugged terrain a *wide* gauge line would run into boxcar figures, the Lilliput would not.

The folks of Bedford and Billerica listened with their mouths open. They evidently thought that George was a god. So, labor pains of money raising shortly racked the Mother State. As Mansfield knew it would, the birth took place. The new Billerica & Bedford Railroad was chartered in May 1876, the first commercial two-footer in America.

In the light of local history it might have been better if those folks had seen in George Mansfield a devil instead of a god, and stuck to their stagecoaches. About the only happy result of this primary venture in the field of bantam gauges was that it ironed out some more kinks which George had missed with his Sumner Heights & Hazelwood Valley, and supplied concrete evidence of narrow gauge economy for more sales talk which followed. The good folks of Bedford and Billerica lost their shirts.

Turning the first Billerica & Bedford sod was a gay and festive event. There were speeches and eats. In fact, I have reason to believe the eats were the last good meal those trusting townsmen had for many a day. Then, two little girls in identical blue dresses toddled a bright blue wheelbarrow up to the site, dug up a few grassroots, with adult help probably, and wobbled the load across the lot. That colorful and cleverly staged act commenced construction of the first 2-foot railroad in America. Everyone was full of sandwiches, beer, and hope.

Construction was quick, just as George had said it would be. One of his yelling-points was the paucity of building problems. Just scrape off the cradleknolls, scatter tiny ties and rails, and there you were—a railroad!

Later, when this Goliath of the Lilliputs tried to explain overdrawing the tiny bank account, he roared about obstacles which taxed the surveyor's skill and the contractor's brawn. It is hard for us to believe that in 1876 the terrain of eastern Massachusetts was as tough and rugged as Manfield's report to the stockholders said it was. He'd spent more money than he said he would. Expenses, he hemmed, had been more than he'd reckoned. Dame Luck, he hawed, had done him dirt. Grades had run to 3 per cent. Curves of 300-foot radius (with 3 inches elevation on the outside rail) had jumped out of the puckerbrush and landed on his right-of-way. There were bridges to cross hitherto unseen streams. One of these was a pile trestle 140 feet long.

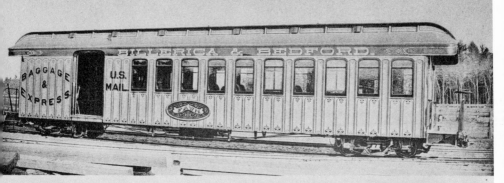

Heliotype Printing Co.   220 Devonshire St., Boston.

COMBINATION CAR,

FOR THE

BILLERICA & BEDFORD R. R.

Gauge, Two Feet.

GEO. E. MANSFIELD, Projector and Manager.

Built by the RANLET MAN'F'G CO., Laconia, N. H.

Weight, 9,000 lbs.
Capacity, 20 Passengers.
Journals, 2⅝ x 5.
Miller Platform.

Length, 40 ft.
Width, 6 ft. 2 in.
Diameter of Wheel, 18 in.
Empire Vacuum Brake.

Ellis Walker

Heliotype Printing Co.   220 Devonshire St., Boston.

BOX CAR,

FOR THE

BILLERICA & BEDFORD R. R.

Gauge, Two Feet.

GEO. E. MANSFIELD, Projector and Manager.

BUILT BY THE RANLET MAN'F'G CO., LACONIA, N. H.

Weight, 5,600 lbs.
Capacity, 12,000 to 16,000 lbs.
Journals, 2⅝ x 5.
Miller Platform.

Length, 25 ft.
Width, 6 ft. 2 in.
Diameter of Wheel, 18 in.
Empire Vacuum Brake.

Heliotype Printing Co.

220 Devonshire St., Boston.

FLAT OR COAL CAR,

FOR THE

BILLERICA & BEDFORD R. R.

Gauge, Two Feet.

GEO. E. MANSFIELD, Projector and Manager.

Built by the RANLET MAN'F'G CO., Laconia, N. H,

Weight, 4,500 lbs.
Capacity, 12,000 to 16,000 lbs.
Journals, 2½ x 5.
Miller Platform.

Length, 25 ft.
Width, 6 ft. 2 in.
Diameter of Wheel, 18 in.
Empire Vacuum Brake.

Ellis Walker

Heliotype Printing Co.

220 Devonshire St., Boston.

BRYANT'S PATENT SWITCH AND FROG.

BILLERICA & BEDFORD R. R.

Gauge, Two Feet.

GEO. E. MANSFIELD, Projector and Manager.

Building crews had toiled into the fall of 1877. Then, the deed was finally done. Eight miles of 25-pound rail costing $38.00 a ton in Boston, was spiked to 24,000 4½-foot-long ties, which cost 12 cents apiece.

We may surmise that those days of experimenting on his Sumner Heights & Hazelwood Valley Railroad had paid off in divers ways, including Mansfield's own design of a locomotive. It's just possible the Hinckley Locomotive Works may have made a suggestion or two. But at their nearby locomotive works the first two engines, the *Ariel* and the *Puck,* were ready and champing at the bit, when the big day arrived. They were coal burners, built to run hind end first. Actually, the *Ariel* and the *Puck* were Forney types, 0-4-4, but in running backwards they became, in effect, 4-4-0's. These engines cost $3,500.00 each and weighed a dite under 12 tons. They had cylinders 8 by 12 inches, and driving wheels 30-inches in diameter.

The Billerica & Bedford Railroad was opened in November, 1877. Scarce six months had passed since digging the first grass root. Presto! Four round trips a day were on the new timecard. George E. Mansfield was General Manager and Promoter. And, the little railroad was doing all he'd claimed it would, except making money.

Trains were running 72 miles a day on 1,500-pounds of coal. Total train expenses were a mere 13 cents a mile, including labor and fuel. The trains ran as steady and smooth as their big *wide* gauge cousins. There was no *oscillation,* Manager Mansfield repeated and emphasized. (I imagine he meant lurching and slamming back and forth, as some of the *Ariel* and *Puck's* successors later did). Crews and passengers alike were amazed and delighted, he jabbered on, by the little trains' riding qualities. The 2-foot gauge was a tremendous success.

The two passenger cars, the combination *Fawn* and the coach *Sylvan*—each 40 feet long and 6-feet, 2 inches wide—had been built by the Ranlet Manufacturing Company at Laconia, New Hampshire, and had Miller platforms and Empire Vacuum brakes. They weighed 4½ tons each.

Ranlet had also built several boxcars and flats, as well as a 60-passenger 25-foot open street car like excursion car, likewise with Miller platforms and vacuum brake.

The rolling stock didn't compare in quantity to the neighboring Boston & Maine's, but it seems to have been sufficient for the available traffic.

That traffic was the Billerica & Bedford's undoing. Actually, not much traffic existed. We may well wonder why the little railroad was ever built. Its active life was only six months. Traffic potentials, which Father Mansfield may not have taken the trouble beforehand to investigate, cast a shadow of cynicism on the undersized project. The thought that he could have engineered the abortive deal for reasons of future promotions or current profit persist.

If George was an idealistic dreamer he might have innocently pressured the good folks to dump their stocking in his outstretched hand. If he was wise to the 1877 equivalent to the cost-plus racket, a less honorable motive might have nudged him on. There's a difference between being a visionary and being a shyster.

Anyway traffic on the Billerica & Bedford Railroad didn't pan out.

That first, and only, New England winter demonstrated the Lilliput's ability in snow and cold. Unhappily, however, it also demonstrated the crushing truth that if this bantam gauge could run on half size expenses it could pile up a full deficit. Come Spring the Billerica & Bedford was broke, and on June 1, 1878, service was suspended.

That was it. There wasn't any wailing about unfair competition. No cussing the dray teams and laundry carts. No howls for a subsidy. Not even a reorganization or hearing before regulatory boards. It just stopped. A couple of the B.&B.'s Lilliput grandchildren followed this hereditary pattern, half a century later.

The next week the property was sold at public auction. Its best part, the engines and cars, went to an otherwise unknown Mr. Brown of New Hampshire, for $9,000.

Thus exploded Gargantua Mansfield's entry into the colorful field of transportation. From the explosion's fall-out, however, came a sounder knowledge and wider sagacity of Lilliput capabilities. Came a more positive sales talk for tomorrow. The fact that the little towns of Bedford and Billerica couldn't support *any* railroad couldn't be held against the fledgling B.&B. It had done *its* part well.

8

SANDY RIVER RAILROAD

Railroad fever was spreading with the air currents, in 1878. Germs and pollen wafted north into Maine. An epidemic infected the good folks of Franklin County. They wanted a railroad.

George Mansfield hustled to Maine. He addressed civic groups in Farmington, Strong, Phillips, Madrid and Rangeley. He had facts and figures to quote. He spread it on like cinder ballast. He glowed about his tiny trains gliding through dale and o'er hill totally free of *oscillations*. If he mentioned the negative problems at home in Billerica—for this happened whilst yet the B.&B. was still running—the Franklin County newspapers didn't print it.

It was like selling cold pop at the county Fair. They lapped it up.

A civil engineer named Thomas Appleton was whistled to the scene. In May, 1878, even before the *Ariel* and *Puck* had hauled the elegant *Fawn* and *Sylvan* to the auction track, Appleton had run his first survey.

He made it from Farmington, Maine, through Strong to Phillips in 18 easy miles of light curves and negligible grades—the famous *Appleton Survey* which old timers up there still talk about, with regret. It was a survey such as railroad builders dream about but rarely find, especially in such rough and rugged country as the Franklin County hills. At least, that was his report to prospective stockholders.

Again came the racking labor pains. Projector Mansfield commuted between his managerly duties in Billerica and his brewing pros-

55

pects in Maine. The Franklin County clientele were rousingly enthusiastic about a little railroad with big promise. But, their enthusiasm slacked off a dite when George passed the hat.

However, farmers none too flush with money, and local tycoons with razor-edge Yankee sagacity pledged free rights of way through their farms and the gratuitous use of their hired men and oxen for a week or two's labor. Most of the hard cash had to be raised outside the State.

The towns of Strong, Phillips, Madrid and Rangeley pledged sizable hunks of town credit as evidence of good faith. The town of Phillips cannily hitched a rider to its $14,000 pledge to the effect that nary a penny would it pay unless rails were laid and trains were running into Phillips by November 20, 1879. Phillips would either have a railroad or it would keep its $14,000!

The situation was static for a year. Then, the birth took place. In March, 1879, the Sandy River Railroad was organized.

The famous Appleton Survey was tossed out because of a $1,500 disagreement in a right-of-way deal. Another survey was run, distressingly different in ups-and-downs from the easy curves and gentle grades which Appleton's transit had uncovered in the brooding hills.

Now for a contractor to get down to grass-roots work. Bids were let, and T.&R. Shanahan drew the lucky number. Work began in June.

Either Old Lady Luck's eyes were twinkling, or someone had played his cards by the calendar. Work on the Sandy River Railroad began at the same time work on the Billerica & Bedford stopped.

The Sandy River needed rails, engines, and cars. The defunct B.&B.'s equipment was for sale. The new Lilliput likewise needed an experienced man to guide its infantile affairs. George E. Mansfield, late of the Billerica & Bedford, was looking for a job.

One of Manager Mansfield's first official chores was to approach the mysterious Mr. Brown of New Hampshire in regard to selling those engines and cars he'd so lately bought at the Billerica auction. Mansfield took leave of Mr. Brown with, so to speak, the equipment in his travel-worn carpetbag. Mr. Brown was staring at $20,000

andy River 2nd No. 2 was a Baldwin Mogul, later the S.R.&R.L. No. 18. Moguls 2nd No. 2
nd 2nd No. 3, and the P.&R. No. 3 were rebuilt to Prairie types, with new and bigger boilers,
n early post-Consolidation years. These engines, S.R.&R.L. Nos. 15, 16 and 18 respectively, had
he Mogul deckless cabs. Here we see the future No. 18 equipped with vacuum brakes, an early
Sandy River feature.

This was No. 3, the Sandy River's third engine. She was built by the H. K. Porter Co. in 1883 in
nticipation of the tonnage about to roll down off the budding F.&M. In her cab window is
Engineer Chris Boston, the victim of Ed West's prank which resulted in Boston and the big 15
anding in the roundhouse ashpit! No. 3 ended her days as Wiscasset & Quebec R.R. No. 1.

The old covered station at Phillips somewhere along in the 1880's. To your left one of the P.&R. passenger cars sits on a siding, and the old, old enginehouse is across the track beyond. The low building to the right of the depot was probably the old car shop. These original buildings stood about where the later structures did.

Lately the *Ariel* on the Billerica & Bedford Railroad, here she is as the Sandy River No. 1 heading a passenger train out of the Farmington depot. Farmington is still there, but the little 12-ton Hinckley, the Sandy River R.R., and the railroad station have long since gone. This picture was taken probably about 1890, after coal had returned as the *Ariel's* daily diet.

worth of Sandy River capital stock, which had somehow got into his trembling hand. A few years later, when the Sandy River was temporarily in the doldrums, Mr. Brown sold that stock back to the Sandy River management for a measly $3,000. The doldrums over, it was shortly back to par, and paid handsome dividends for many years!

Some Shanahans quickly threw up some miles of grade north from Farmington. Other Shanahans began to lay the Billerica & Bedford's 25-pound rail. Soon worktrains were scuffing the Shanahan heels and the Lilliput railroad was streaking through the woods toward Phillips, 18 miles away.

When Mansfield bought the equipment from New Hampshire Brown he shipped the *Ariel* and *Puck* back to the Hinckley Locomotive Works for alterations. Something in that six month's B.&B. adventure must have upset his cab-first idea. The Hinckley people swapped them around to front-enders again. They also switched them over to burn wood for fuel. Wood grew in abundance along the Sandy River. Coal didn't. For the next forty years the little Forneys, now plain No. 1 and No. 2, ran in the direction engines should. Years later the diamond stacks were replaced with straight ones when coal came into favor again.

During the construction days Superintendent Mansfield had a bout with labor. The boys struck. He hurried up to see what the trouble was. It was poor rum. Local bootleggers were rooking the boys on rotgut booze at champagne prices. Management sampled the mountain dew, and strangled in agreement. But in keeping with railroad tradition the big brass hat fired the whole crew, and hired some more. Then, wrongs having been righted, the thud of dirt and the clang of steel once more filled the summer air.

If the bosomy curves of Mother Nature had upset Builder Mansfield when he was laying the Billerica & Bedford track he must have been more unhappy as track unfolded behind Shanahan's steaming Paddies. There was hardly a straight rail, nor a level one. In those 18 miles there were no less than 74 trestles. The one entering Phillips was 850 feet long and forty feet high; another near Strong was nearly as bad. And, plenty more of those 74 were close runners-up.

Eventually, long after Mansfield had departed, these wooden bridges were either filled or replaced with masonry or iron bridges. That huge Phillips trestle was blown down by the wind a dozen years later, and was replaced by a big iron truss bridge which was as solid when the railroad was abandoned in 1935 as when it was set up in 1890.

When the graders reached Strong and the steel gang was a mile or so behind, summer heat had changed to the frosty tang of autumn. Time was running out. Phillips and that coveted $14,000 was still seven miles and umpteen trestles away. So, the Shanahans subleased those seven miles to another son of Erin, Pat Maney by name. With Pat's crew heaving from sun-up to dusk and the Shanahans reeling track out over Strong Mountain things went faster. The big Strong trestle delayed them a week or so, but its lattice-work shortly loomed 40 feet above the Porter Stream and baby engines were nosing steel across to lay on Pat's fresh grade.

A mile or two and 24 hours short of Phillips, simpering Dame Luck dumped a blizzard down. It snowed a foot. Tie and steel gangs waded through it. Only a mile of track and a day of time separated them from Phillips and that jingling $14,000.

Like most good shows this one had a happy ending, too. The evening of November 19, the town turned out. The last half mile was being ironed. Youngsters pitched in heaving ties and rail. Oldsters kept big bonfires leaping into the winter sky. They lit a path for creeping track and showed the excited crowd how work was progressing. Shortly after 9:00 p.m. the last rail clanged down, the final spike was mauled, and a midget engine hissed and snorted into Phillips. The town's support was won!

There was a ringtailed-snorting welcome that night. Horns were tooted and drums were beat. Churchbells rang. The shrill whistle atop the Hinckley's dome split the icy, midnight air. The Lilliput railroad was here.

A few days later, when the Shanahans had surfaced and lined the track a little better, regular trains began to run. Passenger business made news from the start. An old newspaper clipping of the date,

TIME-TABLE.

Sandy River R. R.

MONDAY, OCTOBER 14, 1901.

NORTH.	Train No. 1 A. M.	Train No. 3 A. M.	Train No. 5 P. M.
Farmington, ... Lv.	**11.00**	12.10	4.40
So. Strong, ...	P. M.		
Strong, ... Lv.	12.05	12.42	5.10
Phillips, ... Ar.	12.30	**1.00**	5.30

SOUTH.	Train No 2 A. M.	Train No. 4 A. M.	Train No. 6 P. M.
Phillips, ... Lv.	7.30	8.30	**1.30**
Strong, ... Lv.	7.50	9.10	1.50
So. Strong,.			
Farmington, ... Ar.	8.20	**10.00**	2.20

WESTON LEWIS,
President.

FRED N. BEAL,
Superintendent.

The original Sandy River R.R. going into its twenty-second winter. This was six years before consolidation of the 18-mile run into the Sandy River & Rangeley Lakes.

Franklin & Megantic Ry. STRONG —TO— S A L E M. *P.H.Winslow* G.T.A. 1543	SANDY RIVER RAILROAD. STRONG TO SOUTH STRONG. *J.E.Thompson* G.T.A. 580
SANDY RIVER RAILROAD PHILLIPS TO STRONG *Geo.A.Farrington* G.T.A. 7905	Sandy River & Rangeley Lakes Railroad [B C] KINGFIELD to FARMINGTON, Me. Good for One Continuous Passage within thirty days from and including date of sale. Subject to tariff regulations. 03415 L1 *C.H.Robinson* TRAFFIC MANAGER 9651
Sandy River & Rangeley Lakes Railroad [B C] STRONG to ☐ KINGFIELD, Me. Good for One Continuous Passage within thirty days from and including date of sale. Subject to tariff regulations. 183522 L1 *C.H.Robinson* TRAFFIC MANAGER 5995	Sandy River & Rangeley Lakes Railroad [B C] KINGFIELD to CARRABASSET, Me. Good for One Continuous Passage within thirty days from and including date of sale. Subject to tariff regulations. 03415 L1 *C.H.Robinson* TRAFFIC MANAGER 8735

Tickets were simple on the old Sandy River and the Franklin & Megantic. After the consolidation into the Sandy River & Rangeley Lakes a hint of bigger business crept in and your ticket was only good for thirty days!

announcing the occasion, commented: " . . . The first train arrived with sixteen passengers and a Frenchman."

There was truth in those allegations that you could build a Lilliput railroad for peanuts. When the Sandy River was finished, and folks counted the miles and their money, they found—as Mansfield had told 'em—that 2-foot construction was far less expensive than wider gauges. Excepting iron, the bill for ties, grading, and labor was only $1,500 a mile. And this included the cost of building those 74 trestles.

There were passenger stations at Strong and at Phillips. They were big frame affairs, once popular in northern States, with doors at either end through which the main line ran. The joint station at Farmington was practically identical. The doors were usually kept shut except at train time. Then they would be swung open and the whole train would clank in. While it isn't on record, we can imagine the yawning depot was murky with smoke, betimes. Something like the sprawling trainsheds of today. Or should we say, of yesterday?

These covered depots were popular in those yesterdays, in New England, anyway. One later served the town of Kingfield, when the Lilliput had expanded that far. I believe, too, that Rangeley had one, when its time came.

At Phillips was the little road's enginehouse, shop, toolhouse, woodshed, and its general office. These terminal buildings, or successors to them, stayed at Phillips until the end, 56 years later.

George Mansfield, in spite of his promotional prowess and genius, didn't seem to climb higher on the railroad ladder that promoting the two-footers and holding small supervisory jobs with them. He had lately been General Manager of the few-miled, short-lived Billerica & Bedford. Now he was superintendent of the more-miled, longer-lived Sandy River. But he was its train conductor, too. A position of a different color than the decorous title *superintendent* implies today!

A year or so later, in 1881 or '82, Mansfield dropped out of the Lilliput picture, Sandy River-wise. With his passing Nathaniel Beal assumed his job as train conductor. He also became President. In those balmy days of sweat and callouses there was a closer relation between *officers* and *employees*. Probably it depended on whether you caught him running his train or presiding over a board meeting. This close relation may have had something to do with the Lilliput prosperity which followed.

At Farmington, where the Lilliput tied up with the *wide* gauge Maine Central's Farmington branch, several diamond crossings boosted the narrow gauge over the *wide* gauge tracks and into the trainshed and the yard. That first winter, 1879, while iron diamonds were on order, wooden crossovers were used. They were rough.

The first accident of any importance on the new Sandy River happened on one of them, if ancient yarns are to be credited. This smashup nearly ended the activities of No. 1 Hinckley and her engineer, one Dan Huff.

Trains dropping down to the Farmington covered depot, so this particular yarn is told, had to get rid of the engine first. A brakeman would pull the pin on the tank, the engine shot ahead over one of the crossovers and out of the way into the yard. Then, the brakeman dropped off, threw a switch, and the passenger cars gravitated across the other crossover and into the station, the conductor winding on the old hand brake. This particular day, according to the yarn as told by Nathaniel Beal's son Fred, Engineer Dan Huff, late off the New York & New England, widened on the throttle to shoot ahead of the passenger cars. The galloping little engine teetered onto the old wooden diamond. There, she stubbed her toe. Over she went, into the cindery bosom of Mother Earth, all eight wheels in the air. Conductor Mansfield quickly set the hand brakes, dropped off his passenger car, and dashed over to the upside-down engine. Dan Huff was just crawling out. Seeing Mansfield he roared, "There's yer little jackrabbit, flat on her back!"

This was probably the Sandy River's third wreck. The first was a minor derailment the day of the grand opening, November 20. A week after that one, a work train upset a flatcar which snarled with a misplaced tie.

Sandy River *Old Star,* 2nd No. 3, and finally S.R.&R.L. No. 16. Built by Baldwin for a South Carolina lumber road, the Laurel River & Hot Springs, she was brought north in 1893 first to the embryo Wiscasset & Quebec (which couldn't pay for her) and then to the Sandy River, which did pay for her, quickly. Called *Old Star* because of a big star on her front number plate, she spent most of her days on the F.&M.

In 1907, a year before the Consolidation, the Sandy River bought No. 8 Prairie type from Baldwin. She was the first of this wheel arrangement. The photo shows her as new with builder's striping and paint. The next year she was renumbered S.R.&R.L. 19, which she stayed until the end 27 years later. The 19 had a copper firebox and fluesheets, and was an excellent steamer.

Here's a rare old shot taken at Strong, about 1890. It's No. 3 with a southbound passenger train, on the grade just south of Strong yard. The building in back is the old "covered" depot. F.&M. No. 1 is switching this side of the station. No. 3's train appears to be a passenger extra, as the absence of a baggage car disqualifies it as a regular train.

You may date this picture to suit yourself. It shows a Lilliput boxcar, opposite Phillips depot, being loaded by the courtesy of Old Dobbin. The track in the center is the main line, northbound, toward Rangeley. Years before, a rambling, covered station enclosed this track, and station men had to swing open the huge doors to let trains come in or highball through.

In years to come many wrecks beset the Lilliputs, but no more per train mile than wider gauges had. And, with far less gory results. No passenger was ever killed directly as a result of a wreck, and very few employees.

In the next few years the Sandy River had its ups and downs in other ways, too. Broadly speaking, the Sandy River Railroad was a paying proposition from the start. It was destined shortly to be one of the few American railroads to operate on less than 55 per cent of its gross earnings!

Business didn't develop into voluminous tonnage, measured by today's vaunted standards. But for 70 and 75 years ago a lot of traffic clattered over the midget railroad which George Mansfield had lately lugged up from Massachusetts.

Lumber, pulpwood, bark, and other products of wood such as spools, matches, and dowels, were the biggest outbound items. Inbound came merchandise, tools and machinery, coal and perishables, and feed. Passengers were a source of copious income. Headend business, express and mail, while not earning today's high rate, were another dipperful in the bucket.

When city folks saw the handful of passenger cars in a Lilliput terminal they thought that 2-foot gauge passenger business was less than nothing. Only half a dozen coaches for the whole Sandy River! There was where they got left. The Lilliput's few coaches and fewer headend cars compared favorably with freight equipment. If a hundred freight cars could serve several thriving towns, so could three or four coaches. Remember the Pennsy's 5,000 passenger train cars balance its 170,000 pieces of freight equipment! So it was with the two-footers. They hauled passengers, and made money on 'em.

Another shameful fallacy, popular in the slim gauges' latter days, was that transferring freight from wide to narrow cars was a crippling expense. It wasn't. Any expense is growlworthy, but transferring freight wasn't the major item some standard gauge jingoists howled it to be. Today every scrid of express, mail and L.C.L. freight is transferred plenty of times. Intercity routes, like New York to Chicago are different; through cars are made up to run non-stop between those points. But for every one of those through routes there are still a hundred which don't rate through cars. A bag of mail or shipment of freight from New Orleans to Boston will probably be transferred from one car to another a dozen times. The bulk of such traffic, even in this enlightened day and age, has to "break gauge" just as it did in the days of Lilliput trains. It costs as much, relatively speaking, to handle these transfers today as it did in those yesterdays of "inefficient non-standard railroads." Yet, the bets are a dozen to nothing you've never heard this current subject mentioned before! It made a difference who was handling the megaphone.

One thing *was* more expensive. The small capacity engines and cars. A 2-foot boxcar 26 feet long, six feet wide and 5 feet, 8 inches high, inside measurements, had a cubic capacity of about 900 feet. A 40 foot standard car of today has some 3900 cubic feet. Today's boxcar boasts a capacity of 50 tons. The 2-footer's was fifteen.

Then a Lilliput engine which weighed 25 tons, hauling 8 to 10 loads up 4 per cent grades wasn't hauling ton-miles at the low figure our present *wide* gauge railroads do. A four man crew (working for half size wages) did well to handle a hundred and fifty revenue tons from Farmington to Phillips. Had the Sandy River been *wide* gauge those men could have hauled four or five hundred pay tons.

However, a big wide gauge engine would have cost five times as much to build. She would have chewed up five times more coal with that same train. Heavy track—big rail, big ties, big spikes and fishplates, and twice as much ballast—for the standard size trains wouldn't have been laid for any $1,500 a mile.

The midget Sandy River trains hauled all the freight the area had to offer. The vaunted standard gauge couldn't have done any more. Freight rates couldn't have been boosted to offset the multiplied expenses. Therefore, the Lilliput survived where the *wide* gauge would have dumped its full-fed fire.

Another thing: the Lilliputs, like most narrow gauges, ran where wider tracks would have been hard put to find a toe-hold. If the Sandy River had been made standard gauge, without making costly line relocations, only small engines and short trains could have negotiated its sharp curves and toboggan grades. So, as a *wide* gauge its tonnage would have been reduced to a ton-mile figure similar, in the final analysis, to the bantam gauge.

George Mansfield was right. His two-footers could be built and operated at a cost not much more than the interest charges would have been for the standard plant. Yet, from occult quarters there was beefing and griping about the inefficiency of the narrow gauge, its small capacity, its ton-mile comparison, and the bugaboo of transferring freight.

The Sandy River, in its later years, paid an average of approximately 40 cents a ton—two cents a hundred pounds—for labor at the Farmington transfer! How far would that expense have gone toward paying the difference between building, equipping, and running a *wide* gauge railroad? These boogy-woogies were the good and valid "reasons" for which the Lilliputs, and all narrow gauges, were damned.

In the earlier days, before efficiency was cooked up by some smart men and when people needed railroads of any shape and width they could get, the Lilliputs were considered satisfactory, and even advantageous. They did all the business a wide gauge could have done and did it at half the cost. They made money. They made friends, too, which today doesn't matter so much. Those bantam railroads of the 1880's and 1890's didn't bow to anything. They were as good as the best.

The general picture on the Sandy River didn't change much in the first few years of its life. More cars were added. Another woodshed was built for the big-stacked little woodburning engines, and some track improvements made. One by one those 78 wooden trestles were filled or replaced with iron girders. Then, in 1883, pleasing rumors were in the breeze. Baby clothes appeared, so to speak. A brother railroad was to be born. The *Franklin & Megantic.*

It was winter in Strong, and the trains from the F.&M. and from Phillips waited side by side while their baby Baldwins were down the yard doing something or other. The ball signal indicated whether main line trains or trains off the F.&M. had the right of way into the yard. Several times a mixup let two trains in at once—with a loud bang!

Looking south approaching Salem. The long Salem Turnout was just behind us. The neat station is a house today. Legend says that in the early days there was a covered station here, and one day the agent forgot to open its doors; the train went right through, doors and all! This photo, made in April 1935, shows how the snow hates to leave in the Spring, up in Maine!

9

FRANKLIN & MEGANTIC RAILROAD

Ever since George Mansfield had hustled up from Billerica, tongues had buzzed about midget extensions to this town and that one. Rangeley wanted a railroad. So did Kingfield. Several more places joined in the wishing. Now, Kingfield was to get one.

The birth of the Franklin & Megantic Railroad was attended by less excitement than the Sandy River or the Billerica & Bedford enjoyed. The sensational advent of those bantams had caused a certain maturity to infiltrate the aspiring townsmen. By 1883 Franklin County was ready to build railroads on the coattails of the bustling, flourishing Sandy River. Thus the Franklin & Megantic came into the world.

The F.&M., as it was always called, unreeled its 14½ miles of 25-pound rail as rapidly as the B.&B. Hinckleys had chased the Shanahans five years before.

Construction began in 1884. Leaving the Sandy River at Strong, Maine, it climbed sharp grades and nosed around scenic curves on its ascent to Salem, 8 miles, and to Kingsfield, 14.6 miles. There was even one stretch of 5 per cent near The Summit!

Shortly beyond Salem the Mount Abram Branch switched off. The Mountain Branch, as they called it, was just shy of two miles long and, as its name implied, it ran up to the base of Mount Abram. Logs were its meat. It fed carloads of them to the F.&M. for many years, until the mountain was stripped of every tree which would be big enough to log for fifty years. In the early 1900's the Mountain Branch was taken up.

From Mount Abram Junction to Kingfield the F.&M. followed a more reasonable terrain. It was anything but flat country, but with easier grades and curves.

Generally, the F.&M. was even more rugged than the Sandy River. There weren't so many trestles but its curves were tighter and the grades maybe a bit more sharp. Its scenery surpassed the captivating Sandy River trackorama.

Whereas the Sandy River had been fortunate prosperitywise the F.&M. never reached the point of physical or revenue impeccability. It was usually broke. The track was rough. There was no money to make the improvements the Sandy River had made. Yet, the little F.&M. railroaded heroically and was respected and loved by its townsfolk and neighbors as much as its older brother.

During the Lilliput era there were several seasons of extension talk.

The first concerned the possibilities and advisabilities of building a railroad to be called the Franklin & Somerset (after the two counties it would traverse), from South Strong east to North New Portland. And an extension of this road, to be named the Anson & New Portland Railroad, would continue from the F.&S. still farther east to Anson, connecting there with the *wide* gauge Somerset Railroad.

Talk was all these lines ever amounted to. No eastward trains ever climbed the hills and bucked the snow out of Strong.

One of the F.&M.'s bugbears was snow. The Sandy River had plenty, too. But snow up on the F.&M. seemed to come oftener and faster and deeper, and packed down harder. At least, the F.&M. boys thought so. The Sandy River men might have admitted as much, too, because they usually had to go up with one of their own engines and dig the F.&M.'s two little pots out of drifts.

Deep drifts filled into the worst cuts fiendishly. From that first winter, 1884-85, the Lilliput trains were continually getting themselves lost in snowdrifts and having to be shoveled out by hand. Some of these occasions made railroad history in Franklin County.

One howling afternoon before yours or my day the mixed train blasted out of Strong, Kingfield bound, in a roaring blizzard. On its business end was the F.&M.'s total roster of motive power—both engines. And, a borrowed Sandy River engine made up a three-some. It lacked a much needed snowplow because that worthy piece of equipment was up home in Kingfield, 14½ miles and hundreds of snowdrifts away. Crunching behind the three snorting little engines were a coach, a baggage car, and a box car of horses, in the order named.

Shortly out of Strong the engineers unanimously decided they had too much train. They stopped, which wasn't difficult, and backed back to Strong, which must have been a herculean stunt in that tumbling snow. At Strong they set out the car of horses.

Making a fresh start, with the three engines and tonnage reduced by one-third, with the help of the newly broken drifts the little train did pretty well for a few blinding miles. They got up beyond Stubbs' Meadow.

Drifts, headwinds, and sub-zero temperatures made a progressively harder rail. Just short of The Summit a further reduction of tonnage was made. They dropped the baggage car. The three straining engines crawled up the twisting grades with only the coach and a few anxious passengers. The drifts were deeper. The wind raked down from Mount Abram. Speed slowed to a chuffing crawl. They stalled again.

This time the hapless passengers wallowed through hip-deep snow to the engines. They climbed into the three pint-sized cabs. Anything would go with the passengers by this time, if the engines would only go.

That must have been a humdinger of a trip. Twelve hours after leaving Strong, in a dawn black with whirling snow, the three Lilliput engines broke through the last drift and clanked into King-field. Local history doesn't record what the weary survivors said. Probably nothing. They were lucky to be survivors.

When this kind of snow blankets the track, whether narrow or *wide,* it usually means shoveling. Snow had to be shoveled in those days, up two or three levels. Men with big wooden snow-shovels dug the stalled trains out. Drifts were deeper than a man could sling a shovelful of snow. They would toss it up as far as their reach and the wind would allow, and more men, perched on the sides of the drift, would shovel it up from there. More than once, when the road was shoveled clear, drifts would be higher than the tops of the smokestacks. The Sandy River old-timers told me of a time, years ago on the F.&M., when the shovelers laid a long plank across the top of one of these snow-cuts, and a bantam train puffed under, with room to spare!

So, that was why the train from Strong was twelve hours running to Kingfield that night.

The Lilliputs, however, were snow-eaters who eclipsed even their *wide* gauge cousins. More than once, after an all night blizzard, the "narrow gauge" would wallow into Farmington an hour late, to find the big Maine Central engines hadn't got through yet.

Maine winters used to cost the railroads a mint of money. Times have changed. The climate is milder, even though today that is hard to believe. We still crack the frosty joke that Maine has only two seasons—winter and August.

The F.&M.'s two dinky engines were named. Hinckley No. 1, built in 1884, was the *V. B. Mead,* named for a strong-man backer. The Baldwin No. 2, of 1886 vintage, was the *S. W. Sargent,* who was also a gentleman of position. The *Sargent* was the first of a long line of Lilliput Baldwins. She was also the first of the many tiny engines with outside frames and cranks. This innovation, frames and supports outside the driving-wheels, made them steadier and less disposed to slat around — to *oscillate,* as George Mansfield would say.

These two engines were the only ones the F.&M. ever had. When they needed help, which seems to have been often, they hired a Sandy River engine. The Sandy River's *Old Star,* a Mogul, was used so much up there she was often called "the F.&M. Mogul." While F.&M. power stayed at home the line was often cluttered with engines from Phillips.

According to the old train and engine men whom I knew, the road's passenger train equipment, from first to last, was one bag-

The Franklin & Megantic's second engine, built by Baldwin two years after the F.&M. opened, was
this little outside-frame Forney, *S. W. Sargent,* No. 2. Years later, for a reason lost in her wood
smoke, she had her number set ahead, becoming the No. 3, with a coal burner's straight stack.
No. 2 was the first Lilliput engine with outside frames, and maybe the first one on any narrow gauge.

No. 9 and the F.&M. mixed job in Salem Turnout, waiting to cross the southbound railbus in 1935.
The station is a few rail-lengths behind the combination car. If it were not for those white birches
you could see Mount Abram looming behind the engine, 4,049 feet in the sky. Just beyond this
point the Mount Abram Branch once switched off for its two-mile length to a lumber mill at the
foot of the mountain.

They had snow on the F.&M. They also had *Old Star,* the Sandy River's 2nd No. 2. *Old Star* spen so much time on the F.&M. that she was often called "the F.&M. Mogul." In this picture she started to chase a snowplow off, and was stopped just in time. The man standing in the foregroun was Supt. Vose, father of Orris Vose who later became super' of the S.R.&R.L. system.

One of the steepest grades on the Franklin County roads was this stretch of 5 per cent, on th F.&M. between Strong and Salem. Railroad men could do nothing about Maine topography, bu they certainly did keep their Lilliput track in good ballast and line. This picture was taken on a few weeks before abandonment, in 1935.

n engine and 7 cars tipped over, and not a window cracked! By a slip of the ball signals, Engine o. 7 and a southbound train collide with an F.&M. train, both entering Strong Yard together. hen the two engines met, the No. 7's cowcatcher doubled under her, letting her pivot on it long ough to tip over against the bank. She twisted every passenger car over with her! Just part of the day's work. July 8, 1916.

ne day in the early 1920's they had No. 20 on the passenger train. She was whooshing into rong, Farmington-bound, when her head drivers caught the point of the F.&M. frog. The long- ited Forney couldn't decide whether to go to Farmington or to Kingfield. So, she split the difference—and the switch.

An F.&M. passenger train approaches Kingfield Station, up the stub-end spur from the mainlin
switch. Kingfield is, and was, mainly a lumber town, with novelty mills, dowel mills, and othe
sawmills as the backbone of its economy.

The new station in Kingfield. The old covered depot burned one night, singeing the roof off a
passenger car which was inside. This station, built around the 1920's, became a store when th
railroad went out. The 3-stall enginehouse is just beyond, to the left. Kingfield Yard was on a
short spur off the main line, which was half a mile back to the right.

gage car, a combination, and possibly one or two coaches. Coaches, like engines, were borrowed when business looked promising. No one could say positively that the coaches on F.&M. trains didn't carry *Sandy River Railroad* in gold-leaf on their name-panel. In fact, from along in the 1890's the Franklin County Lilliputs were pretty much owned by the same money. Some connoisseurs of railroad lore stick out their necks by declaring that, by order of the local Wall Streeters, the Sandy River might pay for a new coach which sported the Franklin & Megantic's name. I never found any verification of this from old records or chats with superannuated personnel. And, what does it matter? The F.&M. had passenger cars enough so they could leave baggage cars and coaches sitting in snowdrifts, while herding passengers into engines to ride.

Likewise sparse was its freight equipment. Again, like most shortlines, it used the boxcars and flats of its fortunate neighbors. Some faded old photos show an F.&M. caboose. The rickety old buggy looks suspiciously like the onetime B.&B. boxcar, which Mansfield brought to the fledgling Sandy River.

Stationwise, like the Sandy River so did the F.&M. have two agency stations. Salem, and Kingfield. Kingfield's vintage depot was covered, like those on the Sandy River. In my day the station at Salem was a modern, neat combination building suggesting fairly recent design. Maybe a covered depot served villageless Salem in the early days too. Just north of Salem depot was the long meeting track, Salem Turnout.

Kingfield was a bigger town. It had a main street, and stores, and an elegant hotel. It's all still there, although I mentioned it in the past tense. There are several wood-working mills, too. The old covered depot sat at the southwest edge of the village, with the 3-stall enginehouse and the carshed handy by. The usual team track, runaround, and storage tracks were near, with one or two spurs leading to the mills.

There were a number of woods siding along the line where logs, lumber and pulpwood were loaded. The point where the Mount Abram branch joined the main stem was a place of several names. In early days it was Oliver's Mills. Then it was Mount Abram

Junction. When the Mountain Branch was no more, the point became North Freeman. At Hillside, six miles up from Strong, a siding and a small but neat passenger shelter composed the railroad atmosphere. A mile beyond at The Summit, a watertank, siding, and a sizable pile of cinders made a really pretty scene, in its rustic, forest setting. The cinders, accumulated after the days of wood, were blown from the non-clearing front ends of engines, while the firemen were taking water. As the name suggested, The Summit was at the top of the hill.

The F.&M., again like the Sandy River, was originally laid with 25-pound rail. While Dame Fortune never cuddled the little F.&M. to her bosom as she did the other line, nevertheless the little road managed to relay with heavy 35-pound steel a decade or so later.

Rail weighing 35-pounds to the yard was pretty much the standard for Lilliput railroads. A few, like the Kennebec Central, never relayed the original 25-pound. Others, like the Sandy River and the Wiscasset roads, put some 56 and 60-pound into their spindling track. The 35 was usually ample for the small trains and to their final days two-thirds of all the Lilliput mileage was still laid with it.

As most railroad men know, the weight of rail isn't the only factor controlling track in relation to traffic. Solid well-tamped ties are an important factor. Ballast is an important item. Good workmanship is a big help. When ballast is thin or dirty the track is pretty likely to slide out of line, and its gauge will spread. This was one of the F.&M.'s troubles.

The old boys used to tell how this poor-ballast rough-track pestilence was cured, back in the rough-and-ready days. When the F.&M. was a stripling of twelve or fifteen years of age it came under the control of a Gardiner, Maine, banker. Like most bankers, especially Downeasters, he hated to spend a nickel. His F.&M. railroad was rough and hard-riding. The engines and trains *oscillated* something fierce. The new boss wouldn't authorize a penny to reballast the track. Finally, so much hollering reached his ears, and made 'em burn, that he announced he'd come up from Gardiner and see for himself. The boys got ready.

In order to properly show the old gentleman just how hard his track rode they selected the old rickety caboose for the presidential train. The caboose was not only a hellion to ride in, but it was pretty well shot besides. It never did fly to pieces, but no one was sure it wouldn't.

When the guest of honor was finally ensconced in the killer-caboose, the train highballed.

Yarnsters swore that long before the train plunged over The Summit he was lying flat on the heaving floor. That was partly, they explained, because no one could have stayed right-side-up, and partly because he was getting hell scared out of him at every turn of the 18-inch wheels. His several senses apparently advised him that the lower his center of gravity the better his chances of survival.

Anyway, the Special made it, and in record time. Official approval of betterments to roadway and track were unanimous, the story ended.

The Franklin & Megantic Railroad didn't seem to be as packed with color and roaring romance as its Sandy River neighbor, but what it lacked in that kind of appeal was compensated for in scenic splendor and steam-and-cinders railroading. Its midget trains hammered the tiny rail-joints, bucked Alpine snows, and fed its communities and its connecting line for nearly thirty years, before it finally lost its identity by a total merger with the other Franklin County Lilliputs. As for its extension farther into the northland wilderness, we'll come to that presently.

Breaking Ground For The New Railroad, they called this photo. While it shows the first day's work on the Phillips & Rangeley Railroad, in 1890, it could just as well be used for any of the others. The rocky Sandy River tumbles to the left, and the new grade they're digging is near the wooden covered bridge, leaving Phillips for Rangeley.

Maine wasn't a covered-bridge state. One of its few was this lengthy structure, built in 1890 to get the P.&R. Railroad out of Phillips and on its way. When it was dismantled in 1936 it was still solid. Its lumber was sold for local buildings. The track to the right swings into the old P.&R. yard and to the "Stone Fort," the original P.&R. roundhouse.

10

PHILLIPS & RANGELEY RAILROAD

While the Sandy River and the F.&M. were regaling the citizenry of Phillips, Kingfield, and adjacent regions with profitable rail service, the town of Rangeley was unhappy.

The Sandy River had stopped 29 miles short of Rangeley. The lakeside resort wanted its own railroad. George Mansfield had just the same as promised it one. Rangeley liked the idea of 2-foot gauge. Five years after the F.&M.'s conception and ten years after the Sandy River was built it began to look like Rangeley was coming into its own. A Rangeley railroad began shaping up.

Some Massachusetts lumber barons were behind it. Massachusetts seemed to be the guiding genius behind the Lilliputs. In order to open their timberland holdings north of Phillips these Bay Staters needed a railroad. The local folks were ready and willing to help. In 1889 they chartered the Phillips & Rangeley Railroad.

Naturally it was two-foot gauge.

Ground was broken that same year. Grading crews and steel gangs inched out of Phillips to lay 28.6 miles of as pretty railroad as ever delighted a railroad fan's eye—or the curves and hills of which filled engineers' hearts with dread. It darted through terrain even rougher than the Sandy River's and the F.&M.'s. Alongside tumbling white-water streams and up tortuous 3 and 4 per cent grades the P.&R. climbed and wound through the billowing hills. The last rail clanged down into Rangeley in July, 1891.

73

It was on the P.&R. they laid the *big hill.* The Sandy River boys never spoke of it in those words, but *Sluice Hill* was the toughest, steepest, longest, crookedest of all the climbs on the Lilliput railroads. It began just west of Perham Junction, after two miles of steady 2 per cent had knocked steam down on the hard-working little engines. From its beginning Sluice Hill twisted and climbed and grunted nearly a thousand feet toward the clouds at a fairly steady 4 percent. At the top a long siding was carved out of Mother Nature's buttocks where panting engines could kick off a few cars of their train and careen back toward Perham Junction for some more. Freights often went over Sluice Hill in three or four pieces. In the later days of big engines and heavier loads the boys considered four freight cars and the buggy to be tonnage up the big little hill. One engine, with a good engineer and a better fireman (and all the P.&R. crews were good and better) could switch and slat five or six passengers cars up, and make Rangeley on time.

When the P.&R. was begun, in late 1889, it needed an engine. The Sandy River obligingly handed over its little No. 2 Hinckley, one of the tiny 12-tonners which George Mansfield had toted up from Billerica, Massachusetts. She was sort of a pint-sized boomer. First she'd been the Billerica & Bedford's *Puck.* Next she'd become the Sandy River No. 2. Then to the Phillips & Rangeley R.R. The tiny Forney wasn't called No. 1 on the P.&R., for some reason. She was always the *Bo-peep.* Within a year or two, when the P.&R. had got organized and had taken delivery of two Baldwins and a Portland engine, the number 4 appeared on the Hinckley's cab and nose. But she was still the *Bo-peep.*

Old records make it seem that the P.&R. ordered, or numbered, its new engines without much rhyme or reason. In 1891 two engines were delivered to them, new. The No. 1 *Calvin Putnam,* named for one of the Massachusetts big-wig lumber barons who built the railroad, and the No. 3, a big Baldwin Mogul, which, according to her builder's plate, saw the first light-of-day in March that year, 1891. Her construction number was 11706 and her name was *George M. Goodwin,* another of the Bay State's nobility.

Aboard for Farmington! A P.&R. train, headed by P.&R. *Calvin Putnam,* No. 1, is ready to leave Rangeley, in the late 1890's. The R.P.O.-Express car, next to the engine, later became S.R.&R.L. No. 8, and continued to carry a Railway Mail Clerk until about World War I, when the route was abolished. Plenty of spit-and-polish on this engine and cars!

There was lots of snow in those 28½ miles between Phillips and Rangeley. Here the little *Calvin Putnam,* or maybe the *Bo-peep,* stops her passenger train to show the cameraman just how deep that snow really is. The train was southbound toward Phillips, and the location is Johnson's Mountain, a few miles north of Phillips. Note the vacuum brake dingus atop the engine's cab.

Passenger train at Marbles, ready to leave for Farmington. The date wasn't far from 1895, and P.&R. No. 2 engine, the *Isaac Walton,* is as clean as a whistle. A Sandy River coach and a P.&R. combination will be easy wheeling for the 28-ton Baldwin. It looks like early Spring or late Fall, which probably accounts for the paucity of passengers and no steamboats in sight. It isn't the tourist season.

Sandy River No. 4 and the *Rangeley Express,* in the hole at Phillips for a 1900 meet. The Express, making three round trips daily Farmington to Rangeley, ran the 46½ miles in two hours running time. Fast running for a Forney engine through 16 degree curves and over 4 per cent hills! It was for these crack trains the elegant parlor car *Rangeley* was built in 1901.

This is the bridge built in 1890 to replace one which the wind blew down. On the Sandy River's main line a mile south of Phillips, it crossed the Sandy river at a point called "The Salmon Hole." From the Salmon Hole Bridge to Phillips was the piece of track they laid by firelight, to get the railroad into Phillips by November 20, 1879.

The 16 engine and the big 23 locked horns one day, at the north end of Phillips yard. The 16 got the worst of it. She was coming down from Rangeley with a freight, the 23 was switching. The 16's fireman was down fixing his fire and the engineer, Dana Aldrich, couldn't see around the curve. The man running the 23, Dana Walker, was looking back at switching signals and didn't see the freight train arriving. So, here's how it came out. The 16's pilot seems to be about the only damage.

Dana Aldrich spilled this plow train near Dead River Station in the late 1890's. Ice on the rail. Dana was pinned in the cab while live steam from a broken pipe whistled past his ear 'til the boiler was emptied. While he waited under the Sandy River No. 4 Mrs. Aldrich was presenting him with a baby boy—who later was a fireman, and in a wreck himself.

Here we see luckless Sandy River No. 4 in the ditch again. Engineer Guy Everett was hoofing the Rangeley-bound passenger train a bit too fast, with this result. Apparently the cars oscillated a little too much, and all four of them landed on their rumps. As usual, no one was hurt. Engineer Everett then went to the Maine Central, retiring thirty years later with a right-side-up record.

The *Goodwin* was the very first departure from the Forney engines which had powered Lilliput trains since 1877. She was a Mogul. She was the second engine on the Franklin County roads, and the third of all the Lilliputs to have outside frame. The little F.&M. No. 2 *S. W. Sargent,* 1886, was the first. In 1890 another Lilliput, the Kennebec Central, had one similar to the *Sargent* built. The P.&R.'s *George M. Goodwin* came in third on the outside frame deal. The *Goodwin* was also the heaviest of any Lilliput engine yet built. Her 23½ tons weight and 13x16-inch cylinders put her in a class comparable to the Erie's *Matt Shay* in the matter of heft and wallop.

Whether or not this baby leviathan was Baldwin's first effort in slim gauge engines with outside frames, except for the Forney types, I don't know. She was the first on the Lilliputs, anyway.

That gave the P.&R. three engines. In March, 1893, Baldwin built the fourth. This engine, the *Isaac Walton* No. 2, was a Forney with outside frames, but she differed from her earlier sisters in weight. She weighed nearly 30 tons. And she was designated as a passenger engine.

As I said a minute ago, the numbering scheme doesn't add up. The No. 1 was all right, being built in 1891, although the little *Bo-peep* would have carried that number, you'd think. But the 1891 *Goodwin* being numbered 3, and the 1893 *Walton* being numbered 2, doesn't make much sense today. Especially, when the first P.&R. engine got the last number, 4.

All the P.&R. engine names were for Massachusetts big shots. Excepting the *Bo-peep.* There was no one in Massachusetts by that name.

The new P.&R. had a good supply of passenger cars. The old York, Pennsylvania car builders, Billmeyer & Small, built two coaches and two combination cars. These cars are worthy of mention because they were a little off the regular Lilliput design. Instead of the regulation clerestory roofs they had rounding, arched roofs. Instead of being slung low to the rails, with a single step up to the platform, they were perched up like 3-foot cars, with two steps to the open-end platforms.

This two-step altitude was all right on 3-foot gauge cars but it made the Lilliput 2-footers *oscillate* like the Old Harry. They were shortly dropped down to standard Lilliput height—the car decks 30 inches above the rail.

A few boxcars, 70-odd flats, and some snow fighting equipment, completed the new railroad's rolling stock. The P.&R. didn't own a caboose for several years. Fifteen or twenty years later one of the combinations burned at Green's Farm, on the Eustis road, one night. Its trucks were used under the homemade caboose No. 12, which graced many a P.&R. freight train in later years.

A few years after building the passenger cars, Billmeyer & Small built an express-mail car for the P.&R., identical to the *wide* gauge counterparts, with a regulation Railway Post Office in one end. For years this car handled the Farmington & Rangeley R.P.O. route.

Like many points where one railroad connects with another, the junction at Phillips between the Sandy River and the P.&R. boasted ill-defined limits. You couldn't tell where one left off and the other began. The P.&R. simply started at the north end of the Phillips depot, and kept on going from there. Leaving Phillips village the P.&R. crossed the rollicking, boulder-strewn Sandy River through a long, covered bridge. It was one of the few covered railroad bridges in Maine. When it was dismantled, incidentally, in 1936, its native timbers were still sound and stout enough to bring a good price from local building material suppliers.

Just across the river was the P.&R.'s yard. There were a number of tracks for switching and storage, and a granite roundhouse called "the Old Stone Fort."

Over Johnson's Mountain, five miles from Phillips, was Madrid Station. In Maine they pronounce it with a "short" A, and the accent on the first syllable: *Ma*-drid. Madrid was an agency station for years. It sat in a big, half-circle curve, where the ascending track went half-way around Toothacher Pond. The Berlin Mills Company had one of its huge sawmills here.

After twisting up the curvaceous Devil's Elbow the track dropped sharply down to Reed's Station, another one-time agency. From

Reed's it was steady 2 percent up through Sander's and Perham Junction to the foot of Sluice Hill.

Sanders was a boom town. Then a ghost town. Fifty and more years ago, as old photos show, it was a sizable sawmill village. Houses, store, barns, a sprawling boarding house, and the railroad station and freight house. A big steam sawmill dominated the village. Business boomed. Lumber went out in carloads. Then, the last tree was cut, and folks started packing. A fire broke out, and that was the last of. Sanders. A small, neat flag station was built on the site. Ever after the charred timbers and rusted machinery were hidden by a verdant second-growth of hardwood.

There were frequent wood's sidings. Then Sluice Hill. Finally, after another brisk climb, there was Redington, another ghost town. Redington had been like Sanders, with a mill and houses, barns, depot, and a Post Office. Redington even had an enginehouse once. Instead of being wiped out by fire, Redington just fell into decay. The first automobile to enter Redington was after the railroad had been dismantled. The old grade, bulldozed smooth and wider, was the first road to come into Redington. It's a private road, but you can drive in there today. In the railroad's time you went by train, or walked.

Leaving Redington the track streaked across "Redington Straight", a mile long tangent where little trains used to make up time. Camp Eight was out beyond, then Eustis Junction. Eustis Junction didn't come into existence for a dozen or thirteen years after the P.&R. was built, but it was a busy junction point after 1904.

Dallas was a flag stop, and Dead River Station was where stages and buckboards from the back country met the scurrying passenger trains.

It was near Dallas, shortly after the P.&R. was completed, that a Frenchman fresh out of the woods, saw his first railroad train. He was snowshoeing to Rangeley and came onto the new railroad near Dallas. The snowshoeing was hard work. The freshly plowed and flanged railroad track looked better. He shipped his snowshoes and loped along the hard packed flangeway.

A westbound passenger train frisked up behind him. It was the woodsman's first look at a train. The whistle screamed. He looked over his shoulder. The belching smoke, the plume of steam from the *peeping* whistle, and the threatening aspect of the monster bearing down on him scared the man into a brisk run. The train kept at his heels, whistling angrily. At Dead River Station someone yanked him off the track, and the train clattered by.

"Why didn't you get off the track?" he was asked.

"Whew! If I'd left that good footing the damn thing she catched me sure!"

Between Dead River Station and Rangeley one more flag stop, Gull Pond, or "The Hole-in-the-Fence", completed the P.&R.'s way stations. There were other wood sidings where the trains would stop. But these were the stations which had, or had once had, some importance.

Then Rangeley. Rangeley is a pretty village, half commercial, half summer resort. Each facet of the town's character is intermingled enough so its main street and residential byways seem well blended. The bustling frontier spa lounges on the east end of the Lake. The P.&R. came in from the east and had its terminal on the eastern edge of the village. There was a fair-sized, rambling yard. A 3-stall enginehouse with the turntable in front, the coal shed, and some old cars used for sleeping quarters for lay-over crews, sat at the yard's entrance. The depot was at the west end, on the north-south village street.

Loosely speaking, the 35-pound rails stopped at the gutter. (In those days there was no curb.) Actually, however, the narrow track crossed the street and the spacious lawn of Marble's hotel, to terminate under the shadow of the big 3-story building. There was a small, turreted stone station there, the hotel's very own, *Marble's*. It's still there, today, serving as a shelter for the guests who enjoy the lakefront and the boats.

Fifty years and more ago the Lilliput's varnished trains hauled from the Rangeley depot, across the street and lawn to Marble's, to disgorge the parlor-car elite, almost into their swanky hotel suites.

Here on the Phillips table is old P.&R. No. 2, the *Isaac Walton*, as S.R.&R.L. No. 17, equipped with a new and bigger boiler. This rebuilding boosted her weight to some 30 tons. Although a Forney type without pony wheels, the 17 wasn't as hard on track as her long-gaited, slightly heavier Eustis R.R. cousins, the 20, 21 and 22. But Forneys had a way of knocking track out of gauge, as old section men will grumblingly tell you.

A brisk nor'west tail-wind helps the 16 and her passenger job make time to Farmington. Bound from Rangeley with a passenger train (that boxcar is for express) the 16 engine is wheeling across the sheathed trestle at Fairbanks, three miles short of her destination. The date about 1920. Except for that wind blowing faster than the train was going, a long plume trailing back over the train would have made a bang-up action photo.

S.R.&R.L. coach 20, one of the former P.&R. cars built by Billmeyer & Small of York, Penn. The odd roof distinguished the four Phillips & Rangeley cars from those of connecting lines. When these cars were new they rode several inches higher, with two steps to the platform instead of one. This car now hauls passengers on the Edaville Railroad.

Outside she looks like just another coach. Inside, however, appearances were different. Parlor car *Rangeley* No. 9 was lush with "Victorian splendor," an equal to anything on wider gauge rails. The porter who came up from New York and Washington on the overnight Pullman trains finished his run to Rangeley whisking tuxedos and milady's velvet aboard this product of Jackson & Sharpe Car Company.

Here we are, westbound, puffing slowly over the top of Sluice Hill, climbing up to Rangely. Sluice Hill's three miles of 3 and 4 per cent, plus curves of 12 to 16 degrees, was the hardest pull any of the Lilliputs had. Four freight cars was a load for an engine climbing up. Plenty of brakes was a *must* dropping down the hill.

Baldwin photo of P.&R. No. 2, the *Isaac Walton* at time of construction.

Redington. Kind of a magic name in the rugged Franklin County hills. Until the passing of the railroad Redington could be entered or left only by train—or by a long walk. Freighthouse and depot are on your right. An enginehouse and turntable were once to your left. The big haybarn in the distance fed the many horses which once yarded logs for the big Redington sawmill.

This was Rangeley's new depot, built after the old covered depot had burned. As a bakery, it burned again a few years ago. Out of sight beneath the tar, the rails once crossed the street to the spacious lawn of the big hotel, which boasted a station of its own, Marbles.

Builder's photo of S. R. Baldwin No. 16, to become No. 8 in the S.R.&R.L. consolidation. Builder's records give this inside-framer No. 31826, while the builder's plate in the photo shows No. 31816. Explanations have been lost with the railroad.

Posed for delivery picture is the outside frame Baldwin No. 23754. She went to the Eustis as No. 8, and on to the S.R.&R.L. as No. 21.

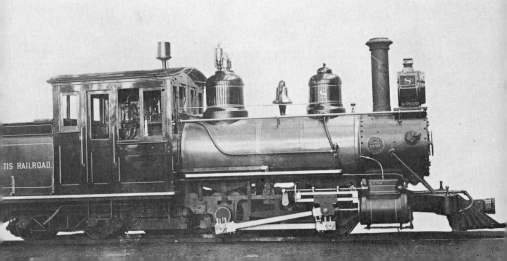

The twenty-ton S.R.&R.L. No. 18, once the Sandy River's second No. 2, steams out of the woods and around a well ballasted curve. Date unknown, place unknown, but from the quiet crew on the flats behind it looks to be near the end of her days.

Marbles Station, looking east toward the Rangeley depot, twenty rail-lengths away. Many a nabob of the Gay Nineties detrained at Marbles for a costly vacation on the Rangeley Lakes chain. Steamers left the wharf at your left, for miles-away points on the big, forest rimmed lake. Today the little stone depot is a boathouse at the hotel.

Coming into Rangeley. The main line ran straight in front of you, the bungalow station being the gray-green building to the left. The bunkcars near the enginehouse were early P.&R. and Sandy River passenger cars. Today a big oil distributor has the old yards filled with storage tanks, the enginehouse has gone, as has the picturesque station.

High water was no obstacle when a Lilliput log train was on the move. Here we see Davenport Flat flooded by a Spring freshet, and a Eustis log train sloshing east to the lumber mills. The date could be around 1910 and the location is about four miles north of Phillips, on the P.&R. main line.

A P.&R. mixed train lets Mrs. Dill off at Madrid Station, around the turn of the century. Caboose 12 had just been built from the bones of a P.&R. combination car which burned one night on the Eustis road. A log "bunk" is seen in the foreground. Madrid Station, five miles north of Phillips, was a busy place in those days, with the big Berlin Mills Co. sawmill going full blast. And Mrs. Dill wouldn't even smile for the photographer!

Yes, there was a Lilliput parlor-car. The *Rangeley* No. 9. This 8-wheeled elegance belonged to the old Sandy River Railroad, but she was always shared with the P.&R. from the time Jackson & Sharpe built her in 1901.

The *Rangeley* was built for the hotsy-totsy, genteel tourist trade. She was identical to those grown-up parlor-cars of Victorian times, excepting she was equipped with two sets of brakes—air and Eames vacuum, so whichever Lilliput engine happened to be hauling her could use whichever type of brakes that particular engine was equipped with. About that period some engines had air and some still had the older vacuum equipment.

She was a chair-car in miniature. Her 20-odd green plush swivel chairs, with a few leather upholstered seats in the smoking end, were comfort de luxe. The plate glass mirrors which studded the walls were a joy to behold. The baby dude-car was well worth the extra fare charged to ride in her.

The time was, in those Golden Days, when a porter who left New York City on the evening Pullman swapped over at Farmington next morning, and continued his vassaldom in pint-sized propriety to the very canopy of Marble's Hotel. The *Rangeley* was the only parlor car on the Lilliput railroads. One or two of the others had a coach which they called a parlor car, but it was not, in the real sense of the term.

It's a pity that George E. Mansfield couldn't have ridden those 46.7 miles on a high-stepping, two-hour train, and seen his Lilliput railroad at its best—even better than his fondest dreams had been. Those first 18 miles which George had built, from Farmington to Phillips, were beautiful, eye-catching miles. But like some other good things, the farther you went the prettier it got. The line from Phillips on to Rangeley, which Mansfield never saw, was prettier with every mile. The 46½ mile run was not only the most scenic, but it was the longest run on any of the Lilliput roads. The Sandy River's next longest was the Strong to Bigelow run, 30 miles.

Engineer Ed West shows no laughter in this picture! He's still shaky, perhaps, from the spill he's just taken on Engine 5, near Carrabasset with an F.&M. passenger train for Bigelow. Even if the Forney No. 5 did wipe the ubiquitous grin from Ed's face she wasn't damaged too much. A few hours later the train was on its way again, grinning at the mess she'd made!

A roaring lumber town—Bigelow, the upper end of the old F.&M. Today nothing remains at Bigelow, except woods, and memories. When this photo was taken, about 1904 or '05, the big steam mill was booming, freight trains were thick, and this little Portland Forney was making two round trips a day to Strong, 30 miles away. Bigelow petered out in the early 1920's, and track was cut back five miles to Carrabasset.

11

KINGFIELD & DEAD RIVER RAILROAD

To go back to the Franklin & Megantic a minute, right after the Phillips & Rangeley was built, the owners of the F.&M. organized a sister company to build track which was actually an extension of the F.&M. from Kingfield north. They dubbed it the Kingfield & Dead River Railroad.

The Kingfield & Dead River was opened from Kingfield to Carrabasset, 9 miles, in 1894. Its primary purpose was probably to open up new forest lands owned by the barons who had a finger in the railroad pies. There was also the hope that the expanding railroad would encourage colonization. Colonization would not only sell cut-over forest land for farms, but create new business for the railroads.

There were also notions extant in those years to build still further extensions. One of them would be built by the F.&M., as followed suit in the building of the K.&D.R., using that venerable midget as a springboard for leaps into the westering haze. It would flitter northwest into the Flagstaff and Dead River country, and maybe even sneak across the border into Canada. It eventually got as far as Bigelow, 15½ miles north of Kingfield and 30.1 miles north of Strong. That Strong-to-Bigelow road was the second longest piece of track on the Sandy River system.

Similar westward-ho projects were dreaming around on the P.&R. Extensions from Rangeley west to New Hampshire, and north into Eustis and Stratton, and the rather juvenile idea—which almost materialized—of wandering north and east to actually connect with its own tail—the F.&M.—at Bigelow. Such an extension would have amounted to a huge circle, around which Lilliput trains could have run in either direction, making a hundred mile run on the grand loop. Those dream railroads which puffed into the wide, blue yonders, did their puffing, for the most part, on paper.

The Kingfield & Dead River was a paper company. The F.&M. owned it. The F.&M. ran it. It never owned an engine nor a car. It had an agency station at Carrabasset, shared with the U.S. Post Office, and the agency at Bigelow. While the Kingfield-Carrabasset section was opened in 1894 it actually wasn't until 1900 that the additional six miles to Bigelow were built.

With the building of the K.&D.R. one branch came into being, the Alder Stream branch. Leaving the main line just north of Kingfield it ran 2½ miles west to a big lumber operation. It wasn't taken up until just before the first War.

Bigelow was another booming lumber town. In the early 1900's it boasted a sizable mushroom village. The neat little station, engine-house, and railroad yard faced the big day-and-night steam sawmill. Regular passenger trains ran for years from Bigelow to Strong, making connections there for Farmington and points beyond. The time was, for awhile, the parlor car *Rangeley* was hauled on these trains. Quite a sporting region developed in the wilderness beyond Bigelow, and the railroad used the *Rangeley* to promote it. An R.P.O. route also ran out of Bigelow, to Farmington, for a few years. In the other direction stage lines and buckboard teams sprayed out to the logging and sporting regions which made Bigelow a short-time bustling terminus.

The Lilliput system was growing. Now, instead of the pitiful 8 miles of Billerica & Bedford in 1877, now, 25 years later, the Franklin County system alone accounted for more than 80 miles, branches and all.

With the expansion in mileage so were bigger engines and larger cars designed.

And, in 1902 the P.&R. people chartered their Madrid Railroad.

The Madrid Railroad (remember to put the accent on the first syllable—*MA* drid) sprouted off the P.&R. just beyond Madrid

Watertank, or Madrid Junction as it came to be known. Running west a couple of miles to Brackett Junction the new road forked. The original construction bore to the left and went another four miles to a logging operation called No. Six. It was in Number Six Township, if I remember right. The right hand, or westerly, switch swung off through fairly level woodland through Madrid Village to several log yards—Littlefield's, Gray's Farm, and Sandy River— nine miles from Brackett Junction.

The Madrid Railroad was another paper company, which actually materialized. Like the K.&D.R., the Madrid was owned lock, stock and both barrels by the P.&R. It never owned anything but a few flatcars which carried its name. Engines, crews and know-how were all supplied by the parent Phillips & Rangeley.

As near as I could ever learn, no scheduled trains ever ran on the Madrid R.R. Times were when a freight train would run in there with supplies, with a combination car on the rear. Sometimes a solid passenger train clattered up to No. Six or through Madrid Village, loaded with woods-crews being taken in to the camps. No open stations were ever established on its 15 miles of road. The Madrid track was maintained to the best standards, and the 35-pound rail was in perfect alignment, to the day it was dismantled. That was Sandy River policy.

The next year after building their Madrid Railroad the P.&R. big shots chartered and built another, and the last, of their extension railroads, The Eustis.

The Eustis Railroad connected with the P.&R. 'way out near Dallas, some 22½ miles west of Phillips, at Eustis Junction.

The time was when Eustis Junction was a hustling railroad site. There was a wye where trains could come off the new line and run east to Phillips or west to Rangeley. An unusually attractive station sat in the wye, facing the main line and the east leg of the Eustis line. The Eustis' track was laid with the traditional 35-pound steel, and according to the Maine Railroad Commissioners' observation as well as my own, it was a stretch of railroad which did credit to its builders.

This road was through more level country. Tracks were straighter. There weren't the tortuous climbs and breath-taking views. It was through the woods. It streaked north 10½ miles to suddenly end at a clearing in the woods called Green's Farm. Green's Farm was the railhead for busy townships beyant and beyond.

For many years regular passenger trains ran on the Eustis Railroad. Some years they shuttled back and forth to Eustis Junction, connecting there with main line P.&R. trains. Other years they ran down to connect with the morning and the afternoon trains for Farmington, and as soon as that train had scuttled away from its wilderness stop, the Eustis train would squeal around the west leg of the wye and run into Rangeley. It would be back in Eustis Junction in time to connect with the Farmington to Rangeley job a couple or three hours later. Old timetables show the Eustis trains making as good running time as their vaunted P.&R. brothers.

One branch switched off the Eustis road at a point near Quill Hill. It ran about a mile into some lumber yards, and a gravel pit, known as Langtown.

Some interesting woods branches radiated from Green's Farm. There was one interesting one which didn't—the line projected to continue on through Stratton to Bigelow to tie up with the F.&M. for the grand loop.

The ones which did were made up of a line leaving Green's Farm at a switch known at different times as Coplin Junction and Stratton Junction. It was the little known Dago Branch. The Dago Branch was strictly a logging line although a common carrier. It ran two or three miles north from Green's Farm to Dago Junction. Here one line switched left and continued two or three miles to the Berlin Mills camps, only a mile or so from the P.&R. station of Redington, with Redington Mountain looming between. It was 22 miles to Redington by rail!

At Dago Junction the other line switched right, following the West Branch of Nash's Stream two miles and a half to Skunk Brook Camp, a logging operation as you might or might not guess from the colorful name.

ctionmen's trackcar and material trailer, at Carrabasset in early 1930's. This car is now in use
Edaville. At the Phillips shop the differential gears were removed and a straight axle installed,
1 which two facing ring-gears were fastened. When a lever moved the flexible pinion to mesh
ith one of these, the car's motion was ahead. When the pinion was thrown to mesh with the
other, the car's direction was reversed, all in transmission "high."

With Mount Bigelow scowling in the distance, the daily mixed train is poised to dash out of
arrabasset for her 30-mile run to Strong, and home to Phillips. Engineer Ed West grins from
e 24's right-hand side as he cracks her throttle for the start. The Carrabasset depot also served
the Post Office. Today, with the railroad and Carrabasset no more, woods have overgrown this
spacious scene.

Things were done the hard way on the Lilliputs. Coaling engines by hand, for instance. Every scrid of the coal used in the day's run had to be shovelled on the tank by the sweating crews. Here the 18 engine is being supplied with a ton and a half, which she used the next day on her 80 miles of Strong to Carrabasset running. The Lilliputs' small cylinders were easy on coal consumption.

It snowed last night, and was drifting bad up beyond Salem and Kingfield. So, the 24 and a full fledged plow train was ordered to clear the line. They had just got back to Strong when this photo was made, and were in to clear waiting for the passenger job so's they could jog home to Phillips— and a belated dinner. Jan., 1935.

For years the 35-pound rails sang and vibrated as log trains squirmed and smoked down the mountain to Green's Farm. Big trees and little ones were chained to log trucks, or *bunks*. These trains, which mostly ran at night, stopped at Green's Farm long enough for crews to inspect the teetering log bunks, to make sure they'd held together coming down the Dago Branch, then with a highball from a dim lantern they continued on down the Eustis road and over the P.&R. to the mills.

The reason the log trains were run at night was partly to lessen the fire hazard. Dew wasn't as inflammable as dry woods and slash. Another reason was to find engines to haul the log trains. The time was when every one of the seventeen baby engines was working through the daytime, and in order to run more trains the little engines had to be worked nights, too.

Those old log bunks were a single unit 4-wheeled truck surmounted by a heavy cross-member, or *bunk,* on which the logs rested. In effect, two bunks supporting a load of logs, amounted to a car. There was nothing but the logs connecting the bunks—no frames or trusses; just logs. If the trees had been tall and the logs cut long, the two bunks might be 40 feet apart. If the logs were sawed short the "car" was short. Sometimes, when extra long logs were chained to two bunks, a middle truck, or "idler" bunk, was chained under the center of the load. This kept the long logs from springing or bouncing, and maybe causing the train to scatter over the midnight landscape.

These "cars" of logs were connected to each other by long wooden poles called *stiff-shackles.* They amounted to a kind of link-and-pin coupling, with the ten foot long stiff-shackle acting as the link.

No air could be fitted to the log bunks, for obvious reasons. There was a hand brake on each one. With rugged brakemen and help from the engine, log trains usually got down the hills without more than routine mishaps. Brakemen had to be half cat and half monkey to scramble over those heaving logs to set hand brakes from bunk to bunk. Nights and rainy weather increased the hazard.

The Dago Branch, or branches, with the fork-shaped Madrid road, were the longest and most important branches the Lilliput had. None of these was a part of any of the far-flung prospects which all seem to have petered out during the dream stage.

It's interesting to speculate on what might have resulted, Lilliputwise, if some or most of those dreams had materialized. A Lilliput empire of tremendous scope could well have developed. These notions of expansion eventually subsided, and a few years later, in the early 1900's, a new wrinkle came into view. Mergers.

12

THE FRANKLIN COUNTY CONSOLIDATION

The Sandy River and the F.&M. had fallen into the hands of the same owners. The P.&R., the Madrid, and the Eustis railroads were, of course, one group although separate companies. It was probably in the cards that these two-footers of Franklin County, Maine, would eventually be merged into one system.

Along 1907 it was noised around that the two owning groups were planning to consolidate the Sandy River, F.&M., K.&D.R., P.&R., Madrid, and Eustis into one company.

So, in January, 1908, the big deal came off. A new system, the Sandy River & Rangeley Lakes Railroad, with some 120 miles of narrowest of narrow track, was born.

For complicated reasons of finance, concerning an issue of mortgage bonds, the Eustis Railroad didn't technically join the Consolidation until 1911. Those bonds came due then, and the bondholders, which were the S.R.&R.L. owners, foreclosed. That ended the Eustis Railroad. It promptly became the Eustis branch, and its three big Baldwin Forney engines became S.R.&R.L. engines. Engines and cars had long been pooled, anyway, so there wasn't much difference except for the paint job.

As a result of the Consolidation the S.R.&R.L. (in spite of new names and ownership it was always the *Sandy River* to Franklin County folks; we'll follow suit and keep on calling it the Sandy River as they still do), owned not only the 120 miles or more of track, but 13 engines, 14 or 15 passenger train cars with a number of

87

heavy-trucked streetcar-type "excursion cars", and more than 150 freight cars not counting all the log bunks. There was plenty of work equipment, too—four or five caboose cars, several snowplows and flanger cars, and some flats for wrecking material and boxcars for tools and equipment. It was the biggest of all the two-footers. None of the others ever equalled it in mileage, equipment, or general perfection.

Operations weren't noticeably changed with the Consolidation. The roads had been one big family too long for a little thing like a merger to effect radical changes.

The engines and cars were all renumbered. A lack of old motive power records has played hob with railroad fans who have tried to reconstruct the locomotive roster in its entirety. Exactly which engines became S.R.&R.L. numbers 1, 2, 3 and 4, will probably never be known. It rests with four engines, through a process of elimination. Old Sandy River R.R. No. 1, the onetime Billerica & Bedford *Ariel;* the P.&R. *Bo-peep,* which had been the Billerica roads' *Puck;* and the two F.&M. engines, the *V. B. Mead* and the *S. W. Sargent.* These engines made up the S.R.&R.L.'s numbers 1, 2, 3 and 4, but which was which is anyone's guess—and guess it must be. From there on, however, the renumbering is accurately recorded.

There is some doubt about the renumbering of the passenger train cars. The old P.&R. cars can never be mistaken because of the unusual, arched roofs which Billmeyer & Small nailed on them. The fact that the Eustis and Madrid roads never owned any passenger equipment, and according to the old Sandy River boys the F.&M. had only a combination and a baggage car, leaves the remaining cars looking logically like former Sandy River Railroad equipment.

The year following the Consolidation some new stock was issued and the money used to build the big 10-stall brick roundhouse in Phillips, and to buy No. 9 engine from Baldwin.

Whether or not other programs of improvement and expansion were discussed is lost in the dearth of records. But there wasn't time for much to be done, because within three years—in 1911— the Sandy River changed owners again.

R.&R.L. No. 6 is something of a boomer engine. Built in the 1890's by the old Portland Company
s Sandy River No. 5 she later became S.R.&R.L. No. 6. Sold in the early 1920's to the Kennebec
entral as their No. 4, she went in 1932 to the W.W.&F. as No. 9. Today she sleeps the days
way on the farm of the late Frank Ramsdell near Putnam, Conn., her high wheeling days
apparently over.

potted in Bearce's log yard, on the Madrid road, is S.R.&R.L. No. 20, one of the ex-Eustis R.R.
orney engines. She was built in 1903 as Eustis No. 7. Here her engineer is Fred Leavett—who
nce ran her off the rails and across frozen ground in a blinding snowstorm! Standing next to the
ab is Conductor Clarence Fairbanks. The date, judging from oil headlights and the vacuum
brake, would be about 1912.

This was years ago, on the Dago Branch of the Eustis R.R. A faint figure 8 on the tank identifie the engine as Eustis Railroad No. 8, later the S.R.&R.L. No. 21, and the date before 1908 Although some flatcars are in evidence too, the picture gives you a good idea of the log "bunks," connected by long wooden "stiff-shackles," in the foreground. Log trains were a hard way to railroad

Log yards were one of the Lilliput's chief sources of revenue. Here P.&R. No. 2, the Forney Baldwin, works among the big timbers in one of the many log yards near the P.&R. main line or branches. No. 2 became S.R.&R.L. No. 17 in the consolidation renumbering. These logs were dogged onto flatcars or logging "bunks" and hauled to one of the several lumber mills on the narrow gauge.

eb. 12, 1923, the Phillips enginehouse burned, catching from the weather curtains on one of the ngines. Burned were engines 8, 16, 17, 18, 19, 21 and 22, the 8 never being rebuilt. The little Jo. 6 hauled the big No. 23 to safety, and the old No. 15 happened to be in the paintshop that ight. No. 10 was at Rangeley, and 9 and 24 were up at Kingfield. Only the 6 and 15 were vailable to work that morning, and the 15, on a plow train, ended her career that day by breaking a driver axle en route to Farmington.

n 1909, shortly after the Consolidation, Baldwin built the No. 9 engine. She was a passenger ngine with 35-inch drivers and 11½x14-inch cylinders, and could run like a deer. Here, Engineer Dana Aldrich has her on the table at Strong, in 1934. Smoke is pouring from a hot tank journal. Dana repacked it a minute later, before heading home to Phillips from a run to Carrabasset on the F.&M.

Sure it's cold, but have patience—the engine will be back in a minute, and we'll be off again. The train was heavy this morning and rolled hard. The engine couldn't quite make the grade. Besides, there's a snowplow train right behind and we're holding it up. So, let's double to the Summit! That's what they're doing, and shortly this end of the train, and the job waiting behind, will be puffing on its way.

Shovelling out. And wind is blowing the snow back again as fast as the boys clear the track. There must have been a story here, because shovelers didn't have to scoop away drifts for the Lilliput engines. Probably one of the cars in the background is derailed, and the men are shovelling snow away preparatory to jacks and rerailing frogs.

New York finance reached its sticky talons into the Maine woods and did some arm-twisting. According to records, during the early 1900's, the New York, New Haven & Hartford R.R. seems to have been a power to be reckoned with. Those old records tell us, "— at the dictation of the New York, New Haven & Hartford Railroad —" the Maine Central bought the entire stock of the Sandy River & Rangeley Lakes for a measly, unbelievable $225,000.

What pressures were behind that "dictation" is beside the point. The fact which concerns us is that in 1911 the Maine Central Railroad became the owner of the biggest and best of all the Lilliput railroads, the Sandy River.

Shortly the Maine Central began making improvements. It began making money, too. It had acquired a slim gauge network which was already in the pink of condition, but under the new ownership it became ever better. Business was on the up-and-up. It was in the heyday of the lumber era, and the Golden Age of rusticating. The forests and mills of Franklin County were spewing wood products out, and the beauties and solitudes of the Rangeley Lakes and the Dead River Regions were sucking rusticators, (or tourists), in. All had to move over the narrow tracks of the Sandy River railroad.

New engines were built. More freight cars and cabooses were added. Miles of heavy rail were laid. Steel bridges replaced the few wooden structures which were left. And, in 1912, the Barnjum branch was built.

Barnjum's Road was a 4-mile, mountain climbing line which left the old P.&R. main line two miles north of Sanders. The switch was named Perham Junction. Climbing heavy grades and writhing curves, it served principally the lumber camps of Walter Barnjum in the town of Perham (*Pay' rum,* they call it.) No regular trains ran on Barnjum's road, but the branch was used until 1932, when the trackage of the P.&R. and Madrid roads was abandoned.

The next year, 1913, the biggest of all two-foot engines was built, the 23.

The big 23 was, of course, a Baldwin. Her boiler was 48-inches in diameter. Her cab and tank lacked four inches of being eight feet wide. Her overhang was almost three feet on each side. A standard gauge engine built to her proportions would be 17 feet wide, with a boiler ten feet in diameter. The top of the stack would be 25 feet above the rails. Yet, the outsized 23 was one of the very best riding of the many Lilliput engines. Oddly enough, the 23 was destined to be the only Sandy River engine—the only Lilliput engine, to be exact —which never rolled over or never was involved in a nasty, or serious, wreck.

This handsome Prairie type was the drag freight engine between Phillips and Farmington. Tonnage from the Branches and down from Rangeley siphoned into Phillips, channelling heavy traffic down the old Sandy River's original line to Farmington. F.&M. trains dumped more cars onto the main line at Strong, filling out the drags from Phillips. That was why they built the 23 with bigger cylinders, bigger boiler, and more weight.

That was where the big Baldwin spent her 22 years, on the Phillips-Farmington road. Only twice did she venture off the high iron. Once she went as a helper over Sluice Hill. Another time she shoved a snowplow up to The Summit, on the F.&M. Those were her two sorties off the heavy 56- and 60-pound steel. In neither of those jaunts did she damage the 35 pound rail nor cause bridges to collapse. But still management feared her hefty bulk.

It was the same with the long-legged No. 10. The Maine Central had Baldwin build her in 1916. She was the biggest of the solid-frame, modified Forney engines. She was a passenger engine. In fact, an *express* engine. She was built for those high-stepping Farm-ington-Rangeley trains. She weighed 38 tons, 45,000-pounds of it on her two sets of 36-inch drivers. There was some sense in thinking the No. 10 should keep off light rail. But the 28 miles of P.&R. 35-pound steel was her habitat. She hauled the expresses down from Rangeley to Phillips, and on over the big rail to Farmington, show-ing no favor or deference for the tiny P.&R. track.

You probably know it anyway, but there's a definite relation between the size of rail and the weight it will carry per set of wheels. Plenty of other factors are also involved, but an axle weight of 15,000 pounds calls for rail weighing 30 pounds to the yard. An axle weight of 18,000 pounds calls for 35-pound rail. A load of 22,000 pounds needs 40-pound rail, and 45-pound steel will theoretically stand up under 25,000 pounds per axle.

The big No. 10 had 23,000 pounds on each set of her high driving wheels. Such "heft" demands rail weighing 42 pounds to the yard. Yet, she ran for years — and ran fast — on the tiny 35-pound steel of the P.&R. No wonder the section men cussed about having to spike-in behind her each trip.

Yet, they didn't dare put the No. 10 onto the F.&M.'s 35-pound track nor onto any of the branches. The big, seductive 10 stayed on the Farmington-Rangeley road to the end.

No. 10 was the only one of the bantam engines equipped with a self-clearing front-end. She had what they called a Hall-Slater Front End, which was so designed that cinders and ash were continually hauled through the flues and blown up the stack. The other engines simply collected the cinders in the smokebox. Several times a day the engineers opened a hand-hole on the side of the smokebox, ran in a long hook, turned a steam blow-off valve and wiggled the hook around inside, keeping the cinders stirred up while the steam pressure blew them out on the other side. While firemen were taking water was a fine time for the engineers to clean out the front ends. Sandy River boys always called it *sparking* the engine. That was how those inevitable piles of cinders accumulated beside every water tank.

Just before the Consolidation the Sandy River Railroad had ordered a 28-ton 2-4-4 rear-tank engine from Baldwin. She was the last inside-frame engine. She was much like the Eustis engines, with a pony truck added. She was built in September 1907, and delivered a month later, carrying the Sandy River Railroad name and the number 16. As a matter of mention, she ran only a couple of months before she was renumbered S.R.&R.L. No. 8.

Following the Consolidation a number of new passenger train cars were built, mostly by the old favorite, Jackson & Sharpe. And new freight cars began to spew out of the fine brick car-shop in Phillips.

Trafficwise, operations after the Consolidation didn't differ much from the years immediately previous. Business was humping. It had been humping for a number of years, which was a major reason for the big merger.

As far as published profits and dividends went, the graph hopped up and down. As in present times, the ups and downs depended as much on what the owners wished to report as on the actual, unretouched net earnings. The fact that the narrow gauge marched on with its program of improvements, extensions, new equipment, and happy purrs indicated that regardless of annual reports the new Sandy River & Rangeley Lakes Railroad was plenty solvent.

The peak year came in 1919. That year the Sandy River hauled the equivalent of six thousand *wide* gauge carloads. One item alone was 70,000 cords of pulpwood—12,000 Lilliput cars or 4,000 standard gauge cars. It would seem from this that without the pulpwood traffic 1919 might really have been a lean year.

This car ratio of 3-to-1 was generally applicable to little cars and big cars. The Lilliput boxcar or pulprack held between six and seven cords of pulpwood. The average *wide* gauge car held from 18 to 20 cords. The standard gauge coal cars held some 40 tons of coal. The slim gauger 15 tons. Some commodities, like grain or cartons of toothpicks from the Strong toothpick mill, would run only two bantams to one full-size car.

In that year, 1919, the Sandy River's gross revenue was $350,-000. In today's inflated figures, and today's high freight rates, this would have amounted to a good $2,000,000. As George Mansfield had predicted, the two-foot gauge could do full size work, and do it at a fraction of full size costs. They were regular railroads in miniature, earningwise, operationwise, and otherwise.

They had Railway Post Office cars, identical in appearance and design to those on the full sized railroads. At one time the *Rangeley Express,* a 2-hour Rangeley-Farmington train, hauled a regulation R.P.O. There were two of these cars on the Sandy River; one built for the old P.&R., and the other a more modern mule-end car built after the Consolidation.

With the Maine Central's purchase of the S.R.&R.L. the operational setup didn't change noticeably. Corporation brass, of course, square-tailed Trout, the most beautiful as well as the gamiest fish known to sportsmen. This

Realistic Fish Story

is no myth, but is founded and illustrated on fact. Such a story is being daily illustrated by those who are so wise as to turn their faces and their steps towards the incomparable

Dead River Region

lying beside and to the east and north of the Rangeley Lakes. Here one encounters Nature in her wild and primeval beauty. Interminable Forests and Grand Mountains, Lakes, Ponds, Rivers and Streams teeming with trout—a region not excelled even by the Adirondacks in the early days.

Trace again on the map your route hither. From Portland by Maine Central Railroad to Farmington; thence Sandy River and Franklin & Megantic or Phillips & Rangeley Railroads to the very threshold of this great sporting preserve.

100-page illustrated guide book on this whole region. Send 15 cents in stamps to

F N. BEAL, Supt., Sandy River Railroad, Phillips.

O. M. VOSE, Supt., Franklin & Megantic Railway, Kingfield.

F. A. LAWTON, Supt., Phillips & Rangeley Railroad, Phillips.

Rangeley Lakes Region.

Now, what are you looking for in connection with a vacation?

Is it trout and salmon fishing? You'll find it here in abundance.

Is it riding, driving or canoeing? Conditions are perfect for either.

Is it pure air and superb scenery? The combination cannot be excelled.

Is it an up to date hotel? These are sure to please the most exacting.

Is it an individual log cabin? There are many attractive ones.

Trace your route on the map, from Portland by Maine Central Railroad to Farmington; thence by Sandy River, and Phillips & Rangeley Railroads—Parlor Car—to the very point shown in the cut, on the shore of

Rangeley Lake

The RANGELEY LAKES and DEAD RIVER REGION MAINE

TIME-TABLE
Sandy River
Franklin & Megantic
Phillips & Rangeley
RAILROADS
IN EFFECT JUNE 10, 1907

MAINE WOODS PRINT, PHILLIPS.

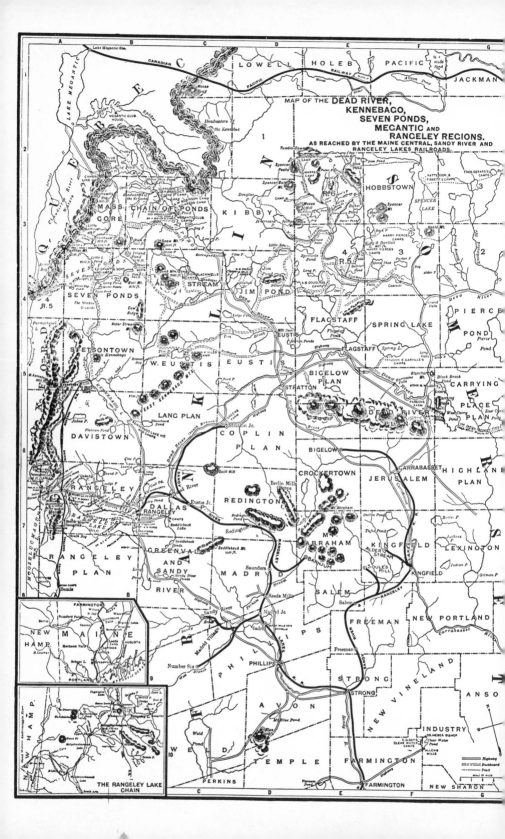

MAP OF THE **DEAD RIVER,
KENNEBAGO,
SEVEN PONDS,
MEGANTIC** AND
RANGELEY REGIONS.

AS REACHED BY THE MAINE CENTRAL, SANDY RIVER AND
RANGELEY LAKES RAILROADS.

Bigelow and Kingfield to Strong.

Nos. of Trains.	†18	*20	†22	†24
STATIONS.	A. M.	P. M.	A. M.	P. M.
Bigelow ....lv.	b10 55	*6 40		†2 00
Carrabasset	c11 18	7 03		2 25
Spring Farm		7 30		3 05
Kingfield { ......ar. { ......lv.	e11 45			
	P. M.			
Mt. Abram Jct.	12 35	7 37	†6 50	
Salem	12 48	†7 51	†7 10	
Summit	12 55	7 59	†7 30	
	f1 00	†8 04	†7 40	
Strong ....ar.	1 20	8 25	8 15	
	P. M.	P. M.	A. M.	P. M.

Rangeley, Phillips and Strong to Farmington, Portland and Boston.

Nos. of Trains.	†2	†4	*6	†10	†12
STATIONS.	A. M.	A. M.	P. M.	A. M.	A. M.
Marbles ....lv.	5 30	h11 35	h6 45		SeeNote
Rangeley	5 35	11 41	6 50		†10 45
Dead River	5 42	f11 47	f6 57		
Dallas	5 44	f11 49	f6 59		
		P. M.			
Redington	f6 08	f12 13	f7 24		
Sanders	f6 28	f12 33	f7 42		
Reeds	f6 38	f12 43	f7 52		
Madrid	6 45	12 50	f7 57		
Phillips { .....ar. { .....lv.	7 00	1 05	8 13		f11 40
	7 05	1 10	8 16	†7 30	f12 10
Hamlin's	f7 10	f1 15	8 20		f12 25
Strong	7 25	1 35	8 35	8 45	2 30
So. Strong	f7 32	f1 37	8 40		3 00
Maplewood	f7 40	f1 45	8 50		
Fairbanks	7 55	2 00	9 10	9 35	
Farmington { ...lv. { ...ar.	8 05	2 10	*9 20		
Portland ....ar.	11 20	5 30	12 15		
	P. M.	P. M.			
Boston { Via Portm'th. ar. { Via Dover... ar.	3 15	9 05	5 10		
	3 30	9 10			
New York, Via Springfield.ar.		*7 36			
	P. M.	A. M.	A. M.	A. M.	P. M.

REFERENCES.
* Daily, Sundays included.
† Flag Station. Train stops on signal or notice to Conductor.
§ Stage connections from Stratton and Eustis.
c Stage connections from Flagstaff, Parson's Farm and Ledge House.
d Fifty minutes for dinner.
e Connects with steamer from all points on Rangeley Lake and beyond.
m Buckboard connection from Seven Ponds, Kennebago and Loon Lake.
  Train 4 Parlor Car. Train 6 Sleeping Car service to Boston.
  NOTE.—Trains Nos. 7 and 12 subject to cancellation on any date without previous notice.

AMERICAN EXPRESS COMPANY operating the express business upon the line of the Sandy River and Rangeley Lakes Railroad, has unequaled facilities for transporting parcels, baggage merchandise, valuables, etc., between all points with speed and safety. Rates always as low as those of any other responsible express. The American Express Company issues Money Orders, Drafts, Travelers Cheques, Letters of Credit and Telegraphic and Cable Transfers, payable in all parts of the world.

Boston, Portland and Farmington to Strong, Phillips and Rangeley.

Nos. of Trains.	1*	†3	†5	†7	†9
STATIONS.	P. M.	P. M.	A. M.	A. M.	A. M.
New York, Via Springfield.lv.		*8 00	9 00		
Boston { Via Portm'th. lv. { Via Dover .... lv.	●10 00	3 00	8 55		
	A. M.	A. M.	P. M.		
Portland	*1 25	8 40	1 00		
Farmington ....ar.	4 35	11 55	4 10		
Farmington ....lv.	5 25	†11 55	†4 20		†11 00
Fairbanks	f5 30	f12 00	f4 25		
		P. M.			
Maplewood	f5 35	f12 08	f4 33		
So. Strong	f5 37	f12 12	f4 35		
Strong {	5 55	12 25	4 50		1 40
Hamlin's {	6 00	f12 30	f4 55		
Phillips { ....ar. { ....lv.	6 15	12 45	5 10	SeeNote	2 15
	6 15	1 03	5 13	†7 40	
Madrid	f6 30	f1 08	f5 28	8 10	
Reeds	f6 38	f1 10	5 28	8 22	
Sanders	f6 48	f1 23	f5 45	f8 35	
Redington	f7 08	f2 02	f6 05	9 15	
Dallas	f7 27	f2 02	f6 25		
Dead River	f7 28	f2 18	f6 27		
Rangeley {	7 43	g2 20	6 43		
Marbles { ....ar.	g7 46	g2 20	6 45	10 15	
	A. M.	P. M.	P. M.	A. M.	P. M.

Strong to Kingfield and Bigelow.

Nos. of Trains.	*15	†17	†21
STATIONS.	A. M.	P. M.	P. M.
Strong ....lv.	*6 00	4 55	†9 30
Summit	f6 20	5 17	f9 55
Salem	6 26	5 23	10 05
Mt. Abram Jct.	f6 32	5 28	f10 15
Kingfield { ......ar. { ......lv.	i6 46	5 42	10 45
	7 46	5 45	12 00
			P. M.
Spring Farm	n8 14	†6 13	12 35
Carrabasset	q8 37	†6 35	1 05
Bigelow ....ar.		†7 36	
	A. M.	P. M.	P. M.

The time between 12.00 Night and 11.59 a. m. is shown in light face type. Between 12.00 Noon and 11.59 p. m. in dark face type.

All trains run daily, except Sunday, unless otherwise specified.

REFERENCES.
* Daily, Sundays included.
† Flag Station. Train stops on signal or notice to Conductor.
‡ Stage connections for Lodge House, Parson's Farm and Flagstaff.
§ Stage connections for Stratton and Eustis.
e Connects with steamers for all points on Rangeley Lake and beyond.
f One hour for breakfast.
g One hour for dinner.
h Parlor Car included. Boston to Rangeley.
k Buckboard connection to Loon Lake, Kennebago and Seven Ponds.
n Private conveyance may be engaged by writing Proprietor Stage Line, Flagstaff, Me.
q Private conveyance may be engaged by writing Proprietor Stage Line, Carrabasset, Me.
● Sleeping Car Boston to Farmington.

SANDY RIVER AND RANGELEY LAKES RAILROAD

TO AND FROM THE

RANGELEY LAKES AND DEAD RIVER REGION

LOCAL TIME TABLE

IN EFFECT

JUNE 23, 1913

MORRIS McDONALD,
President & General Manager
PORTLAND, MAINE.

F. N. BEAL,
General Passenger Agent.
PHILLIPS, MAINE.

ADV. FORM 2.

SANDY RIVER and RANGELEY LAKES RAILROAD

FROM RANGELEY

Nos. of Trains STATIONS	†4 A.M.
Rangeley lv	†8 45
Dead River	†8 52
Dallas	9 01
Eustis Junction	9 07
Redington	9 39
Perham Junction	
Sanders	f10 01
Reeds	f10 13
Madrid	10 20
Phillips ....(ar	10 40
Phillips ....(ar	10 50
Avon	f10 56
Strong ....ar	11 14
Strong lv	11 14
South Strong	f11 19
Maplewood	f11 37
Fairbanks	f11 37
Farmington ....ar	11 47
Farmington lv	†1 50
Portland ....Oar	†5 50
Boston, via Portland	†9 55
Boston, via Dover	†9 15
	P. M.

FROM BIGELOW

Nos. of Trains STATIONS	†18-14 A.M.	†20 P.M.
Bigelow lv	d9 05	†3 40
Carrabasset	g9 30	4 05
Kingfield ....(ar	10 00	4 35
Kingfield ....(lv	10 05	
Mt. Abram Junction	f10 18	
Salem	f10 30	
Summit	f10 30	
Strong ....ar	10 52	
Strong lv	11 14	
South Strong	f11 19	
Maplewood	f11 25	
Fairbanks	f11 37	
Farmington ....ar	11 47	
Farmington lv	†1 50	
Portland ....Oar	†5 50	
Boston, via Portland	†9 25	
Boston, via Dover	†9 15	
	P. M.	

REFERENCES.

† Daily, except Sundays.   () Restaurant.
f Stops on signal or on notice to Conductor.   —— Train goes no farther.
d Stage connections from Stratton and Eustis.
g Stage connections from Flagstaff, Parson's Farm and Ledge House.

SAVE THE FORESTS

The State's 15,000,000 acres of forests furnish varied employment for many thousands of her people. They protect water powers of great and increasing value and form the Playground for the Nation.

DON'T START FOREST FIRES

DON'T drop lighted matches, cigars, cigarettes or live pipe ashes where they may set fire to inflammable material.

DON'T throw out lighted cigar stubs or matches out of the car window.

DON'T kindle a camp fire in dangerous places, near logs, rotten wood, leaves, nor at a distance from water.

DON'T leave your camp fire until you are sure it is out.

If possible, put it out. If you cannot do this, spread the alarm by notifying the nearest fire warden. Also wire the Forest Commissioner at Augusta, Maine.

PREVENTION OF FOREST FIRES IS TO EVERYBODY'S ADVANTAGE

WON'T YOU HELP?

WINTER SCHEDULE

SANDY RIVER AND RANGELEY LAKES RAILROAD

NARROW (2 FEET) GAUGE

IN EFFECT SEPT. 28, 1919

LOCAL AND THROUGH

TIME TABLES

TO AND FROM THE

RANGELEY LAKES

AND

DEAD RIVER REGION

MAINE

From 12.00 Night to 11.59 a. m. is shown in light face type.

From 12.00 Noon to 11.59 p. m. in dark face type.

All trains run daily, except Sunday, unless otherwise specified.

F. N. BEAL,
General Manager,
PHILLIPS, MAINE.

SANDY RIVER and RANGELEY LAKES RAILROAD

TO RANGELEY

Nos. of Trains STATIONS	†3 A.M.	†5 A.M.
Boston, via Portland lv		†9 00
Boston, via Dover lv		†8 50
Portland ....Olv	e2 45	†8 10
Farmington	†12 10	†5 30
Farmington lv	†1 10	6 10
Fairbanks	f1 20	
Maplewood	f1 29	
South Strong	f1 33	
Strong	1 40	
Strong lv	1 40	6 10
Avon	f1 50	
Phillips ....(ar	2 10	†6 30
Phillips ....(lv	2 40	
Madrid	f2 50	
Reeds	f3 00	
Sanders	f3 01	
Perham Junction	f3 55	
Redington	f3 57	
Eustis Junction	4 02	
Dallas	f4 15	
Dead River		
Rangeley ....ar		
	P. M.	P. M.

TO BIGELOW

Nos. of Trains STATIONS	†15 A.M.	†13-†17 A.M.
Boston, via Portland lv		
Boston, via Dover lv		
Portland ....Olv		e2 45
Salem		†8 30
Farmington		†12 10
Farmington lv		f1 10
Fairbanks		f1 20
Maplewood		f1 29
South Strong		f1 33
Strong ....ar		1 40
Strong lv		1 45
Summit		f2 07
Salem		2 13
Mt. Abram Junction		2 18
Kingfield ....(ar		2 32
Kingfield ....(lv		2 35
Carrabasset	†7 50	g3 03
Bigelow	8 25	
Bigelow ....ar	†8 45	
	A. M.	P. M.

REFERENCES.

† Daily, except Sundays.   () Restaurant.
f Stops on signal or on notice to Conductor.   —— Train goes no farther.
d Stage connections for Stratton and Eustis.
g Stage connections for Ledge House, Parson's Farm and Flagstaff.
e Sleeping Car Boston to Portland.

The AMERICAN RAILWAY EXPRESS COMPANY, which operates over this road has unexcelled Travel, Financial and Express facilities.

For information consult the agent at any office of the

AMERICAN RAILWAY EXPRESS COMPANY

went out and Maine Central braid assumed those executive positions. Local supervisory personnel held its own. Decisions and plans of a major character were now handed down from Portland, but they were carried out by the Sandy River veterans.

The splendid shops at Phillips, rebuilt and revamped after the Consolidation, did all the locomotive repair work. The adjacent car shop could build freight cars, and it did all the car repairs, keeping the equipment in the pink of condition.

At the time of the Consolidation, by some mutual agreement between the little roads involved, the boys protected their seniority more or less. This arrangement survived under Maine Central control. As far as the innocent bystander could see, the two roads— the S.R.&R.L. and the Maine Central—were as separate as if no relationship existed.

Part of the Maine Central's good work was to rebuild a number of engines. The old P.&R. No. 2, now the 17, got a new boiler, air brakes, and other refinements. Electric headlights appeared about as soon as on the Maine Central itself. The three Mogul engines, old P.&R. No. 3 and Sandy River Nos. 16 and 18, not only got new and bigger boilers, but emerged from the operating room as Prairie types, with roomy, open-deck cabs. Instead of being cramped up in the deck-less cabs of the old Moguls, the engine boys now had cabs to work in which were nearly as big as those of *wide* gauge engines. The Forney and 2-4-4 engines, by virtue of their type, could not be converted to open-deck cabs. The crew had to be wedged between the cab-side and the boiler jacket to the final days.

Those engines which hadn't previously been equipped with automatic and straight-air brakes, were now fitted with them. The engines bought after Maine Central control came from Baldwin with either H-6 and ET brakes or something very similar. By 1916 all the rolling stock had likewise been fitted with air.

The Maine Central also built the narrow gauge several beautifully proportioned cabooses, which had no equal on any railroad, anywhere.

The old covered stations had disappeared, excepting the one at Kingfield. Modern depots of typical Maine Central pattern replaced them. The last of the old-time covered buildings to go was the one at Kingfield. It burned one night. Combination No. 14 was inside, as was the practice, and came near burning too. Willing hands and rugged backs pushed her out, as shirt-tails smoked and flickered. She lost her roof, the clerestory type, and ever after skulked at the rear of the trains with the ugly, flattish, swayback top which replaced it.

To this day, on the Edaville Railroad where Combination 14 still rides, that same unlovely roof is much in evidence.

The two Sandy River depots which didn't follow Maine Central artistry were the new ones at Kingfield and at Rangeley. Rangeley's old covered station went by the board in relatively recent years, along with the one at Kingfield. While the replacement buildings were different from each other, they were more on the modern pattern. The Kingfield station, used as a store after the Lilliput's demise, resembled the current *ranch house* fad. The one at Rangeley was fancier, more on the elegant bungalow style. This later became a bakery, when the narrow gauge was no more, and in recent years, burned.

Fires hit the Sandy River on numerous occasions. Enginehouse fires seemed to lead the trend. The big roundhouse in Phillips burned at least twice. The original wooden house was badly singed, and resulted in the fine brick, "fire-proof" 10-staller being built in 1909. It, too, experienced a major conflagration in early 1923, although quickly rose again from its ashes. In that fire several engines were badly scorched. Nearly all the Sandy River engines had been burned at one time or another when the several enginehouses burned.

Early in that peak year, 1919, the Sandy River bought its last engine, the 24.

The trim 24 was as neat an engine as ever slipped a driver. Her dimensions were similar to the 16, 18 and 19, except for being four tons heavier. Baldwin must have stood off and viewed this finished product with a flush of pride.

Except for being a coal hog, comparatively speaking, the 24 engine was economical. She was smart. She rode well. She could roll a mean driver when some fast running was in order. Folks who remember the final years of Sandy River operation remember the 24 as being the engine most frequently seen.

When the 24 was ordered from Baldwin the Sandy River people jotted down a few specifications and measurements for the builders to follow. In line with the other little Prairie types they specified that the new engine's tank be 84 inches wide. At least, that's what they *thought* they jotted. But someone's foot slipped. Instead of writing a legible 84 *inches,* 8-feet, 4-inches was written. That is exactly one hundred inches, or 16 inches more than they meant to order.

In due time Baldwin shipped the little Lilliput to Farmington, Maine on a big, *wide* gauge flatcar.

The Sandy River had a track there which was elevated to standard flatcar height. When new engines and cars arrived, down through the years, the big flatcar was nosed up against the narrow gauge bulkhead, and the midget equipment was nudged off the flatcar onto rails of the pint sized system.

When the brand new 24 was trundled off the big flatcar onto her new home rails, someone may have noticed that her tank wobbled a wee. *Oscillating,* George Mansfield would have put it. Maybe no one did notice, just then. They were all too excited about the 27-ton engine they were getting. But it wasn't long before they did notice. The 24's tank was a little too wide for the Lilliput track.

They knew from her trial runs they had a tankful of trouble there. When the tender lurched over a low-joint or from fast running, the water sloshed back and forth. That made the tank *oscillate* to the concern of the usually lionhearted Lilliput boys. By careful running, however, and keeping the tank full of water, mishaps were side-stepped for several weeks. Then, like lightning, trouble struck one day.

They were hauling a pulpwood train out off the Madrid Branch. The mettlesome 24 was chuffing down the 35-pound rails, a bone-in-her-teeth, so to speak, when she trotted out onto the Madrid Village girder bridge. Maybe a joint was low. Or perhaps the water was low in her tank. The bantam tender began to *oscillate.* Back and forth it teetered. Then—its tiny wheels cleared the rail and off she went, *ker-smash!* down onto the ties.

The tender trucks banged and splintered over the bridge ties, shaking the bridge like an earthquake. Away it went, the whole shebang—bridge, the 24, and a string of loaded pulpwood racks, into the river!

The engine crew was pretty much shaken, especially the fireman. Conductor Clarence Fairbanks and the brakeman, riding the tops a few cars back, saw what was coming and slithered off into the bushes. The shock of the wreck rattled houses in Madrid Village, a quarter of a mile away.

As usual, the wreck was quickly picked up. The 24 was still more quickly hustled to the shop to have sixteen inches sliced out of her oversized tank. From then on the little Baldwin was as good an engine as the best of them.

Of course, she was on the ground other times. What engines weren't, on *any* railroad? A winter or two later she was plugging up to Rangeley through six inches of new-fallen snow. Approaching Sanders' watertank there was ice over the rail, hidden by the new snow. The 27-ton engine couldn't crush it, so she rode up on it, and stopped seconds later crosswise of the track.

Another engine, the 22, skun the 24 to a frazzle, as far as getting crosswise of the track went. One snowy, winter day a train was in on the Madrid branch, with the big Eustis Forney hauling it. Snow was deep. More was blowing with the ubiquitous wind. Fred Leavett was running the engine, and Clarence Fairbanks was conductor. The snow got deep, and the rail harder. The 22 had no ponies to break a track for her driving wheels, and shortly Fred Leavett had the throttle wide open and the lever in the corner. She stalled. Hossing her back and forth didn't help. Wading around in hip-deep snow, trying to shovel snow which blew in faster than they shoveled it, didn't help, either.

But, "We'll shovel her out!" Fred barked.

After an hour's scooping snow the boys finally got a hole down to the rail. Or at least, to the bottom of the wheels. There was no

The result of a silly blunder—engine, train, and bridge, down in the stream! Through a slip in specifications the 24 came from Baldwin with a tank 8 feet, 4 inches wide. That was too wide. The water sloshed and the tank teetered. This time it teetered off the iron, as luck would have it, on the Madrid Village bridge. The bridge, all hands and the 24 landed in the shallow river below.

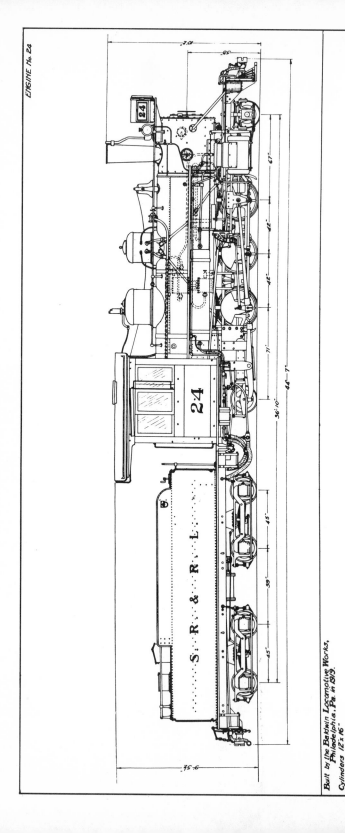

ENGINE No. 24

Henry D. Crittenden

Built by the Baldwin Locomotive Works,
Philadelphia, Pa. in 1919.

Cylinders 12" x 16"
Drivers 32" dia.
Boiler Pres.   lbs.
Total Weight   lbs.
Tractive Force   lbs.

Drawing of S.R.&R.L. No. 24 by Henry T. Crittenden. Photo of the same engine taken at the Baldwin Works in Philadelphia in 1919.

Date on this old print says May 29, 1923. It shows the Bigelow-bound passenger train through the bridge at Kingfield, with the 18 engine holding up one end and the parlor car askew on the rear. A baggage car and a coach repose in the icy waters of the Carrabasset River. No one was hurt.

rail there. The 22 was off the track. Some hurried and worried exploration on the part of Conductor Fairbanks revealed the unheard of fact that the 22 engine was not only off the track but was out in a field some fifty feet away from the track! She had been plowing over the frozen ground for a couple of hundred yards, with Fred working her wide open and wondering why she rolled so hard.

One winter's day in 1914 the Madrid branch was the locale of another horrid incident, reminiscent of Lilliput ruggedness and the cussedness of Maine winters.

A 22-car freight train, with two engines, was working the branch. While switching in Madrid Village one of the engines went off on the hard-packed road crossing. The thermometer was 43 degrees below zero. It was snowing and blowing. The conductor telephoned Phillips for help. The wrecking train headed in, but stuck fast in the snow half a mile from Madrid Village.

It was so cold nothing could be done but keep the engines from freezing. Master Mechanic Caswell froze his nose and both ears while walking 200 yards to Charles Smith's store.

Next morning two more trains were sent in to rescue the first two—a total of five locomotives!

Perhaps one of the oddest mishaps occurred years before, on the F.&M. A small tornado hit the Kingfield-bound passenger train, and actually blew the baggage car off the track and down over the dump.

Another wreck which looks bad in photographs but didn't seem to disturb anyone much at the time, happened around 1916. Southbound trains coming into Strong from Phillips and Rangeley had an across-the-valley glimpse of the ball-signal at the west end of Strong yard, as they drifted down Cook's Grade onto the Strong Trestle. In that quick glimpse the engineer's eagle-eye could see whether the balls were set for him to enter the yard, or were set for an F.&M. train to enter. With the help of this preview he could govern his approach to the yard accordingly.

This day Engineer Dana Aldrich was hightailing a passenger train for Farmington. As his No. 7 Forney slithered down the hill

Dana caught the glimpse of the half-a-mile-away signal with the balls set for him to enter the yard. He let his train roll.

Old Lady Luck was capricious that day. She had some fun with Dana Aldrich. In the minute it took his train to career across the trestle, around the big curve, and up the winding grade to Strong yard, an F.&M. train had hollered for the balls. The agent had accommodatingly changed them to let him in. Two trains were dusting into the yard with an obscuring hill and curve between them.

The two engineers saw each other in time to shut off and apply their brakes. But not in time to prevent a resounding crash. Dana's No. 7 got her cowcatcher pushed in under her by the impact, and the little 18-ton Forney promptly climbed up on the crumpled cowcatcher. She teetered on its point. Then she toppled over against the cut. Like dominoes, every baggage and passenger car twisted over in suit.

Not a soul was hurt. And, they said, not a pane of glass was cracked.

Eight years later a similar head-on happened as Dana Aldrich with the 16 engine was about to enter the west end of Phillips yard, with a freight train from Rangeley. Steaming around the long curve into Phillips, Dana was on the outside of the curve and couldn't see too far past the nose of his engine. The fireman was down on the deck fixing his fire. The big 23 was switching pulpracks up ahead, and moving slowly toward the oncoming freight train. Her engineer was watching back for hand-motions and didn't see the Freight job rounding the curve onto him. However, both engines were moving slowly when they hit. The big 23 didn't bat an eye. The 16 was caught just right and *oscillated* onto her side, like a hound-dog catching an after-dinner nap.

The 16 probably holds the all-time record for an engine doing a complete *oscillation* of this kind. She had stopped at Madrid Water-tank one day, in the sharp curve. There was plenty of elevation on the outside rail. The boys were squatting beside her, examining an overly-warm journal when they got the shock of their lives. The 16's tender wheels were slowly rising off the outside rail. The wheels rose higher. It was apparent that she was in danger of upsetting.

And, that's just what the baby Baldwin did—upset, tender, engine, and all.

To this day the boys never knew what caused it. She had been standing there several minutes, which should have allowed any sloshing in the tank to calm down. The fact still remains, the 16 actually tipped over while standing still!

Everyone concerned was satisfied if engines did their *oscillating* and upsetting while standing still—or moving at a crawl. There were plenty of curves, 15 and 16 degree curves, too, which would have been miserable places to take a spill. Those 28½ miles from Rangeley to Phillips were full of them.

Oddly enough, it was on this long run of tight curves and heavy grades that the two-footers hung up their best speed records. Most of them were in the days of 12 and 18 ton Forney engines, too. When venerable Ed West and affable Dana Aldrich used to whisk their miniature passenger trains over that run in 56 minutes, including station stops, it was really honest-to-God fast running.

It was something to brag about when an engineer high-wheeled 'em from Farmington up to Phillips, 18 miles, in 27 minutes. It was a damsite better when a little Portland engine yanked the *Rangeley Express* from Farmington to Rangeley, 46½ miles, in two hours.

If you peruse a Sandy River timetable, especially one of later years, you will get the impression that two-footers didn't go very fast. You'd be wrong. They did. That timetable schedule, averaging 18 miles an hour or so, will mislead you. They clipped by plenty of mileposts a minute to a post. That gait, of course, wasn't the rule. The ordinary running speed was from 30 to 45 miles an hour and the advertised schedule took into account the leisurely station stops. In later years when earnings began to slack off and track maintenance slacked with it, speed was reduced in proportion. Plenty of Lilliput mileage saw some fast running right up to the last, especially on the Sandy River.

It was on the Rangeley run, in the fifty-years-ago days of the *Rangeley Express,* that Conductor Bob McMullen had to stagger up through the badly *oscillating* coaches and a baggage car or two, to the front platform where he could shout across the stubby coal-pile to Dana Aldrich, perched jauntily on the righthand side of No. 10's streaking cab.

"When Dana got onto that big No. 10 engine," Bob used to tell, "he didn't realize how fast he was running. The 10 rode like a cradle. He'd haul us so fast the coaches were jumping up and down. Passengers were scared. I'd have to go up there time after time and slow him down!"

Dana would snort when asked about it.

"No. 10 engine," he'd stoutly declare, "was as steady and safe as anything on *wide* gauge roads. I knew she was safe when she was running fast."

Bob never said she wasn't safe. But those cars full of passengers didn't know it.

There were times when the little trains didn't fare so well.

The time Engineer Frank Hodgeman was heading north with a passenger train, for instance. He had the No. 8 engine, a high-wheeled, inside-frame Baldwin. The inside-framers were prone to *oscillate,* anyway, in spite of George Mansfield's brags. Hodgeman was letting her out. Coming up through Fairbanks station something went wrong. The No. 8 *oscillated* too much and over she went. Hodgeman was killed, or might as well have been. He died a few hours later, one of the few slim gauge railroaders to ever die in an accident.

Before that, way back in 1904, Engineer Guy Everett took a similar spill with little Portland engine No. 4 and a long passenger train. He was headed toward Rangeley, too. He was cuffing the wind, as Hodgeman had been. Everett stayed right side up for more than a dozen miles. West of Strong, whizzing up crooked Cook's Grade the old *oscillating* began, and before you could say, "Jack Robinson!" the No. 4 had slewed over on her side, twisting every one of the passenger cars over with her. No one was hurt. But Engineer Everett was soon working down on the Maine Central, where track was twice as wide.

Don't get the impression that wrecks were the rule on two-foot roads. They weren't. The two-footers had wrecks aplenty, but train-mile for train-mile they didn't go off any more than the standard-gaugers did. It was rare, too, for anyone to be hurt when a spill occurred.

Faded photographs and the yarns of old timers bring up the subject of wrecks more often than reminiscences of smooth running and routine performance. Recollections of men riding a slithering engine down the dump, or scampering over somersaulting boxcars, are more dramatic than thousands of miles of uneventful railroading.

Dana Aldrich ran Lilliput engines close to a million miles, and so did Ed West and Charlie Hodgeman and a number of other old heads. They all got plenty of scares, just the same as *wide* gauge railroad men do. One of Dana's clearest recollections is of the night, 60-odd years ago, when he was nosing a snowplow from Rangeley home to Phillips. It was in the night. Dana was in a hurry. Mrs. Aldrich was due to present Dana with a son before morning.

The little P.&R. No. 1 *Calvin Putnam* was purring past Dead River Station, the plow spraying snow clear over the fences. Suddenly the plow rose up on some ice. She dived for the woods. The engine followed her. In a second the plow, engine and the flanger car were in a nasty, steaming heap at the bottom of the fill. Dana was under the whole shebang. He was pinned in the cab, a bent reverse-lever jamming his leg against the boiler-butt. Live steam from a broken pipe roared inches past his face.

"I thought my time had come," he told me forty years later. "To make it worse," he went on, "reports of the wreck were garbled and someone notified my wife that I'd been killed. The boy was born before she knew the difference."

As a sequence, years later when the 24 engine broke through the Madrid Village bridge, as a result of her tender being 16 inches too wide, that boy was her fireman!

The old non-air log-bunks were responsible for some crazy episodes. Occasionally they piled up in matchwood wrecks, and other times their antics were fearsome but had happier endings.

When the night log trains were running down off the Dago Branch a funny thing happened. Funny to hear it now, but not so jolly to the boys who figured in it.

Conductor Clarence Fairbanks was in the caboose, behind a string of logs. His brakeman was cautiously crawling over them, setting some hand brakes for the approaching descent down Sluice Hill. He felt the little buggy gathering speed. This shouldn't be, not on Sluice Hill. The night was pitch black. The log train was shortly making passenger train time. Fairbanks crawled out, too, and managed to set enough brakes to hold them. The little Baldwin up ahead was using her straight-air to advantage, too. Finally they reached the foot of Sluice Hill in one piece, and tearing past Reed's Station the speed slackened in the heavy upgrade of The Devil's Elbow. When the train stopped everyone began to hunt for the missing brakeman.

His feeble cries led them to him. Back on Sluice Hill he'd been crawling over one of the stiff-shackles connecting the log-bunks when its slatting motion had thrown him off balance. Quick as a flash he'd grabbed the pole with both arms and legs, and flipping underneath he had swung suspended like a pendulum.

In that precarious position the brakeman had ridden the length of Sluice Hill, the ties scrubbing his back, shoulders, and rump. When they found him he was still holding like grim death to the stiff-shackle, every stitch of clothing stripped from his body except his shirt collar and his shoes!

Another one of those log trains gave a brakeman something to remember. Clarence Fairbanks was running that train, too. Fred Leavett was hauling it with the 18 engine. It was pitch dark and they were dropping down Sluice Hill, and the brakeman had worked the length of the train tying down hand brakes. He was crawling back, releasing the brakes, toward the caboose. From the cupola Fairbanks saw the brakeman's twinkling lantern suddenly soar off over the treetops. That could mean only one thing. Fairbanks rushed out and began setting brakes again. After passing Reed's Station and running halfway up The Elbow with the brakes set, Fred Leavett took the hint, and brought the train to a stop. They walked back, watching in the lantern light for signs of the brakeman.

Again the victim's feeble groan guided them. They heard it just as they were walking past Reed's Station. Following the sound in the darkness it led them up to, and *under,* the wooden platform. And there he was, well under the platform, alive, and not too much the worse for his miraculous tumble.

It seems that when he'd fallen from the logs, the momentum had slithered him along the shoulder of the ballast and slid him up under the station platform.

There were other near-misses, galore. One time on the heavy grade of the Barnjum branch a cut of freight cars slipped their brakes and shortly gathered speed down the 3 and 4 percent toward Perham Junction. As in all good melodrama, a Rangeley passenger train was shortly due at the switch.

It arrived, and stopped. The conductor was examining the register book when he heard the roar of flying wheels up on the mountain. Guessing right, he waved a frantic highball and his engineer snaked the coaches off the switch in the nick of time. The hurtling freight cars left the curve, took to the air, and disintegrated on the spot where seconds before the passenger train had stood!

The same thing happened up on the F.&M. A northbound passenger train had stopped with a God-given hotbox between Kingfield and Carrabasset. While cooling the box the boys heard a rapidly approaching roar. Being good railroad men they guessed right, too. While the engineer was backing his passenger cars away from approaching doom the other boys were frantically throwing some ties across the rails. The runaway tore into view. Three box cars, which had got loose at Carrabasset a few minutes before, hit the pile of ties, leaped into the air, and somersaulted into the field. The passenger train was saved!

Then, typical of the stalwart little Lilliputs, the passenger job highballed for Bigelow only a few minutes late. The runaways had jumped the track so neatly that not a bit of damage had been done— to the track.

One years-ago derailment happened right inside the Phillips roundhouse. Ed West, the old prankster, dreamed up one of his everlasting jokes. Engineer Chris Boston was about to ease the No. 15 engine out of the house. Smiling diabolically, Ed West placed a sizable nut under each of the 15's six driving wheels—a nut in front and a nut behind each one, trigging them completely. Boston climbed up in the cab. Ed West climbed out of sight, to watch. Boston opened the cylinder-cocks and cracked the throttle. She hissed and shivered. He inched it out another notch. She trembled again. Then, impatiently, Boston widened on her, expecting probably that she'd leap out of her stall onto the table. Instead, the big nuts trigging her midget drivers, she leaped straight into the air. Ker-smash! she came down into the pit.

Thus did accidents and personalities play their parts in Lilliput operations, as well as such grim matters as meeting expenses and staying in business.

Business held up splendidly during the roaring 1920's. Private autos and trucks were just beginning to appear in backward Maine. But, progress was encroaching and passable roads were beginning to be built in Franklin County, Maine.

Whether the Maine Central saw the hand-writing on the wall, and knew that there was no time like the present, or whether it actually lost some money, doesn't matter any more. In 1922 they let the interest slip on the bonds, and the bondholders squawked. As a result, in 1923 the Maine Central sold its Sandy River stock, terminating 12 years of paternal control.

This control was bought by a Gardiner, Maine banker Josiah Maxcy, and lumberman Herbert Wing of Kingfield. These two owned it until the end, twelve years later.

When these two took over the Sandy River they appointed Orris Vose as superintendent. The title was a misnomer. Actually Vose was general manager of the then-115 or 118-mile system. Why the title Superintendent was selected by the owning tycoons was a mystery.

The first job Vose had on his hands, the day he became top man of the line, was to pick up a wreck at Kingfield. The northbound passenger train went through the pile-supported girder bridge just north of the Kingfield switch. The 18 engine got across, leaving only her tender hanging in the gap. A baggage car and a coach were pretty well toward the Happy Fishing Grounds, while the parlor-car was still hanging to the mainland by the skin-of-her-teeth. No one was hurt, of course. With the experience gained from this baptism, Orris Vose launched on a career as guide, counsellor, and mortician of the S.R.&R.L. for the next twelve years.

Orris had come to the Lilliput as no stranger. His father before him had once been superintendent of the old F.&M. Orris had worked as a brakeman and a fireman up there. On one occasion, while acting as engineer, he had the dubious honor of upsetting the 16 engine, *Old Star,* at The Summit.

For a while after returning to independent control the railroad continued to make money. Not so much, but a comfortable profit. Even as late as 1930 the total revenues were a tidy $131,506.00; and those, remember, were 1930 dollars. The 1959 equivalent in deflated *dinero* would amount to some half million dollars. That year the Sandy River hauled 9,781 passengers and 49,640 tons of freight.

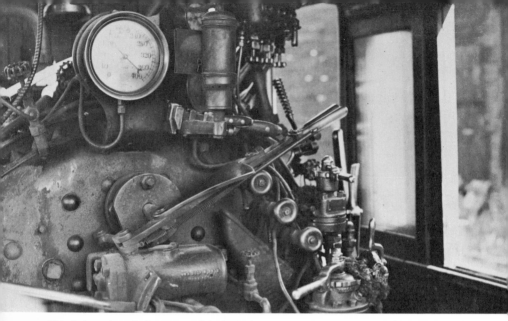

This is how the 24's business end looked to engineers and to railroad fans who were lucky enough to ride her. The 27-ton midget had everything the big engines had, except an automatic bell-ringer and steam heat. And like frolicsome kittens, these Lilliputs were ten times more appealing and fascinating than the full-sizers were.

Three coaches stored on the Wilbur Track at Phillips. Old coach 18, and "new" coaches 21 and 22 weren't used so much in later days. The time was, however, when their little journals were rarely cold. The 21 and 22 now run on the Edaville Railroad. Coaches averaged 40 feet long and their one-person seats held some 28 passengers.

13

RAIL CARS, JITNEYS, RAIL BUSES

But little by little revenues and passengers and tonnage fell off. By now the timetable didn't show three round trips of the *Rangeley Express* between Farmington and Rangeley. They had been cut back first to two trains, then to one. No more passenger jobs ran on the Eustis branch. The logging trains didn't rumble their nocturnal descents off the Dago branch any more. In fact, the last train out of Green's Farm was in 1919. Freights continued to use that part of the Eustis road to Langtown, however, as long as the Rangeley end of the system operated.

Over on the F.&M. the line was cut back from Bigelow to Huston Brook, nearly down to Carrabasset, in 1925 or '26. Regular passenger trains shortly disappeared between Strong and Carrabasset, mixed jobs emerging from Vose's economy moves.

The major reasons for the early decline on the Sandy River was the fact that one of the heaviest items of revenue had been lumber and pulpwood. As far as long lumber went, the region had been pretty well cut off. While there were still millions of board feet of timber standing on the rugged Franklin County hills, and innumerable cords of pulpwood, the diminished supply no longer amounted to a boom period. The Sandy River was still doing a fine business but not the overflowing volume of a few years past. While no one thought of the calamitous possibility in those golden days of the 1920's, actually the little Sandy River was checking out.

Only two years after the Maine Central sold, experiments were begun with gasoline railcars.

The first of these conversions was a Model T *jitney,* as the boys called it. You may remember them—the 1925 equivalent of today's *ranchwagon.* The high, wagonish vehicle was fitted with flanged wheels, plus some side-irons of a railroad motif to prevent the wheels falling off in case something broke, and was put to work as a supplementary passenger service on the P.&R. Its success, mechanically and economically, inspired converting two more Model T's to mechanize the maintenance of way crews.

Several of these cars were built, or converted, in the Phillips Shops, and were paragons of their kind. Most of the credit for their excellent design and ingenious construction belongs to Master Mechanic Lee Stinchfield, who lay awake nights devising and fabricating these automotive marvels.

Shortly the appellation *jitney* gave way to *railbuses,* as the motor railcars were ever after called. The railbuses were used not only for maintenance crews but for emergency crews and firefighters, for special train service, and for carrying the U. S. Mails when passenger trains no longer made appropriate schedules. One, a sedate Model T touring car of 1926 vintage, was the private inspection car of Orris Vose.

Either the success of the railbuses, or a worsening passenger train situation set Superintendent Vose and Master Mechanic Stinchfield to thinking in terms of bigger and better rail wagons, the 1926 equivalents of today's Budd Cars and Talgo Trains. Shortly there emerged from the depths of the Phillips' shop the first railbus of full-train-proportions. Reo No. 4.

The Reo Motor Company furnished the engine and radiator. That was about all. Stinchfield and the Lilliput shops did the rest. Reo railbus No. 4 took over the Rangeley-Farmington varnish. She held in her Stinchfield-designed body, all the passengers who by now were taking passage on the Lilliput train to and from Rangeley. In her trailing 4-wheeled vans rode the mail and express. At first two men, an engineer and a conductor, crewed the monoxide marvels. Later only one man was used. He could be either an engineer or a conductor, according to seniority.

The Farmington diamond layout in 1934, with Me.C. No. 284 leaving for Portland with Train 24. The Sandy River railbus No. 5 is under the canopy, ready to leave as soon as the wide gauge train is clear, and the red ball is hauled to the masthead for clearance of narrow gauge trains. The diamond in the foreground is the one from which old No. 1 engine is supposed to have toppled, in 1879.

Big Reo bus No. 5 on table at Phillips, with trailer attached. These buses were easy riding and capable of 45 or 50 miles an hour speed. The No. 5 was scrapped after the Sandy River quit, but the smaller No. 4 was bought by railroad fan Edgar Mead, and presented to his favorite Lilliput, the Bridgton and Harrison Ry. It is now in use on the Edaville Railroad.

One weakness of the converted Model T's was inability to cool the water while running backwards. Frequent stops were necessary to refill the steaming radiator. This water stop was at the Cascade Brook, on the P.&R., high up on Sluice Hill. To the immediate left of the photo the brook makes a sheer drop of 90 feet, a Niagara in miniature!

The two jewels of the motor car conversions were railbuses Nos. 4 and 5. No. 4, to your left, was a four wheeled car with five rows of seats, for 15 passengers. Express and mail were carried in the trailer. Later a double truck was put under the front end. Bus No. 5, to your right, was a double-truck, easier riding car, and besides six seats for 18 passengers, she had a mail-express compartment. On the long Rangeley run No. 5 also hauled one or two trailers.

Two converted Model T's at Avon, Maine, in 1933. The car at right is a section workcar, in to clear on a section of temporary, light railed track made especially as a "jigger track" for quickly moving trackcar off main line. These cars not only saved the Sandy River a lot of money as transportation for track crews and materials, but also in rushing fire-fighting crews in quicker time than steaming up a locomotive and getting a crew together.

No. 10 engine, complete with her pony-plow, heads a Farmington to Phillips mixed train through Strong, in 1934. The two balls at the masthead give mainline trains the rights. The F.&M. swung sharp to your left here, and on a long curve it straightened out for the hill climbing jaunt to the north.

This cold, smoky scene was snapped in January 1935, and shows one train, hauled by the approaching No. 24, lugging snow out of Strong yard, to be dumped over a fill up the track aways. Another train, the F.&M. mixed, is now turning its engine on the table, down that right-hand track. Strong was a roaring railroad town when two or three Lilliput trains landed there at the same time.

Looks cold, doesn't it? It was. Especially riding the flanger car coupled to the tail of the little combination. The train, sitting in front of Phillips station, had just come up from Farmington, on Jan. 1, 1935, and snow and ice plastered its sides. With the blower cracked, No. 10 is ready to leave again, on another southbound bout with another winter's day.

The Phillips yard, roundhouse and depot with the noon passenger train steaming in from Farmington, in 1935. Railbus 4 and the 24 engine's tender are in front of the 10-stall brick roundhouse. The adjoining building is the car shop. The train is on the main line, which passed the station and continued on to Rangeley. To the right is the Wilbur Track, a team track and storage.

These railbuses, so far, had all been 4-wheeled cars. Their riding qualities left something to be desired. Although Stinchfield's spring-hanging and axle supports were more than M.C.B. requirements could have demanded, the buses rode hard. They banged every rail-joint. They surged back and forth, like Forney engines, crowding the rail first on one side then on the other. They were surefooted and never were derailed, but still, they rode hard. Passengers sometimes gritted their teeth and swore softly.

So, Reo No. 5, a double-truck 8-wheeler was born.

The No. 5 was longer. She held as many passengers as her older mate and also incorporated in her length a baggage-compartment for mailbags and parcels. She, too, hauled one or two 4-wheeled trailer cars. This bus went onto the Rangeley run, the No. 4—contemporaneously equipped with a 4-wheel truck forward to improve her riding qualities—was relegated to the F.&M. run.

For years these two railbuses, the 4 and the 5, handled all passenger train schedules, excepting one or two mixed jobs, on the Sandy River. They were good, too, in winter snows. But from freeze-up time in the fall until the first of April they were stored, and steam trains took over again. This was partly because Maine has blizzards which stall even steam trains on occasion, and at such times the buses wouldn't have a chance. And too, in sub-zero weather, with a howling gale driving the cold through any wall which wasn't thoroughly insulated, the unheated buses were not exactly attractive to the traveling public. The conventional wooden coaches, with their hotwater heaters, were.

The one exception to winter storage was Vose's railbus, the so-called inspection car. That jet black hotrod might be seen anywhere, anytime, wherever there were midget rails to carry it. Often it was pressed into service to carry Dr. Bell, the community's surgeon at Strong, to Rangeley or Kingfield for an emergency operation. Vose has pushed the Model T over the hills to Rangeley in roaring blizzards—snow halfway up her radiator in places, and succeeded in getting there. Vose once declared, with a confidential wink, that he could put that railbus through any snowdrift a baby Baldwin could wallow through!

The railbuses were no slouches when it came to turning a mean wheel. If bantam Baldwins could hang up speed records, so could Henry Ford's product. Vose nearly scared a train crew to death, bringing them home from Redington. The boys were in a hurry, because it was Graduation night at the high school. Vose promised to get them home in time. He did. They dropped down the sixteen crooked miles from Redington to Phillips in twenty-three minutes. That included the hairpin curves of Sluice Hill and The Devil's Elbow.

There were times, too, when both Engineer Ed West, and Conductor Bob McMullen were running the Reo 5 on the Rangeley job, they had the speedometer on 60 more than a little of the way.

The big Reos used the conventional transmission and differential, a chain and sprocket running to the other axle of the rear truck. They had no reverse but the slow truck reverse. The Model T's, however, sported a Stinchfield innovation which lifted them out of the mundane passenger train class. The result of Stinchfield's lying awake nights was to remove the innards from the Model T rear end, installing a solid, full-length axle, and to it riveting the two ring gears some four or five inches apart. The driveshaft might be called *floating,* because it could be moved by a lever to engage its pinion gear with either one of the ring gears. When the pinion was meshed into one ring gear the car moved ahead. When it was engaged with the other it moved in reverse. Thus, in high gear the car might go ahead, or backwards, according to the desire of the operator. It need not be turned. It would go one way as fast as the other. The only kink Stinchfield never ironed out was the failure of the Ford cooling system when the car was running backwards. The engines would boil.

As a tribute to Stinchfield's and the Sandy River shop's ability, one of the last jobs to be done there before it was dismantled, was to convert a full-size highway bus for use on a standard gauge railroad—the Maine Central's line from Oquossoc to Kennebago.

However, even the economies and efficiency of the motor passenger trains couldn't overcome the trend of slumping business. As the depression approached, lumber and pulpwood traffic was down. The once lush vacation travel to the Rangeley Lakes resorts was moving by private automobile. Trains weren't earning much more than enough to pay the road's operating and maintenance expenses. The owners weren't getting a penny of interest or dividends on their $340,000 stock and accumulated $190,400 funded debt. The Sandy River was in a bad way.

Except for the railbuses, only a mixed job was working out of Kingfield covering the F.&M., and another mixed made the run between Phillips and Farmington. The Rangeley line and the branches were handled by freight extras as business was offered.

Of course, the depression had a lot to do with it. If the road could have held out until the pre-war boom, it would probably be running today. But it didn't. Trucks were hauling pulpwood, too. They were beginning to haul lots more than pulpwood, skimming the cream off the general freight traffic into Strong, Phillips, Kingfield and Rangeley. The situation was serious.

Then one day the bigwigs got their pates together. Something must be done. After days or weeks of pondering they came up with an idea. They would cut the cards, gamble. It would be either life, or death.

They announced their plans to abandon operations a few days hence—in July, 1932.

So, abandon they did with the blessing of the various regulatory bodies, and the few faithful friends who knew about the scheme. The morning of July 9 dawned on a usually bustling railroad yard which was strangely silent. No little Baldwin was fuming across the table. No midget trains were being made up. Not even a railbus was in sight. The Sandy River was dead.

During the rest of the summer the folks who were in the know kept a sharp watch. They watched the trucks and the expression on the faces of business men whose traffic could have kept the Sandy River going. Their wishful thinking was, in the light of later years, pitiful. Their hopes weren't fulfilled. They had lost.

The gist of the scheme was that, if the road was shut down for nine or ten months, the community economy might be so severely affected that folks would be jarred to their senses. If trucks might fail to handle the transportation business, especially during the rugged

Maine winter ahead, maybe merchants and mill owners would be mighty glad when the little railroad gave them another chance, and resumed operations the following spring.

The scheme was a good one, the gamble was clever, but the Lilliput lost.

Came mid-April, 1933. The Sandy River started up again.

However, it wasn't the same. Some folks still think that Orris Vose made a disastrous blunder by dropping the most promising part of the line. All track north of Phillips was abandoned.

The once prosperous P.&R., the Madrid and Eustis and Barnjum branches, which had once siphoned thousands of tons of freight onto the high iron from Phillips to Farmington, were struck off the map, closed forever. The folks who took a dim view of this move—and some of them were railroad men themselves—saw the Sandy River's last chance to survive, jettisoned by closing those feeder lines which might have once more originated enough traffic to make operation profitable.

A few people, partisans of the narrow gauge, even went so far as to say that the owners would prefer a quick cleanup at scrap price than the then-dubious chance of the little road staging a comeback. Owner Maxcy was a banker. Owner Wing was a lumber baron. The potentials of their Lilliput railroad were peanuts to these men. Maybe they were glad to be rid of their liability. A hard thing for some of us to remember is that everyone doesn't take the sentimental slant about railroads, especially little ones, that some of us impassioned romanticists do. To many of us a railroad is a living, precious be-trothed. To others it's a business property which, when no longer lucrative, must be dumped. The fact that those slim gauge lines beyond Phillips might have produced revenues, but currently were not, so were abandoned, makes the Maxcy-Wing group appear more sensible than sentimental.

Whether the loss of the feeder lines, tapping an area of some three hundred square miles, was responsible, or if it was simply and inevitably in the cards, business didn't return to the Sandy River when it reopened in April 1933.

Train service was good on the surviving 42 miles of road. The big Reo railbus No. 5 made two round trips a day between Phillips and Farmington. The smaller No. 4 tied up at Kingfield, leaving there in the morning for Strong, to connect with the Phillips to Farmington bus. It turned and ran back through Kingfield to Carrabasset, returning to Strong to connect again with the Phillips to Farmington afternoon bus. When that car returned from Farmington, Phillips-bound, that late afternoon, the No. 4 left Strong for Carrabasset again, finally deadheading home to Kingfield in the early evening.

A freight train left Phillips in the morning, ran to Farmington, back to Strong, up to Kingfield and Carrabasset, back to Strong, and home to Phillips that afternoon. The next summer its caboose was swapped for a combination car and it became a mixed train, offering still better passenger service.

When the road reopened the railroad boys all agreed to help finance the experiment by accepting wages which amounted to about one-third their regular pay. Trackmen, train and engine men, station agents, shopmen and carpenters were paid $2.00 a day, $12.00 a week. Superintendent Vose drew double that amount, $24.00 a week, as did also Master Mechanic Stinchfield. Auditor Clarence Roy, later of the Springfield Terminal Ry. in Vermont, drew about the same. The Receivers, as the two owners were officially called, drew similar salaries. It wasn't much, and every Sandy River man did a full and efficient job of railroading for the miserly stipend. It was in depression times, of course, and besides being lucky to have a job at all, a family could live for a fraction of what it costs us today. That $12.00 a week tax-free wage was probably equivalent in buying power to a gross earning today of five or six times as much.

Track and equipment were maintained in the usual excellent condition, although it was due as much to coasting along on its previous perfection as anything. One track crew, riding a Model T railbus, took care of the big iron between Farmington and Phillips, 18 miles. The other crew, also with a railbus, looked after the 24 miles of 35-pound track from Strong to Carrabasset. And, as long as the Lilliput ran those tracks were in a splendid condition which many of today's Class 1 railroads might envy.

The meager shop force kept engines, cars, and railbuses in their usual trim. That was the only condition those fellows knew how to keep it.

But, spending was cut to the minimum. When the 21 engine broke a driver axle she was nosed into her stall in the Phillips roundhouse, and left there. Another engine was fired up to take her place. The 21 was never repaired. The 16, 19, 22 and 23 were out of service for tubes. While except for Government inspection rules these engines were ready to run, they never were retubed and never ran again. After the 21 broke her axle the 9, 10, 17, 18 and 24 were left in service and were periodically alternated in use, until the end.

On this basis, though on its knees and moribund, the little Sandy River operated and actually made a profit.

That is, it made a profit before funded debts and interest charges on an investment covering 120 miles of onetime line were deducted. Those charges caused the books to show a loss of nearly $40,000, and an operating ratio of 158.37.

When winter came, in late October 1933, the railbuses were put away and steam came out again. Once more the sights and sounds were reminiscent of the Sandy River's golden yesterdays. The little No. 9 and the big No. 10 had pony-plows fitted to their noses, and alternated hauling the mainline mixed train. Likewise bedecked with pony-plows were the Forney 17, and Prairie types 18 and 24. Usually the 17 and 18 alternated on the F.&M. job, while the 24 hauled the extras and was a general standby engine. These were in no wise hard-and-fast arrangements. Any engine might be on any of the trains, anytime. But this is the general idea of how they were used.

Business was fair that fall and winter, but woefully under the woeful figures for 1930-31. Big snowplows on powerful trucks, supported by willing and unwilling taxpayers alike, kept the highways open. Pulpwood trucks, freight trucks, and private autos continued as in summer months. Even old Mother Nature seemed to enter into the fiendish machination to butcher the struggling Lilliput. The vigorous winters for which Maine is famous—or infamous—levelled off into mild, weak seasons which made highway plowing and traffic relatively easy. An old-fashioned winter, the likes of which had once kept triple-headers busy dragging a baggage car and a coach through the drifts, would have spelled finis to highway competition that winter. The Sandy River would have come back with a bang. But, Mother Nature chortled malevolently, and the tiny Baldwins chuffed through the silent hills, hauling little else but ghost-freight of the past.

Everyone hoped for a miracle. And no miracle came.

There was brave talk of tomorrows which would come. The F.&M. rail was showing signs of wear, and they talked of picking up the little-used Eustis steel and relaying the F.&M. There were rumors galore of reopening the P.&R. to Rangeley. But it was all nothing but rumor.

With the spring of 1934 the railbuses came out again in mid-April, before the snowdrifts were melted. The baby Baldwins went back to their stalls to sleep—excepting one to haul the mixed train. Business continued about like the year before. Some of the railroad boys thought it picked up a little.

Shortly all hopes of reviving the P.&R. vanished when Superintendent Vose put crews to work breaking up the branches. A Model T railbus, rebuilt during the winter with a Model A motor, began picking up the rails. The Madrid lines came up, and Barnjum's road, and the Eustis. Then, the P.&R. Some of the steel went West for worm-proof telephone poles. More was cut up for scrap, for Japan. In any event, it seemed more profitable to preside over junking the lines than trying to run them.

A few years after the Sandy River had gone, and pre-war business began to surge upward, there was reason to believe that had the Lilliput system been kept intact it would have staged a glorious comeback—even in spite of owners who may not have wanted it. Other bankrupt railroads came back. The war boom, with gasoline rationing and shortages, kicked more than one surprised railroad up the steps to solvency. Business in Franklin County spiralled. There is little doubt if, had the Sandy River system been available, it would have been snowed-under with traffic. But, the Lilliput was dead.

With the winter of 1934 came the same train changes and programs of the year before. Steam trains covered the 42 miles with excellent service. Men worked for the discouraging $2.00 a day. Those men—engine and trainmen, trackmen, shopmen—were an abbreviated roster of the old Sandy River, the F.&M. and the P.&R. of years before. The big difference being there were fewer names.

Up on the F.&M. the steady hand of Charlie Hodgeman handled the throttle on the eighty mixed-train miles a day. Hodgeman had fifty years of service. He was as able an engineer as ever blew a whistle. Behind him, in the combination car, rode Conductor Herbert Walker, another old-time F.&M. man. Fireman Hershal Boynton, once an engineer, and Brakeman Flave Vose, the superintendent's brother, were both old F.&M. men.

Out of Phillips on the Farmington run Conductor Bob McMullen ran the train. Bob was a P.&R. man with forty years of Lilliput railroading. Brakeman Clarence "Son" Fairbanks was also an old conductor. Up ahead, perched on No. 10's right-hand seat, Dana Aldrich rode, as perky and confident as in the P.&R.'s Gay Nineties. Firing for him was veteran P.&R. engineer Ed West whose twinkling eye and sly smile had kept pace with forty years of practical jokes and superb railroading. In days of old it had been Dana Aldrich and Ed West, each hauling one end of the famous *Rangeley Express,* who had tied for the speed record over the 29 crooked, hilly miles between Phillips and Rangeley. Each had run it in fifty-six minutes!

It had been on that Rangeley run that Bob McMullen had often staggered up to the front platform, where he could shout across the stubby coalpile to Dana.

Oldtime engineer Fred Leavett, who had once hauled the log trains down Sluice Hill and ran Forney engines through the snow across frozen ground, did odd jobs around the enginehouse and shop, and did a little spare running now and then. Joe Boston, an old conductor, did carpentering and car-shop work with veteran shopman Nat Harnden. Roadmaster Hal White, an oldtime trackman, with his busful of crew—some of them old-timers, too—kept the perpetual curves in perfect line. Even in these last days the midget trains streaked through the woods at 35 or 40 miles an hour, reasonably free from the *oscillations* which Father Mansfield had once emphasized as a selling point for the two-foot gauge.

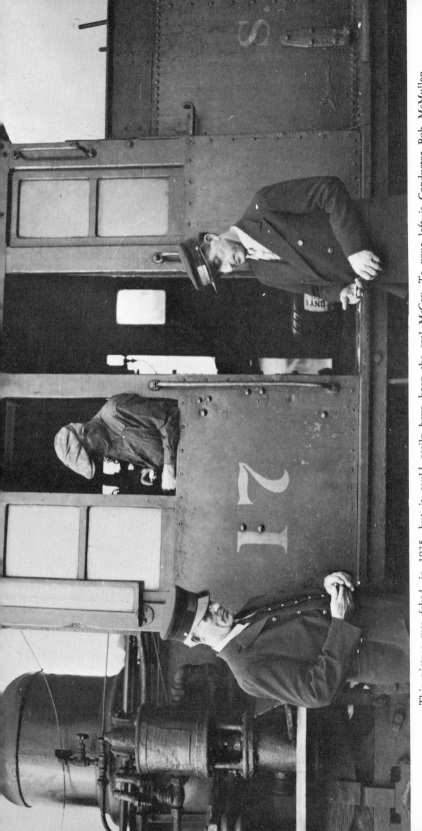

This picture was faked, in 1935, but it could easily have been the real McCoy. To your left is Conductor Bob McMullen, longtime boss of the *Rangeley Express*. Engineer Fred Leavitt is in the 17's cab, and Brakeman Clarence "Son" Fairbanks completes the foursome which had, thirty years before, handled the *Express* together.

Graveyard Train—last Sandy River run, June 29, 1935, stopped in the woods on Strong Mountain for a last drink from a trackside spring. The trim No. 24 engine—24 tons of original beauty—is trailed by combination No. 14, the car which lost her clerestory

This picture actually is historic: it shows veteran Ed West blowing cinders from the 24's front end at the end of the final run —June 29, 1935, when the Sandy River dumped its fire for all time. Only one engine, the 10, had a Hall-Slater self-clearing front end. All the others had to be blown clean at the end of each trip. The cloud of steam to the 24's left is loaded with the cinders she'd gathered during her last, long mile up from Farmington that day.

The F.&M. and the Sandy River were wrecked with steam. No. 18 with a winch-car and so[m]e flats is picking up the 35-pound F.&M. rail, nearly down to Strong. The old man looking on, [at] your right, helped lay this rail 35 years before, when it replaced the original 30-pound steel w[ith] which the F.&M. was laid in 1884. The date, August 1936.

Like the open graves of the World War II concentration camps is the macabre scene at Howlan[d] Pit, between Phillips and Strong. Five hundred tiny freightcars were nosed into the pit, burned, a[nd] their metal salvaged for junk. The twisted, blackened mass to your right is all that remains of ha[lf] a thousand Lilliput cars. Today a new highway location runs over this site.

Agent "Pansy" Newell at Strong was an old station man, as was Agent Leary at Kingfield. The agents at Phillips and Carrabasset were comparatively new men, hired when no old-timers wanted to work for $2.00 a day.

Many another old rail dropped in at train-time when he could, and helped with the switching, or slung a scoopful of coal on a popcorn fire, to keep his golden memories bright.

From her kitchen window near the track, Celia Whitney Smith waved at every passing train. For a lifetime she had been a Sandy River bookkeeper. Her husband, Procter Smith, had been an old Sandy River man years before.

Then there was the farmhouse between Phillips and Strong where a member of the Hamlin family had waved at every train for 56 years. The old patriarch, Grandpa Hamlin, had lived there when the Sandy River Railroad was built, in 1879. He and his children and their children kept the tradition warm. When the last train passed the Hamlin home—the scrap train, picking up the rails—three generations were out there in the yard, waving their last goodbye.

At another trackside farm, Cecil Voter's Collie *Prince* had for seven years raced the train from pasture fence to potato patch, without fail. When the scrap train inched its way by, leaving two ugly scars behind, Prince stood there and whined.

So, in its latter days the long-loved Lilliput railroad was handled by the old men who had handled it for years; and attended by other old-timers who had loved it along with them. Unlike so many communities, where a railroad is just an impersonal part of the landscape and economy, the Sandy River's neighbors took a warm, lively interest in it. During its lush years they had watched the frequent trains with delight. When business dwindled and the trains were fewer, they watched with a tug of alarm in their hearts. Now, that a figurative death-pallor tinged the Lilliput's complexion, they worried and fussed, and were perpetually looking out their windows for the train they feared might come no more.

The end was near. In the spring of 1935 you could feel it. The midget was holding its meager business. It was actually making a tiny profit. But something was about to happen. Either a streak of luck, or the end, was sure to come.

It was the end, as things turned out.

In May vague rumors wafted on the breeze. Nothing definite. One was that some rich men had bought it, and the Sandy River's future was secure. Another, that the receivers, Maxcy and Wing, were going to dump some new money in, and stage a comeback. Still another rumor whispered that the Lilliput would be scrapped.

That one was the truth.

Most of the strangers poking around Franklin County had the look of junkmen. Two or three may have had honest intentions. But the junkmen won. Maybe their intentions were the soundest, from a dollars-and-cents point of view.

An auction was advertised for May. Something like the auction fifty-seven years before when the infant Lilliput, the Billerica & Bedford, was butchered on the block. This auction in May 1935 was butchery, too. The Sandy River went for $20,200.00.

That happened May 18. By the terms of the sale the road would be scrapped if the Maine Public Utilities Commission gave permission.

When this news appeared next day a weak protest rustled from the lips of a few business folks along the line. They hadn't even rustled during the years the Sandy River was laboring up the grade, her exhausts lame and weak, needing help right then. Now, with junkmen already climbing the fence, they weakly demanded the matter be reconsidered.

Another rumor whispered that this protest scared the two lucky junkmen. They feared, it was said, their $20,200.00 might be tied up in a road they had to run. Twenty thousand dollars was more money in 1935 than it is today. Anyway, these two eager beavers quickly and suddenly sold their bonanza to a nationally big scrap iron firm. Rumor had it that the two original junkies took a $200.00 loss as an incentive to the larger firm to snatch the threat off their heads.

The big scrap company didn't bother with Public Utilities and I.C.C. permissions. As soon as their purchase was complete and legal

—recorded duly in Book 258, Page 545 in the Franklin County Registry of Deeds as of June 28, 1935—they wired Superintendent Vose to cease all operations the following day, June 29.

That was it—the end of the Sandy River.

The next morning the little 24 engine and combination car 14 (the one which lost its roof in the years-ago Kingfield fire) clattered out of Phillips on the final, common-carrier trip.

The Reo railbuses ran as usual, too. Bus No. 4 on the F.&M., and Bus 5 on the old mainline run. The 24 cleaned up the cars at the way-stations and sidings as well as it could. The parlor car *Rangeley,* long stored in the Kingfield enginehouse, had been hauled to Phillips a short time before. The last few loads of pay freight were taken to Farmington.

Dana Aldrich eased them into Phillips station that afternoon exactly as he'd done some twelve thousand times before. Clarence Fairbanks cut off the engine and it chuffed down the runaround, onto the table. Instead of helping push the heavy table around, Dana walked quickly into the enginehouse.

Ed West, the merry twinkle gone from his eye, took over. He moved her to the cinder pile, opened the handhole on the side of her smokebox, attached the cinder pipe to her blowoff valve, and *sparked* her for the last time. She clanked slowly into her stall. Silence filled the car-jammed yard.

During the remainder of 1935 the scrap people cut up a few of the out-of-service engines—the 22 and 21, the 16, the 19, and the wreck of the 20 over in the Old Stone Fort, along with the long rusting No. 7.

Price tags were put on everything. The pint-sized Baldwin engines were offered, ready to run, for $250 each. Only the 24 was sold. A railroad fan bought her and built a shed for her protection, but in October 1937 finally sold her for scrap.

All the passenger car bodies were sold, mostly for camps, play-houses, or chicken pens. The elegant parlor car *Rangeley* was sold, for $200, to Dr. Bell who had her left on four lengths of rail where the main line crossed his spacious lawn in Strong.

Most of the cabooses and a few boxcars too were lifted off their trucks and taken to farms and camps nearby. The Lilliput railroads were enjoying a lot of railroad fan popularity then, but it was Depression times, and money was tight. The folks who were interested spent time shedding tears instead of spending money buying the bantam engines and cars.

Winter came again. For the first time since 1878 the unbroken snow mantle lay cold and deep over Franklin County fields and woods. The lonesome grave of the Sandy River showed as a winding streak of deathly white.

Early the following spring, 1936, while the snow was still on the ground, Dana Aldrich and a helper or two began hauling boxcars out of Phillips yard. A two or three mile jaunt down the high iron and the train stopped alongside Howland's Pit, a big gouge in the earth where countless yards of gravel had been taken for resurfacing the Sandy River in times gone by. The boxcar bodies were toppled off their trucks into the gouge. That fire burned continually until nearly five hundred cars had been reduced to scrap metal. On the return trips to Phillips Dana would haul a long, macabre string of headless car trucks. The cutting torch at Phillips made short work of them.

In early summer the "wrecking crews" were formed. Dana Aldrich was hired to run the engine, because the wrecking boss decided to dismantle the road with steam. The 18 engine was selected to haul the funeral train. The little No. 9 was kept for possible use. A few flatcars, one equipped with a Ford motor and a winch for hauling rails aboard the flatcars, made up the train.

While wrecking was in progress the remaining little engines were hauled out of their comfortable stalls, stripped of their cabs, jackets, domes, and fittings, and put to the cutting-torch. The 10 and 17, and the big 23 moved reluctantly out into the sunshine, and next day they were gone.

The F.&M. was wrecked first. Because an early spring freshet had taken out the bridge at Kingfield—the same one the passenger train fell through a dozen years before—one of the Model T railbuses was trundled around the washed out bridge and rerailed just beyond.

They used her for picking up and hauling the steel and other scrap between Huston Brook, a mile or so above Carrabasset, and King-field. Then steam took over.

It was on August 13, 1936, that the last F.&M. rail was ripped loose at Strong. The train quickly moved to Phillips, to begin there the next morning.

Slowly, but surely, they moved down the big iron. They left Howland's Pit behind, and the charred bones of a half a thousand Lilliput cars. They passed the Hamlin Farm, where the Hamlins waved their last farewell. Strong was left behind. It was late September when the procession moved at last into Farmington.

When the last rail was up, and Maine Central freight trains rumbled out for Portland and the scrap markets beyond, only the little engines 9 and 18 were left for *processing*. The job didn't take long.

The Reo railbus No. 4 had lately been purchased by a railroad fan and presented to the neighboring Bridgton narrow gauge. The big Reo No. 5 was bought for a song by a Farmington lumber mill, to be used for moving boards and bolts around his millyard track. Boilers from a few of the best engines were sold to sawmills and canning factories nearby. One of these incidentally, the boiler of the high wheeled No. 10—complete with her Baldwin's builder's plate —turned up in a Portland, Maine machinery dealer's yard as late as 1954.

All that's left today of the once-flourishing Sandy River is a few of its buildings, and miles of bush-grown, brooding grade.

At Strong there is hardly a trace. Station and freight house were moved and new buildings built where the tracks used to run. An addition to the toothpick mill has overflowed the old F.&M., blotting out its approach to Strong yard.

At Phillips the station, almost untouched, now serves as a civic hall. A few feet away the big brick shops and roundhouse have become a factory.

Some of the way stations up the P.&R. are still there, as camps or shelters for logyard teams. The enginehouse and station at Rangeley are gone, and an oil dealer's tanks sprawl over the onetime rail-road yard. But you may still see the tiny stone station on the hotel grounds, which was once Marble's, the end of the P.&R. Today it is a lounging nook for hotel guests, close by the wharf used by vacation-ing outboarders.

Up on the F.&M. the Salem depot is a summer camp, and the new station at Kingfield is a store. The town of Kingfield uses the three-stall enginehouse to garage the town's trucks.

The depot at Carrabasset is a tumbling ruin, not only the railroad yards but the area that was once the village of Carrabasset lies buried deep in 20 years of bushes and trees.

The Sandy River is gone. But they say, and there are folks who will swear to it, that on windy nights when the sky is black you may see a pencil of light flickering among the trees, and vaguely hear on the treetop wind the sweet, shrill whistle of a Lilliput train.

14

BRIDGTON & SACO RIVER RAILROAD

Along in 1879 the good folks farther down in western Maine, 80 odd miles south of the Sandy River, got grandiose notions about having a railroad.

The town of Bridgton (they spell it minus the *E*) was, and still is, a flourishing summer resort. The rusticators had to flourish fifteen miles to and from the nearest railroad. The Portland & Ogdensburg Railroad, from Portland, Maine west through the White Mountains to St. Johnsbury, Vermont, passed through the town of Hiram. There was no transportation thither and hither better than a buckboard jolting behind a team of horses. Half of Bridgton's habitues jolted up from Hiram on the buckboards.

Then, there was a canal, too. The other half steamboated up for the summer by way of Sebago Lake and various rivers and locks. Before the P.&O. was built the Cumberland & Oxford Canal came all the way from Portland. When the railroad poked west toward Vermont it paralleled the canal to Sebago Lake, so that part of the waterway fell back to lily-pads and eel-grass. Sebago Lake railroad station became the breech, while the muzzle scattered passengers all along the lake shore and clear up to Long Lake, which was studded with such favored resort towns as Bridgton and Harrison.

Those far off events of 1879 have dimmed with the years. Nothing has come to light which actually declares that a rapport existed between railroad-hungry Bridgton and the towns which were lately enjoying the advantages of the new railroad along the tumbling Sandy River.

However, old newspaper clippings of those Bridgton days are lurid with the name of George E. Mansfield, "inventor of the 2-foot gauge system of railways", as was unfailingly added. So, railroadingly speaking, it might seem that Mansfield was getting around, even while building the Sandy River.

Not much is known about George Mansfield. Many letters of inquiry were mailed to all the likely places, and many unlikely ones, before writing this book in hopes of telling you a little about the unknown man who "invented and promoted *the Mansfield System*". But every inquiry ran off into the weeds and petered out. However, in the light of history, it looks as if George either did some fancy promoting along with his managerial duties in Billerica and in Phillips, or that his "invention" was so currently popular with wouldbe railroad builders that they ferreted him out of whatever remote neighborhood he was railroading in at the moment.

Anyway, he had a hand in the Bridgton & Saco River Railroad.

During its embryonic stage there was, as usual, the hassles and wrangling, the cussing and discussing, the meetings and handshaking, speeches, baby-kissing, and numerous impulsive false starts.

The false starts on the Bridgton project may have been weak accidents in the overall scheme, or maybe they were actually designed to bring order out of chaos. Few railroads ever did go where their promoters said they would.

During the Bridgton hassles there were folks who thought the best route would be running east toward Portland, using the towpath of the abandoned Cumberland & Oxford canal some of the way. This would tie Bridgton by rail with Maine's largest city, some thirty miles away. It might well have been the best, too, in the light of later events.

As often happened in other places, these embryonic dreams collided with opposition. It came partly from the steamboat people, partly from the buckboard men, and not a little from the Portland & Ogdensburg Railroad. Those steamboats plying Sebago and Long Lakes were doing a gold-mine business. The owners had no desire to see a new railroad shoplifting their passengers and freight. They had little use for the iron horse which spattered calamity on canals and wagon roads.

The stages and freight wagons which billowed through dust and wallowed through mud from the P.&O. at Hiram up through Denmark, Bridgton and Harrison could see no prosperity for themselves harbingered by a competing railroad. Likewise did the Portland-to-Vermont railroad company take a dim view of losing lucrative traffic to direct from Portland-to-Bridgton trains. These opponents bared their dentures and snarled.

When tooth-baring and snarling became especially formidable there was talk of discarding the Portland-Ho idea, and running the new railroad from Bridgton north. The old Atlantic & St. Lawrence, or Grand Trunk, was up there. Its station at Norway, Maine was only 15 miles away.

In some ways that Grand Trunk connection would have been all right. The Grand Trunk would have been a good route to Portland, besides the route would have given the new railroad two or three other towns to serve. Even today the Grand Trunk offers a better freight route from the West, and this advantage could have been exploited by the new line, as far as its far-flung commerce went.

However, this proved to have been another false start. As time and speeches and meetings went on, eliminating the illogical, the politics, the petty prejudices, and other schemes which destiny had fore-ordained, the new railroad began to take shape.

As we've seen, George Mansfield was around. Somewhere along the way from 1879 to 1881 he sold his "Mansfield style of railroad" to the crowd. Someone else sold them the route which they decided on—south from Bridgton to a point on the P.&O. a mile east of Hiram depot.

In July 1881, the Bridgton & Saco River Railroad was chartered.

The name *Saco* is an old Indian word. The river which tumbles down through the hills, to the Atlantic Ocean at Biddeford, is the Saco River. It is pronounced, by the way, *Saw' ko*. The Bridgton & Saco River Railroad would terminate on the trembling banks of the turbulent river.

The B.&S.R. Railroad, the third of the Lilliputs to be born, was chartered in 1881 and construction was started from the *wide* gauge at Hiram a year later, in July 1882.

It would have been about this time that George Mansfield did a Houdini from the Sandy River pages. Apparently he disappeared in order to quickly reappear in the history of the B.&S.R. He seems to have been pretty much the guiding hand in raising this third Lilliput from the hassling stage to materialization as a swashbuckling, operating railroad.

Mansfield also brought some boys from the Sandy River to help him.

One of these men, John Marcque, became something of a legend in Bridgton. Mr. Marcque was born in 1850, in St. Francis, Quebec, of French-Canadian parents. He was one of fourteen children, of whom several became railroad men. In 1867 he began railroading on construction trains of the old Androscoggin Railroad. In March 1879 he fell in with Inventor Mansfield someway, who appointed him as a locomotive engineer on the fledgling Sandy River Railroad. Shortly, because Mansfield recognized Marcque's ability, he made him Sandy River roadmaster as well as engineer. The early Lilliputs may have had something there—their habit of combining "official" capacities with menial jobs! Two years later, on Sept. 6, 1883, John Marcque followed Inventor Mansfield to the B.&S.R. as engineer of the construction train.

Mansfield did things in a hurry. He built the 16-mile Bridgton & Saco River in six months. Marcque ran the first train into Bridgton almost before he'd learned the road. As a yellowed newspaper clipping eloquently relates, "On January 20, 1883 Engineer Marcque had the felicity of running the first train over the entire roadbed."

We aren't hypercritical, of course, but let's hope the laymen's expression, "—entire roadbed—" didn't mean what it sounds like!

The Marcque clan liked railroading. Two brothers, Joseph and Lewis, didn't come to the B.&S.R. They stayed with the Sandy River and for many years were section foreman and section-hand, respectively, there.

Like Engineer Marcque, another lifer on the Bridgton line was M. M. Caswell. Mel Caswell, as his initials might imply, was Master Mechanic. He worked from the beginning to the declining years of the little railroad's life. In the final days Uncle Mel didn't do much railroading, because he was close to 90. But he was still a familiar figure around the narrow-gauge.

The first passenger train ran into Bridgton January 20, 1883 (some old clippings say it was the 21st), and regular service was set up a few days later.

As another and further proof of the validity of *the Mansfield System* of building railroads, the B.&S.R. was built for $10,000 a mile as compared to $20,000 and more which contemporary *wide,* or standard, gauge was costing.

One item of interest in those early Bridgton & Saco River reports, and an item about which Lilliput opponents of later years either were ignorant, or ignored, was the fact that transferring freight at The Junction was an expense which amounted to *one-eighth of the interest on a wide gauge investment!*

In other words, the additional $160,000.00 which a standard gauge railroad would have cost would have run up an interest charge of $9,600.00 a year. The total cost of transferring freight in those early days was less than that amount, not to consider the ten cent ties, the 25 percent as much ballast, the smaller rail, less coal, and many, many other one-half and one-third expenses for the two-foot gauge. Inventor Mansfield had been right in his promotionalizings.

While the B.&S.R. was preparing grade and ties on which to lay the 30-pound rails the Hinckley Locomotive Works was building a couple of 13-ton Forney engines. They were similar to the ones it had built four years earlier for the Billerica & Bedford Railroad. They had cylinders 9 x 12 inches, driving wheels 30 inches in diameter, and carried 140 pounds of steam. They cost the new railroad $3,000.00 each, according to a newspaper report of the time.

There were two coaches, 45 feet long over the Miller platforms. They were six and a half feet wide and seated 30 passengers. Finished in solid mahogany and controlled by vacuum brakes, one was named

Mount Pleasant and the other *Pondicherry,* the original name of the town of Bridgton. There was also a combination car, ten "platform cars", five boxcars, and a caboose. From the newspaper clippings, these were all built by the Laconia Car Company of Laconia, New Hampshire.

Besides the $166,000.00 the new railroad cost to build, the equipment was on the books as costing another $26,000.00.

Loosely speaking, like the Sandy River the B.&S.R. was a paying proposition from the start. Most of the early Annual Reports announced not only a profit for the year but a substantial nestegg as a surplus from preceding years. This happy happenstance wasn't always the case with *wide* gauge roads which were new in those same years. Enormous interest charges often bankrupted them before the first pay day.

Like all Maine railroads—all New England railroads, in fact, and perhaps most all the railroads everywhere—The Bridgton & Saco River did a booming business in forest products. Lumber, pulpwood, dowels and shovel-handles and shingles, and even bark for tanneries provided lush earnings in early years.

Passengers, too, were profitable. Soon after that first train "ran over the entire roadbed" more coaches were needed. Two more were bought, making a total of four. Then, two baggage cars, one fitted with a Railway Post Office compartment, were added. The B.&S.R. didn't seem to go in for the open excursion cars which characterized the Sandy River's overflow equipment.

The ancient newspaper clipping, which featured Engineer John Marcque, had some interesting things to say about the B.&S.R. and its doings. After the stock "commercial", "—it was constructed and is run on the Mansfield System, its inventor and promoter being George E. Mansfield of Greenfield, New Hampshire—" the clipping gets down to business and makes some solid comments anent the B.&S.R.

"If any of the passengers who desire information about this queer railway have time to chat with Engineer Marcque a few minutes before the train starts, they might learn some curious and interesting

Photo by Hugh G. Boutell

e of the very rare photos in existence of B&S.R. No. 1, taken in front of the Bridgton engine-
se prior to 1909. The first twenty-odd years of her life saw few changes in appearance. The full
size headlight and the big bell seem to go well with her diminutive lines.

S.R. No. 2, the 12-ton Forney which Hinckley built in 1883, posed with her engine crew at
Maine Central depot at Bridgton Junction. Wide gauge freights beyond are at the transfer
1 where wide and midget cars exchanged freight. No. 2 later went to the W.W.&F. as their No. 5.

Photo by Hugh G. Boutell

An early train, southbound, at Sandy Creek on the B.&S.R. The tiny diamond-stack engine
either the 1 or the 2, in either case a Hinckley Forney. By the position of the sun this tr
would appear to be the down train in the morning. Date probably around 1883; the grade a
building looks new.

B.&S.R. No. 5, snapped July 24, 1907, when the little engine—the last the Portland Compa
ever built—was but one year old. No. 5 survived more than twenty years after this picture w
taken, being retired only a dozen years before the railroad itself was done.

Photo by Hugh G. Bo

facts about Bridgton's odd little railroad. He could tell them as to the road's history being untarnished by any record of loss of life or limb. He could state that his little 26,000-pound locomotive can draw a well loaded train of cars up so heavy a grade as 4 percent; that his engine and train can easily and safely round so sharp a curve as 20 degrees at the rate of 25 miles an hour; that the seeming recklessness of trying to run a train on rails only two feet apart is an entirely safe performance so far as any danger of a tip-over is concerned, by reason of the nearness of the cars to the ground and consequent lowering of the center of gravity; in short, that the three essentials of safety, speed, and comfort are thoroughly assured."

Besides being a plenty long sentence, we could secretly guess that maybe George E. Mansfield himself wrote that piece for the paper!

"He could also state," the report goes on, "that such a road can be built for a little more than half, and its running expenses are only one-half, that of a broad gauge road; for corroboration of which he would refer to President William Berry, Treasurer Perley Burnham, or General Manager Joseph Bennet, all of whom have been officially connected with this railway from the start."

So, there you have it. No wonder George Mansfield sold his system of two-foot gauge railways. While we may wrinkle our little noses at the verbiage, history did prove these declarations to be true.

The two Lilliput engines scooted back and forth around those 20 degree curves and up the 4 percent hills at 25 miles an hour, and faster, piling up not only enviable safety and comfort records, but a pleasing surplus as well. Now and then a few more cars were added, as freight and passenger business increased. There must have been times when things were in a muddle, when one of the little Hinckleys had to go in for repairs.

Nine years after the B.&S.R. was opened, in 1892, another locomotive was bought, the Portland Company No. 3, a Forney like the others. No. 3 was more powerful, having 10½x14-inch cylinders, and weighing 18 tons.

When the different Bridgton engines were retired is a matter of conjecture. The No. 3's arrival didn't catapult either of the Hinckley engines onto the junkheap. It was a dozen or fifteen years later when No. 2 was sold to the W.W.&F.

Another nine years sped by before the fourth engine came. Business was really good. Three engines weren't power enough to assure Bridgton of the frequent and uninterrupted service it demanded. No. 4 was likewise a Forney type, but much heavier than her predecessors—28 tons. She had 11x14-inch cylinders and a boiler as big as a barrel—a *big* barrel. In order to keep the larger boiler where it belonged, the cab sat farther ahead, and the steam-dome was inside the cab. Her whistle and pops poked up through the cab roof. No. 4 differed still more from the others in that she was built by the H. K. Porter Works instead of by the more popular builders. Porter had built, you'll remember, one other Lilliput engine 'way back in 1883, the Sandy River Railroad No. 3. Why more of our Lilliput railroads didn't buy from Porter is a mystery. Porter built excellent and beautiful engines, second to none. But three were all they ever sold to the two-footers.

Five years later No. 5 came to Bridgton, in 1906. No. 5 was a Portland Company engine but the B. & S.R.'s first 2-4-4RT. That is, she was a Forney with a rear tank like the others, except she had pony wheels for better riding and to be easier on track. And, she is said to have been the very last engine built by that famous builder of so many fine locomotives. She also had the reputation, among her engine crews, of being one of the hardest riding and hardest steaming engines any railroad ever had!

The following year, 1907, the first Baldwin engine came to the B.&S.R., No. 6.

Just as No. 4 had been built in a joint order, and was identical, with W.W.&F. No. 4, so was No. 6 a mate to an engine Baldwin built for the Sandy River, its No. 8. Whether there was anything more than coincidence in these two occasions of two roads buying engines which were mates, no one seems to know. Anyway, there was no financial or managerial relationship between the roads involved. Perhaps Baldwin designed this engine and a good salesman sold one to both the Sandy River and the Bridgton road that same summer. No. 6 was a 2-4-4RT like No. 5. Engine crews didn't brag too much about No. 6's riding qualities, either. The inside frames made the engines teetery—made them *oscillate,* as Mansfield would have said if he'd admitted it at all. The little 12 and 18 tonners didn't flip and roll so much, because of their light weight and scantier dimensions. But the larger the engines became the worse they rode. That was the major reason that later ones were all of the outside-frame design. No. 6's mate on the Sandy River, the No. 8 over there, cut up the same didos. She was the engine which tipped over, scalding her engineer to death, you'll recall.

So far all the B.&S.R. engines had used inside valve-gear, the Stephenson link type. In fact, until several years after this, all Lilliput engines sported the inside link motion. Outside gear didn't come until 1913 when both the Sandy River and the Bridgton roads bought new engines, equipped with Walsheart.

The B.&S.R. had also been adding more cars, along with more engines. It had been adding substantially to its traffic. This expanding tonnage was so promising, in fact, that 29 years after the Lilliput was built, in 1912, the big Maine Central which was currently getting control of shortlines in Maine and New Hampshire, gobbled up the Bridgton & Saco River.

But before that—we're getting ahead of ourselves a little—in 1898 the long struggle of Harrison people was rewarded by their getting the railroad extended from Bridgton five miles to Harrison.

Harrison, like Bridgton, was a summer resort. Even in those days before the State of Maine sold out to the out-of-Staters many Maine towns were in the *rusticator* business from June to September. So it was with Harrison. People swarmed into town on the lake steamers and by buckboard. A few came via train to Bridgton and team to Harrison, too many of them were coming up the lakes by steamboat. The railroad tycoons in Bridgton didn't like the looks of those over-crowded steamers. They were afraid someone would fall overboard and get drowned. They decided, at long last, to spend a few dollars and build their railroad up to Harrison, and thereby avert any tragic drowning accidents. It might also help swell the coffers of the railroad, too, by diverting that traffic to the B.&S.R.

This extension, as it was called, was approximately five miles long. Bridgton was Mile 15.8 and Harrison became Mile 20.7. One station was on the extension, North Bridgton, and the final couple of miles was along the shore of Long Lake.

Long Lake presented something of an obstacle. Near its northern end Harrison was on the wrong side of the water. So, the extension went across a long pile trestle. As soon as it hit solid ground again it was in Harrison Village.

A neat terminal was built in Harrison. It was smaller than the yard down at Bridgton, but just as attractive and totally adequate for the activities with which Harrison traffic could fill it. There was a fine depot, with varnished hardwood interior. A 2-stall engine-house with the table in front, and a carhouse were built. Those passenger cars, in 1898, had to be run under cover every night.

Harrison had a corn-shop, which contributed carloads of canned corn for hungry folks in the outside world. A coopershop added some more freight. A grain mill and outgoing lumber filled more midget freight cars. The summer rusticator boom, with all its baggage and indirect supplies, was a lush business. Excursions in cahoots with the steamboat company, which the railroad hadn't yet put out of business, were extra money. That five mile extension, laid with 35-pound rail, was a good investment for the B.&S.R.

Those rail-water excursions were fun, too. They must have been, or so many people wouldn't have taken them. Folks from Portland, and beyond, would come up to Sebago station on the Maine Central train. There they would race out to the wharf, many of them loaded with picnic baskets, to the waiting steamboat. The trip up Sebago Lake was sightly and exciting. Sightly because of the rugged, wooded shores with their backdrop of hills. Exciting because the company staged an Indian attack at a bluff called Frye's Leap which the steam-boat passed nearby. Some hired hands, painted and befeathered, would rush into view when the steamer was scant yards away, yelling and war-whooping, and brandishing guns. The shots they fired at the helpless passengers did no harm, because they were blanks. But many of the excursionists didn't know it.

rthbound along the shore of Hancock Pond, midway between Bridgton and the Junction. Just
ond the cottage is the Hancock Watertank. One time in the 1920's a train got stuck here in ice
snow, and stayed nearly a week before it was dug out. The crew lived on bread from the express
car and water from Hancock tank.

he only 2-foot gauge tankcars were two which ran on the B.&S.R. These actually weren't true
nkcars, but tanks put onto standard flatcars. And, they weren't railroad cars; they were owned by
e gasoline company which supplied Bridgton with gasoline and fuel oil. One car was 5,000
gallons and the other 3,500. Both are on the Edaville Railroad today.

A passenger train, headed by No. 8, 2-4-4T Baldwin, just arrived at Bridgton Jct. The 8 was slightly heavier than the 7, weighing 38 tons, and was the very last Lilliput locomotive built, coming in 1924. Like the 7, No. 8 now hauls Edaville passenger trains around the cranberry bogs and except for some fancy paint to attract the holiday crowd, she's not materially changed since her B.&S.R. days.

Arriving at Harrison in mid-afternoon the crowd would troop ashore and over to the depot. The afternoon train took them down to Hiram, or Bridgton Junction, where the eastbound Maine Central train landed 'em back in Portland by early evening. These round-the-circle jaunts lasted up to the latter days of operation on the Harrison extension.

In the earlier days there were several way stations which had agents. An agent and an assistant or two were kept at Bridgton Junction, besides the crew which transferred the freight. South Bridgton and Sandy Creek were agencies, as were Bridgton, North Bridgton, and Harrison. There were flag stations and small yards at Twin Lakes, West Sebago, Perley's Mill and Ingall's Road. In later years all these were flag stations, the only agencies being at Bridgton, North Bridgton, and Harrison.

In 1900 another new baggage car appeared. The B.&S.R. listed that year three engines, two coaches, two baggage cars, fourteen box and 23 flats, besides such work equipment as snowplows and flangers.

As we've already seen, No. 4 engine came in 1901. Another coach in 1904. No. 5 engine came in 1906 and the next year No. 6 was bought. No. 2, one of the original Hinckley midgets, was sold to the Wiscasset, Waterville & Farmington Ry. in either 1906 or 1907. Most likely in 1906 when No. 5 was built. According to old-timers, No. 2 wasn't paid for by her new owners, and finally some B.&S.R. folks went over to Wiscasset and lugged one of its coaches home, to square things. At any rate, the Bridgton road had a former W.W.&F. coach, which lends strength to the legend.

In 1906, according to old Maine Railroad Commission reports, the equipment was fitted with three-fourths size Climax automatic couplers. Then, in 1911, the year before the Maine Central got control, another coach was added, at a cost of $1,500.00.

There another proof of Lilliput economy stares you in the eye; where could a *wide* gauge coach be found, even in 1911, brand new for only $1,500.00?

Then the Maine Central moved in.

The big road made many improvements. It made a lot of money, too. One of the improvements was No. 7 engine in 1913. No. 7 was the B.&S.R.'s first outside-frame, outside-gear engine. She was built the same month as S.R.&R.L. No. 23, and these two introduced Walsheart valve-motion to the Lilliput roads.

The Bridgton & Saco River had been paying dividends for years. When the Maine Central took over there was a hefty surplus in its treasury. Old newspaper accounts, some of them obviously not on the *wide* gauge's side, openly and belligerently declared that the Maine Central robbed the Lilliput. These columns boldly accused the wide-gauger of deliberately voting itself 20 percent dividends from that chunky surplus. The Maine Central either didn't bother to tell its own side of the story, or the paper which printed the defense hasn't come to light.

In 1916 the narrow-gauge's balance sheet showed a total earning of $60,615.00, which wasn't bad in the days of $3.00 a ton coal, $3.00 a day crews, and five cents a mile passenger fares. Total expenses for that year were $46,851.00. $13,000.00 was paid in interest and dividends. The operating ratio was 76 percent. The tiny trains hauled 34,000 passengers and 30,000 tons of freight.

Another event in 1916 was the resignation of Joe Bennett as President, General Manager, Superintendent, and what-have-you. Bennett had been with the little railroad 33 years, ever since it was built. He was succeeded in most of those official capacities by Everett Crosby.

The biggest year, revenuewise, the B.&S.R. ever had was 1921.

In 1921 its gross earnings were $112,000.00.

It was sometime in these years that the Railway Post Office route was abolished. For years the two round trips daily had hauled the R.P.O. car, which didn't pay as high a mileage rate as it would today, but still was a pretty penny when the 80 miles a day were added up. From then on, until the end, the railroad continued to haul mail on a closed-pouch, storage basis.

Three years later, in 1924, the very last Lilliput engine was built, the last for any of the two-foot roads. Baldwin built her and she was numbered 8. She was slightly heavier than the 7, weighing approximately 38 tons. Why the Bridgton & Saco River never followed the Sandy River's and the W.W.&F.'s lead by buying any separate-tender engines, is a mystery. All its locomotives were single-unit, or Forney types. The ones with the added pony truck were not, of course, true Forney types, but perhaps we can use the term loosely to distinguish them from the Moguls and Prairie types which abounded on the Sandy River, and appeared on the Wiscasset line.

Also in 1924 those crotchety newspapers were beefing that the Maine Central had already collected 85 percent of its investment in dividends taken from the road's treasury. Other people there were who thought the two new engines, the miles of heavy 56-pound rail and the improved roadbed compensated to some extent for depleting the rotund surplus which had thus dwindled year by year.

After all, the Maine Central hadn't bought the narrow-gauge's capital stock at par value for sentimental reasons. Nor were business deals of this kind particularly frowned on in those lush days of high-finance railroading.

Something must have gone sour, however, for three years later, in 1927, the holders of some mortgage bonds got their fur up. By process of mortgage holders legal privilege they took over control from the wide gauge owner. Temporary receivership was ordered by a court. The Lilliput railroad tightened its belt, so to speak.

The next year, 1928, a new company was chartered, the Bridgton & Harrison Railway, for the purpose of operating the property. Nearly two years passed before the various and probably necessary legal hurdles were achieved and the new company stepped into the picture. In June 1930 the new Bridgton & Harrison Railway Company acquired some railroad to go with its hitherto unpropertied title. It bought the Bridgton & Saco River Railway for $27,000.00.

Business had fallen off unbelievably. In 1930 the freight earning was only $15,628.00. Passengers — 1,646 of them — paid only $891.79 for the esoteric privilege of riding the Lilliput trains. Mail and express revenues totalled $6,415.62, or a grand total income of $22,946.00 as compared to the $112,000.00 of only nine years before.

The Lilliputs half-size expenses were only $25,204.00, an operating ratio of an unhealthy 109.84, but even so that gross revenue was short of the meager income by some $2,000.00. The 1,646 passengers and the 7,396 tons of freight simply wasn't enough for even a half-cost two-foot gauge.

We have to keep the vague recognition in mind that when a railroad reports expenses which are bigger than earnings, there probably isn't any out of pocket loss. It's usually due to the system of bookkeeping. When the Sandy River reported a $40,000.00 loss in 1934 or '35 the little road most certainly didn't take $40,000.00 out of its bank account to make up an actual loss. The $40,000.00 was a "loss" because it was a desired sum which the road didn't earn. In most such cases desired dividends on capital stock, or some such item. Neither railroads nor other enterprises are likely to stay in business if expenses are actually and truly greater than gross income. So it probably was with the Bridgton & Saco River Railroad in 1930. All of which doesn't mean, by a long shot, that things weren't discouraging, Lilliputwise.

Traffic on the Harrison extension had slumped in proportion. Maintenance on those five miles had slumped beyond proportion. The heavy engines had raised havoc with the light, 35-pound steel. Derailments were becoming uncomfortably frequent. Shortly after the new B.&H. Railway took over, the big No. 8 engine hit a soft spot in the track going up one day, and quicker than you can spit she was over on her side in the ditch. It's a credit to the feline characteristics of Lilliput railroaders that Fireman Howard Whitney and Engineer Phil Marcque landed in the lap of Mother Nature before their bantam engine did. The baggage car tipped over, too, but the coach stayed right side up.

So, three months after taking over the 20 miles of miser-gauge railroad, and renaming it the Bridgton & Harrison, the track between those two towns was unceremoniously abandoned.

Cutting back to Bridgton didn't save the day. Old Lady Luck was in her well-known sour mood. Nothing seemed to improve, and lots of things got worse, including business and general maintenance. Due to her cussedness some drastic changes in policies and practices were tried.

Came the then-popular experiment with some kind of automotive substitute for trains which most shortlines and some big ones fooled with in those changing times. The neighboring Sandy River had hit the jackpot with its super-duper railbuses. The B.&H elected to follow suit.

The B.&H. either didn't have the genius and shop equipment which turned out the splendid Sandy River buses, or it didn't have time to bother with such extravagant elegance. Its first automotive product which passed as a self-propelled motor passenger train, left much to be desired by both passengers and crew.

This rig, the Chevrolet radiator being the only feature which was recognizable, replaced steam mixed trains part of the time. Either one of the two round trips each day was made with the motor rig, or as in later years the motor was the regular equipment, a steam train running once, twice, or three times a week when enough freight showed up at Bridgton Junction to justify the cost of running a steam job.

Still matters got worse. In 1933 freight earnings had dropped to $10,478.00. Passenger fares slumped to a mere $309.57 for hauling 810 people. The total revenue for that year was only $15,918.00. Expenses were $15,761.00 and most of it was honest figuring. Mighty little time was wasted, at that late date, in adding non-existent depreciation of equipment or the dividends which would have been paid if the capital stock was to pay 6 percent. There was a meager $157.00 clear of expenses for that year, 1933. It was not so much the $157.00 profit which was scary as it was the unbelievable decrease in freight tonnage and passengers—6,292 tons and the rock-bottom 810 passengers. Those figures amounted to the proverbial handwriting on the wall. The B.&H. folks could read.

Of course, the depression was on, by now. That didn't help. If there hadn't been any depression the chances are the Lilliput railway still wouldn't have been doing much better. The trend was in full swing.

Railroads themselves weren't wholly free from blame for this trend. High passenger fares weren't offering irresistible lures to the rails. Trucks, flexible and convenient and less rigid and unyielding,

made patronizing them attractive. The old wail about unfair com
petition, subsidized highways, regulation, and the unions may hav
had some merits. But there were other causes for the trend whicl
Depression Age railroads didn't talk about.

In those depression times, like today, much passenger travel i
for pleasure or business combined with pleasure. Often your ow
auto adds aplenty to both. When two people were traveling togethe
the auto was a lot cheaper than the three or four or five cents a mil
for a ticket.

The freight field had similar advantages. When a canning factor
or lumber mill could load a car of its freight on a big truck this after
noon and have it delivered to the consignee's plant tomorrow, a
opposed to a railroad boxcar being a week in transit, the advantage
of the truck attracted a lot of traffic, depression or no depression
Unhappily, with today's railroad woes ringing in our ears, this sam
situation is still true.

The Lilliput railroads felt this situation painfully. All railroad
did. Shortlines were hit the hardest and probably our Lilliputs wer
hit still harder because by the very virtue of their full-size-servic
versus half-size-expenses no standard gauge shortline would hav
survived as long as the midgets did.

Moreover, their status as originating-delivering railroads, with
out any "bridge" or intermediate tonnage left them in a bad fix. Tha
was the kind of a how-dee-do the Bridgton & Harrison was in, th
first of the 1930's.

Beefing and wailing and cussing the other fellow didn't help
Cussing didn't bring tonnage back. Cutting off trains and curtailin
service wasn't a remedy. All the little B.&H. could think of was t
grit its teeth and keep on puffing while there was a lump of coal o
the tank.

In the illuminating light of hindsight miracles can be done
Maybe in some cases a shakeup in officialdom might have helped
Maybe a greater effort to have served the public instead of demand
ing that the public serve the railroad would have been effective publi
relations. This could be equally effective today.

So, probably the two-footers were predestined to go, just as some shortlines and even some big roads which are checking out currently, were predestined to go. Maybe the whole railroad industry is on skids, but because you and I can't do much about it, maybe it's better to simply call it The Trend. Be that as it may, the Lilliput railroads felt the trend severely. As we've just seen, the B.&H. was doubled up with cramps all through the 1930's, and was pretty nearly crippled along the tail-end of its losing struggle. But, they kept on railroading.

Sometimes for days on end only the railbus would be operating, for mail, express and the random passengers. Then, if 40 or 50 tons of freight arrived at The Junction a steam engine would hustle down, or maybe that morning an old-time mixed train would be out again.

The Bridgton road had several special spouts from which seasonal revenues dribbled. One was the Summer Camp Specials. Being a summer resort community, all the rusticators weren't sedate adults. Mobs of 'em were kids. Many summer camps abounded—and still do— in the woods around Bridgton and Harrison. When city schools closed for the summer lots of the higher salaried folks shipped Junior and Sister off to camp, up in Maine. Along the last of June these camps swamped the B.&H. Long passenger trains creaked off the weedy storage tracks and rumbled toward the Junction for their loads of juveniles. Often, when a single camp was opening, a couple of trips were necessary. Another train would have to go down when the two passenger trips were done, to haul up the stacks of trunks and duffles and other equippage for the summer fun. This process was repeated again just before Labor Day, when the rising generation left the wilds of Maine for drab civilization again. Multiplied by ten or a dozen camps and the Camp Specials were a welcomed squirt of extra money, especially in the last years.

Another lucky happenstance, which the other two-footers missed out on, was the Railroad Fan trade.

In the late 1930's, when the Railroad Fan movement was really flourishing and those *flourishistas* realized that the Bridgton & Harrison was the last of the famed Lilliputs (the 200-miles-away Monson Railroad was still running, but didn't pack the appeal the B.&H.

did), there began the many excursions from Boston to Bridgton. Not necessarily Boston; but most of them originated there. Sometimes it was a jointly sponsored, bona-fide excursion, with the Boston & Maine, the Maine Central, and the Bridgton & Harrison railroad running it. Other times the group simply arranged to hire the narrow-gauge for the day, and take their own time browsing through the car-jammed yards, inspecting every railroad item in sight, and finally the leisurely, never-to-be forgotten ride to the Junction and back on their own special train. No arbitrary, unyielding rules prevented them from each having a turn riding the tiny Baldwin's cab. Often it was the only time many a fan of the 1930's had even been on an engine.

On those excursion days not only a steam engine was brought out for admiration as well as locomotion, but usually old Uncle Mel Caswell was brought out, too. Uncle Mel was the last tie with the Lilliput's beginnings. He was about 90 years old and had been the road's first Master Mechanic. The fact that he had retired many years before didn't dim his memories, calm his enthusiasm, or in any way detract from his own and the fans' delight in having him a part of the holiday!

These Fan Trips were welcomed by the B.&H.'s owners, rather than frowned upon as is the case so often when big roads are earmarked for See-the-Railroad fan trips. The town of Bridgton was the principal owner. And at least half the town welcomed the healthy earnings from these excursions as well as the potential which they suggested for future rusticators to the vacation resort.

True to public ownership, Bridgton was about equally divided in its sentiments concerning the little white pachyderm which it owned. As road and equipment fell into more disrepair and earnings sank to new and newer lows, the townsmen took sides. Figuratively anyway, they arrayed themselves in two formidable, opposing lines, sleeves shoved back and dentures bared.

The rightist-group, captained by First Selectman Lester Ames, cheered for the wobbling two-footer and demanded that the town's voters keep it running, even if a small subsidy became necessary. There was gold in them thar hills, they shouted.

dgton Yard. The track boys could have done good service here, with a lining-bar or two. The
pound rails seem a little out of tune. This photo is looking north, toward the bumper post.
main line to Harrison switched off a few rail lengths behind us here. Today a new school and
playground have been built on the old railroad yard.

"Campers' Special" about to leave Bridgton Junction behind No. 7 engine in the golden days
of July, 1935.

The Bridgton road survived to see the boom in railroad fan interest. Fan excursions fed its starv[
treasury the last few, final years. Here, in Bridgton in 1940, a fan trip waits to return the cro[
to the eastbound Maine Central train for Portland and Boston. Passenger trains like this, howe[
were the rule a quarter of a century earlier.

B.&S.R. No. 8 and mixed train rattling into Bridgton yard after a pay-trip up from the Junct[
August 31, 1937. By then the B.&S.R. had become the B.&H.

Photo by Hugh G. B[

The leftists, or negative group (not actually sourpusses and cranks) were progressive. They had advanced from the buckboard and steamboat days, passed the transient railroad period, and were now determined to lead their fair town into the ways of modernity if not righteousness and economy. They demanded that the voters vote to dispose of the derelict eyesore to whomever would buy it, preferably a junkie who would clean it up and leave Bridgton spotless and pure for the lucrative rusticators.

For several years the bloodless strife surged back and forth. First the pro-railroad Amesites were in power. Then the junkity group would steal the votes. When the junkiters were in power they would make strenuous efforts to dispose of the antique anachronism which was such a shame to their side of the town. But the followers of Lester Ames managed each time to thwart their progressive antics. Several times groups of railroad fans tried to organize to buy the property. A few individuals who were money-blessed came, looked around, but went away again. The ardent and devoted fans were the most likely prospects for making the purchase but the boys never seemed to have any luck when they passed the hat.

Passenger business would, at that 1939-40 date, seem to be the source from which revenue must necessarily come, no matter who was to run the railroad. Those fares would have to come from tourists, rusticators, and fan groups. Local travel was gone with Dobbin. Besides, there was no place for local people to go if they did ride. By now the Maine Central had taken off its Bartlett to Portland train, down in the morning and back at night, which would be the only direction Bridgton folks would be going, if they went at all. So, outsiders attracted by Bridgton's various charms would simply have to ride the trains.

Freight was getting to be a thing of the past. It's hard to understand what kind of an economic hop-over took place in these rural communities, all the way from depression years up to the present. All small towns of 30 years ago were on the receiving and sending ends of quantities of freight. Coastwise, even the onetime fleets of island steamers were loaded with it. Today the volume doesn't exist. Trucks are not filling rural highways in sufficient numbers to be carrying the freight which in 1920 or '25 was moving in railroad "waycars". Islandwise, no small power boats are trucking it, and the island steamers have gone. Yet, like the inland communities, the island towns still thrive and prosper—without the commerce of yesteryear. So it was in Bridgton, twenty years ago. Freight which once filled several midget boxcars each day, now didn't exist any more.

Besides, Bridgton and its surrounding towns, had become "summer resorts". Maine, as a State, had some years earlier abandoned the efforts to be an industrial region, and had gone into the tourist business. The word *Vacationland* is even stamped in big letters on our automobile license plates! Whether it's a town or a whole State, when it goes into the "summer business" it promptly loses whatever industrial importance it may have had. "Summer people", especially the halfway rich ones, object to smoke and smell and the sight of uncouth workingmen. Bridgton had suffered this stroke more or less by 1930. Its textile mill had closed, and local year-round business had pretty much shut-up-shop. Where hardly fifteen years before the B.&S.R. had earned a round hundred thousand dollars from freight alone, by the middle 1930's there simply wasn't any appreciable volume for anyone, railroad or trucks. So, if anyone but a junkman bought the Lilliput it would have to be run as a tourist attraction. And tourist attractions are unpredictable gambles. Probably that's why no one bought it for such use.

At one particularly vitriolic town meeting the Progressives won. The town voted to sell its stock, at once.

An option to buy it was promptly taken by a Massachusetts junkman. He was willing to gamble $20,000.01 of his hard earned money.

There followed months of petitioning the I.C.C. and the Public Utilities Commission for permission to abandon. Last minute frenzied efforts to *Save the Narrow Gauge* kept pace with abandonment proceedings. Bridgton's weekly newspaper advertised Sunset Excursions *a la the railbus*. As ever, the *News* was loyal to the two-footer.

A few folks enjoyed the round-trip rates, and pleasant suppertime ride to the Junction and back. Their fares probably helped a little.

About this time a Connecticut railroad fan, who was summering in Bridgton and giving generously of his time and labor, donated one of the splendid railbuses once belonging to the Sandy River. It was an immense improvement over the rig which had been doing the two-round-trips-daily honors. This ex-Sandy River No. 4 had room and comforts for more passengers, it rode reasonably well, and held a lot more inducements to sunset-excursion riders. Still, traffic didn't fill the car.

This sort of thing couldn't go on for long. It didn't. Finally, in 1941, the resistance movement ceased. The Progressives made their date with Fate. Regulatory permissions were granted. The Bridgton & Harrison Railway stopped.

That was September, 1941.

Precipitation that fall was probably the greatest ever recorded. It was a wet autumn. Wet from the torrents of tears which were shed by railroad fans throughout the land. Autos from about every state in the Union dusted over the back roads to watch the wrecking crew, headed by the little Baldwin No. 8, inching down toward the Junction, taking the 56-pound rails as it inched.

All the equipment had been hauled to the Junction in the few days between the abandonment date and the start of dismantling. It was stored in the tiny yard down there.

That junkman made money, even if scrap iron was cheap in 1941.

Several fans, with a little depression money to spare, bought pieces of equipment. One man bought several coaches, a tankcar, and the snowplow for museum pieces. A couple of youngsters from Ohio scraped up a thousand dollars with which to cross the outstretched palm, in return for a title to No. 8 engine.

From the lush cranberry fields of Plymouth County, Massachusetts came a fan with a little more money, Ellis D. Atwood, and paid through the nose for the remaining cars and No. 7 engine. He also bought the 35-pound rail on which the cars were stored.

Even then, the junkman cut up some of Atwood's purchases, until a watchman was hired to prevent further piratings.

Ellis Atwood didn't know for sure just what he wanted of these cars and a hefty 35-ton engine. But he had ideas. His ideas eventually materialized, a whole war later, in the now famous Edaville Railroad.

By late fall, 1941, the Bridgton & Harrison was gone. Tears stopped flowing. We were rapidly becoming involved in a Gargantuan struggle for power, World War II. Frivolities were brushed aside as the sky began to fall, and the little railroad faded into the encroaching verdure, forgotten for the next few years.

B.&S.R. combination No. 25. The origin of this car isn't a matter of absolute record. Some said she was the Railway Post Office car—when the road had one—others opine she was a rebuilt coach. Another claim is that, during Maine Central ownership of the road, the Me.C. built the car at the Thompson Point shops. Anyway, about 1935 she was sold and became the Mayfair Diner in Bridgton's town square.

15

SIXTY YEARS OF THE TWO-BY-SIX

The third Lilliput railroad to stretch its stubby legs in the Victorian woods of Maine was the six-mile Monson Railroad. *The Two-by-six,* they called it—two feet wide by six miles long.

Hard on the sweat and clatter of the Bridgton & Saco River's building, and while yet the Sandy River folks were still panting from their three-years-ago exertions, the little Monson line was born. It had been chartered in late 1882.

A paucity of folderol attended its conception. Its birth was hardly mentioned in the local newspaper. There was no golden-spike ceremony. It was simply built, and that was the first that was heard of it.

Within eleven months the Two-by-six was open for business. That was in October 1883, scarce eight months after the Bridgton road's opening.

As far as history reveals itself, this was the first two-footer with which that ubiquitous inventor and promoter, George E. Mansfield, hadn't identified himself. His name doesn't pop up in the Monson Railroad annals, although at the time he was very much in evidence as Superintendent of the B.&S.R., only 120 miles away. The furious steamboat and buckboard boys of Bridgton were probably keeping him in the house at night; and his newborn Lilliput could well have had him walking the floor.

The Two-by-six was built for grim utility. It was a burro of labor from its start. No flags were flown nor trumpets blown during its half century of work. Shortly after it was opened there were

145

flurries of talk about extending it hither and yon, but in sixty years of operation it never got beyond the miser confines for which it was originally intended—a railroad to connect the village of Monson to the *wide* gauge Bangor & Piscataquis Railroad (now the Bangor & Aroostook's rapidly fading Greenville branch), to get the lucrative Monson slate on the first stage of its journeyings to markets of the Western Hemisphere.

Of those brief flurries of wanderlust-talk, the first was an 1883 flutter to keep on laying 30-pound rails clear into Greenville, a dozen or fifteen miles further on.

Maybe the woods were too thick. Anyway, they forefingered on the map in the opposite direction, imagining how the tiny rails would look if they ran south, to tie up with the abuilding Sebasticook & Moosehead Railroad, creeping up from Pittsfield, Maine.

Oddly enough, this was the first of two times that a Lilliput railroad looked lecherously at the Sebasticook & Moosehead as a means of furthering its respective dreams of empire. Ten years later the Wiscasset & Quebec likewise aspired to use the S.&M. in its Northward-ho!

Piscataquis County legend has it that several miles of roadbed was actually graded south from Monson Junction toward Wellington, 20 miles away, before the Two-by-six got over its random movements and settled down to growing up on its half-dozen miles of midget track. That ended Monson ideas of spanning the world.

They say that heredity crops out in later generations. Maybe it did with the Monson Railroad. The Monson's chief reason for existing was to haul Monson slate. We will remember that the great-grandpop of all narrow gauge lines was the hoary Festiniog Railway in Wales—George E. Mansfield's inspiration to thread America with Lilliput railroads. The Festiniog existed primarily to haul slate. Now, half a century later, in 1883, the Monson Railroad was also built to haul slate in Northern Maine.

The Two-by-six left the Bangor & Piscataquis Railroad at a point still called Monson Junction, a mile west of Abbott Village, some dozen miles east of Greenville. From the Junction the meandering little line ran northerly to Monson village, exactly 6.16 miles.

The Monson No. 1, G. S. *Cushing*, built by the Hinckley Locomotive Works in 1883. Exact date of photo unknown, but wood fuel indicates it between 1883 and 1890.

Monson Railroad No. 1 was an 1884 Hinckley Forney, typical of those midgets with wh[...]
Hinckley equipped the early Lilliputs. This engine, the *G. S. Cushing,* was originally a woodburn[...]
The straight stack and the extended front end dates the picture between 1900 and 1913, when [...]
No. 3 was bought. As with several of the other Lilliputs, Massachusetts people financed buildi[...]
the Monson Railroad.

When No. 3 was new. Nearly half a century ago the little Vulcan came to the big North woo[...]
resplendent in silver tires and gold stripes. She had a headlight then, and her bell was where b[...]
were supposed to be. Her all-steel cab was the first to appear on the two-foot engines, and [...]
fashioned at the proper height to crack skulls and part a man's hair in the middle.

From the tiny yard by the Monson depot a righthand spur dropped down a steep grade to the more extensive yard where the Monson Slate Company's quarry, mills, and storehouses were. Continuing on, it poked through the forest past another small quarry and mill to a third slate operation. This spur was a total of two miles long, measured from the Monson station to its farthest extreme. That was where the mileage quoted in old *Official Guides* came from, 8.18 miles.

The Two-by-six was laid with 30-pound steel. When the last train was run sixty years later the rails were still in excellent condition, as far as wear was concerned.

Like most of the two-foot lines, the founding fathers were out-of-Staters. Its first president was H. A. Whiting of Wilton, New Hampshire (a town neighboring George Mansfield's home in Greenfield, New Hampshire). G. S. Cushing of Lowell, Massachusetts was the first manager. He was also a lucky fellow who had one of the original engines named for him, the *G. S. Cushing* No. 1.

Again history lets us down, and not much is recorded about the Monson's early years. We might as well assume they were routine, uneventful years. The midget railroad did, however, figure in one calamity of a sort. It shortly piled up more red ink than all the other two-footers combined. Probably there was an inside story to explain it, but that explanation is still inside, and probably always will be. About every year of its early existence the Two-by-six accumulated a rugged, robust deficit. Later years of its existence didn't help. By 1916, for example, this deficit had swelled to $186,000.00. It was hard to see how a six-mile, two-foot gauge, half-as-expensive railroad could have lost that much money, and still have done a lucrative business too. Nor, why no action was taken during those years to correct whatever was the trouble.

Anyway, it's all water out of the stack now. The calamity couldn't have worried the folks who owned its $70,000.00 worth of capital stock. So, it needn't worry you and me, now, 75 years later!

When the Monson Railroad was some twenty years old the Monson Slate Company bought it. Very likely the slate company may have owned it all the time, indirectly. Probably no shortline railroad ever needed a reliable parent more than the Monson Railroad did, along in the early 1900's.

The following years weren't marked by any spectacular events. It seems to have been plain, down-to-earth railroading (in more ways than one), with the little train making two, three, and even four round trips a day from Monson to the Junction.

In those days—in fact, up until comparatively recent years—the B.&A. ran four passenger trains a day between Greenville and Bangor. The little Monson rattler met each one, and often scurried home to Monson and back before the next one came along.

It's hard to believe that a small village like Monson, Maine once poured $1,000.00 a month into ticket sales. It did. The tiny Laconia-built combination car, scarcely 30 feet long, bulged with passengers in those Golden Years. Even as late as 1916, when automobiles had pretty well established themselves, the little Two-by-six hauled 7,589 people and earned $2,656.31 doing it.

That same year, 1916, the Monson Railroad's total revenue was $15,062.00. Passengers account for $2,656.31 and $11,022.12 came from moving 13,249 tons of freight. Mail paid $272.28 and Express $936.59. There were 2 engines, one passenger car, 22 freight cars, and 16 employees. The investment, so-called, in road and equipment was $79,726.63 and $70,000 worth of capital stock was shown.

That year the funded debt had swelled to *wide* gauge proportions, $186,491.94. But $4,205.80 was paid in interest. The very good operating ratio was 71.67.

A three man crew was always the train personnel. An engineer, fireman, and conductor was plenty. Many times Superintendent Harold Morrill was the conductor. Other times he pinch-hit as engineer. This arrangement of an "official" also acting as a crew member smacked of Mansfield's practices on the lines which he promoted. If the idea had clicked, and been practiced more widely, the big brass of today's railroads might have a better idea of what the troublesome labor element is up against.

nd the stub switch is the Monson's yard, depot, general office, and enginehouse. The spur
e quarry switched right just beyond the boxcar. The snow spreader waits on a siding to your
for winter to come. The village of Monson is a short way to the left of the photo, on the
auto road to Moosehead Lake.

the final days, in 1944, Monson engines were coaled by hand from a wide gauge coal car.
photo was made at Monson Junction, and the car of coal is on the Bangor & Aroostook's
old Bangor & Piscataquis line to Greenville.

Photos of the Monson Railroad seem more appropriate if taken in winter. This view shows far on each side the snow spreader winged the snow. It left plenty of room for the next bliz and the next. Otherwise the narrow track would shortly have been at the bottom of a canyon, with nowhere to put the rest of the winter's snow.

Boxcar No. 2, link-and-pin coupler and all. The handbrakes were the only brakes the "two-by-railroad had, and brakemen lived up to their name on these little trains. They plied their t with a wooden brake-club such as we've read about in Grandpa's day.

Often Superintendent Morrill would sell tickets to a stationful of people, and minutes later, as conductor of the train, would collect these tickets the length of the Laconia combination, and snap them with his ticket punch.

Even after the advent of the Detroit horseless carriages passenger business was good through the long, hard winters of northern Maine. Winter up there is no picnic. They say it makes you tough. Nearer the hellish truth is the fact that you have to be tough to live through them.

The locale of the Two-by-six is a hundred miles from the cold-tempering ocean. Fifty and sixty below zero is no novelty in northern Maine. Neither is six or eight feet of snow. The two-footers were adept at boring holes through those deep-hard-packed drifts, even when their *wide* gauge connecting trains became stalled in them. The Monson Railroad was in the worst climatic location of any of the Lilliputs, snowwise and coldwise. The little Two-by-six, like the other midgets, burned thousands of cords of wood and thousands of tons of coal battling the eternal snows of Maine winters.

Somewhere along the years, probably in the early 1900's, the Monson engines were changed from wood burners to coal. Straight stacks replaced the sombrero-like sunflower stack which Hinckley put on them.

Those straight smokestacks were about the only mark of progress to ever show up on the cocky little line of the big North Woods. Its link-and-pin couplings never surrendered to Janneys or automatics. Neither air nor vacuum brakes ever pinched the tiny wheels. Never did heavier rail replace the original 30-pound sticks. No split switches followed the ante-bellum stub switches with their so-called banjo switchstands. Except for a few new freight cars, and a layer or two of slate ballast, the only new things the Monson Railroad ever got were engines 3 and 4.

Along 1911 or '12 one of the Hinckley engines, it may have been No. 1 or maybe it was No. 2, konked out. They ordered another. This time the Vulcan Iron Works got the order. Why the trend was ignored and a baby Baldwin wasn't favored, is unanswerable. A Vulcan she was, No. 3. No. 3 Forney put in her appearance in 1912.

Six years later, in 1918, her sister, the No. 4, was born. She was likewise conceived and delivered in the Vulcan Iron Works. These two almost identical engines lasted even longer than the two 1883 Hinckley creations, although they were usually spoken of as the *new* engines.

The 14 years between 1916 and 1930 saw a lot of changes, other than airbrakes and automatic couplers and split-switches, on the Two-by-six. Passenger travel and earnings decreased by 60 percent. Instead of raking in $2,600.00 for hauling 7,600 passengers, the Monson Railroad carried only 2,157 people in 1930. Those people paid a measly $900.63. That was about one-third as much and as many.

The same $70,000.00 stock was shown in 1930 but the holy-tearing funded debt was finally absent. Maybe the parent Monson Slate Company, which had officially bought the railroad some years before, had wiped it off. It's pretty sure the little Lilliput didn't pay it off from earnings.

Freight revenue in 1930 was higher, due to increased rates, but the tonnage had gone down. The 9,127 tons of freight had paid $14,216.00, nearly 30 percent more than 1916, although tonnage had decreased nearly 40 percent.

Mail and Express pay had also gone up by 1930. The two items dumped $3,275.00 on the ledger. Total income for that year, 1930, was $18,395.00 compared to the $15,062.00 of fourteen years before. But, where 1916's expenses were only $10,994.95 the figure for 1930 had rocketed to $16,222.00. Still, interest and dividends of $4,206.00 were paid and the operating ratio was still favorable, 88.22.

However, there was, in far off 1930, a scrawl on the proverbial wall which boded no good to the Monson Railroad, nor to any of the Lilliputs for that matter. The historical fact that finally the Two-by-six outlived all the others didn't mean it was the last one to feel the effects of the changing times.

In a short three years, from 1930 to 1933, that proverbial hand-writing blazed like a row of fusees. In 1933 that same property investment was still on the books and the $70,000.00 capital stock hadn't changed. But everything else had.

Freight earnings had plummeted down to only $3,280.00. That was for hauling 2,024 tons of freight. Passenger fares had gone through the cellar-bottom, loosely speaking. Only 209 people had ridden the Lilliput train that year, and they might as well have stayed at home. Their fares added up to just $39.80. The decimal is in the right place; thirty-nine dollars and eighty cents!

Mail and Express earned $1,065.56, making a total gross revenue for 1933 of $4,585.64. Expenses were $5,597.00. The upside-down operating ratio that year was an unhappy, un-Mansfield-like 217.13. No dividends or interest were mentioned.

We could have sent condolences to the family that Christmas. It didn't look like the Monson Railroad would be around much longer. The fact that it hung on another eleven years, watching its Lilliput mates cross the River, was due to the reluctance of its industrial parent to give it up.

Through the rest of the 1930's there wasn't much further change. There couldn't be. Crews were reduced until only the three trainmen were left, and Superintendent Morrill. Those trainmen acted also as track crew and transfer stevedores at the Junction. More than before Morrill would run the engine while the regular engineer was busy at a more important chore.

In 1938 all passenger service was abandoned. Passengers, such as there were, had been riding over the highway in the company's platform-body truck as often as on its train. The discontinuance of passenger service may not have been such a calamity to Monsonites as it is to city-commuters who lose some trains today. From 1938 the train ran only when there was freight to haul. Most of that freight was slate, by 1938.

In Monson those 900-foot deep slate quarries still did an excellent business. Slate, quarried deep down in the cool subterranean tunnels, was moved to the elevator shaft by electrically operated two-foot trains, of the typical mining variety. Few people other than workmen ever saw these trains. Many of us have stood at the shaft opening, like the top of a mammoth well, and looked down hundreds of feet to the perpetual snow and ice at the foot. We watched platformlike boxes loaded with big hunks of raw slate being hoisted up by a surface derrick. We have wandered through the sprawling, dusty stone-cutting sheds where slate slabs were worked into the products which went all over the Americas. But the tiny railroad down there never came up. We never went down!

Another important event—important for the Monson Railroad—occurred in 1938. Superintendent Morrill retired.

H. E. Morrill had been with the Two-by-six about all his life. He had been pretty much the guiding hand, plus handling not only the supervision but two or three other jobs for most of that time. Knowing Morrill and the Monson, his retirement seemed like an impending deathblow to the railroad. However, in the weeks and months which followed, the little road hung on. It had suffered about all the death-blows there were, so one more didn't make much difference.

A few months before he retired, Superintendent Morrill had said, in answer to a question, "Do we hear anything about abandonment? No. We won't until it's gone, and that will be the end of it." That is just how it finally happened.

As the years wore on, and the Monson Railroad wore out, the little train ran to Monson Junction less and less frequently. Sometimes a week would pass without tiny 18-inch wheels polishing the rusty rails. Smaller shipments of freight went down in the company's highway truck. Maybe even the folks in Monson didn't know which trip might have been the last one.

In the fall of 1943 embargo notices were sent out to other railroads. This wasn't because there was much danger of any freight being shipped, or billed, on the narrow-gauge, but because such a procedure is demanded by law. It is a step preliminary to cancelling tariffs and abandoning service.

The Monson Railroad was to be abandoned. That was how it happened. We didn't hear anything about it until it was done. And, as Morrill had prophesied, that was the end of it.

That winter, despite northern Maine's wicked disposition, the junk crews "wrecked" the Two-by-six. They wrecked it about the same way other junkmen had wrecked other Lilliputs. They ripped up the ancient rails. They burned cars for the metal. What couldn't be reduced to usable scrap was destroyed.

...son 4 and the tiny 1883 Laconia combination car pose outside the Monson enginehouse one ...noon in 1935. The 4 is a coal burner, and the wood in her cab is for building a new fire ...day morning. Monson engines were never turned. They ran down to the Junction, and backed home. The road's only turning facilities were two midget tables for snowplows only.

...only reason Monson No. 4 has a number on her cab is because the photographer cut one out ...white paper and stuck it on there with pin grease—for identification purposes. He hadn't dis-...red at that time that the 4 had two stirrups in her cab step, and the 3 had only one. No. 4 was a 1918 Vulcan, steam brakes, 10-inch cylinders, and weighed about 18 tons.

The gauge got a little wide here. The Monson Railroad was affectionately called "the two-by-s
and it was pretty necessary to keep the "two" end of it tight. This one-man section crew has b
"spiking in" the 30-pound rails after someone discovered the railroad was in danger
standard-gauging itself.

All but the two engines. Engines 3 and 4, instead of being put to the torch as so many bigger and better Lilliput engines had been, were block-and-tackled onto *wide* gauge flatcars and billed out to Rochester, New York, the junkmen's seat of operations. By a miracle, or a whim of Fate, they were spared.

Why the junkmen paid good money in freight charges to cart two eighteen-ton two-foot locomotives 'way out to New York State is still a question. It was lucky, however, that the notion took him when it did. The two baby engines were destined to run again on Ellis Atwood's backyard Edaville Railroad!

So, the Monson Railroad was the last survivor of the colorful little railroads, the final line to check out. Thus did 67 years of pint-sized railroading in the United States come to an end.

From the Billerica & Bedford Railroad to the little Two-by-six, from the first 8-miler to the last 6-miler, the short, fascinating era of the Lilliputs had burst into being, "like a proud burst of music" in 1877. It had bloomed and boomed through those 67 years, maybe with George Mansfield's enthusiasm and faith as an impetus. It had wilted, withered, and died in 1943. . . . And maybe gone to seed, with his fond benediction.

MONSON RAILROAD

1937-1938

PASS ___ Mr. W. L. Bowen, _____

_____ Belfast and Moosehead R. R. _____

UNTIL DECEMBER 31, 1938 UNLESS OTHERWISE ORDERED,
ON CONDITION THAT HE ASSUMES ALL RISK OF ACCIDENT AND
DAMAGE TO PERSON OR PROPERTY

NO. 1

SUPT.

KENNEBEC CENTRAL
RAILROAD CO.

=== TO THE ===

National Soldiers' Home,

Connects at Gardiner with Maine Central Railroad, Androscoggin & Kennebec R. R. and Boston Steamers. Summer Schedule in effect May 16th, 1925.

UNAVOIDABLE DELAYS EXCEPTED.

WEEK DAY TRAIN SERVICE

READ DOWN					READ UP			
1	**3**	**5**	**7**	Number of Trains	**2**	**4**	**6**	**8**
A. M.	A. M.	P. M.	P. M.		A. M.	A. M.	P. M.	P. M.
7.40	10.40	1.05	4.00	Lv.Randolph Ar. 8.50		11.35	2.00	4.50
f7.52	f10.52	f1.17	f4.12	Chelsea f 8.38	f11.23	f1.48	f4.38	
8.00	11.00	1.25	4.20	Ar. Nat' Home Lv. 8.30		11.15	1.40	4.30

SUNDAY TRAIN SERVICE

	P. M.			
No. 1	1.50 Leave	Randolph	Arrive	5.25
	1.58	Chelsea		5.13
	2.10	National Home	Leave	5.05

Sunday Train No. 1. will not run when Ball Game is cancelled. Sunday service subject to change without notice.

BAND CONCERT

Every day except Monday, at 4.00 P.M. by the National Home Band, B. W. Thieme, Leader.

BASEBALL GAME

Every Sunday at 2.45 P. M. (Weather Permitting)

f Stops on Signal or Notice to Take or leave Passengers.

The Express Business is Operated by the American Railway Express Company.

E. L. Bussell, General Manager.

16

THE TOGUS ROAD

When the Sandy River and its brother lines, and the Bridgton & Saco River and the Monson Railroad had been built and established as going concerns, several years passed without further Lilliput pregnancies. It wasn't until 1889 that the next one was born. The Kennebec Central.

The Kennebec Central Railroad always seemed to be the baby of the family. It wasn't the youngest, but it was the smallest. That's probably why. We remember that a few years later, during the Wiscasset road's childhood, there were rumors and rumors of rumors of branches which might be laid westward to various points on the Kennebec River. Two or three of these dream-projects involved our little Kennebec Central Railroad, as a conspirator.

Except for two or three post-natal brain-throbs for wandering elsewhere the Kennebec Central was built pretty much for one, definite, specific purpose: To serve the National Soldiers' Home, in the town of Chelsea, Maine, which still goes by its hundred year old name, *Togus.*

If Togus hadn't been there, the Kennebec Central wouldn't have been.

In 1889 talk was rife in the proper circles, of building such a line. It would begin on the banks of the deep-water Kennebec River at Randolph, Maine, which is directly across the river from the City of Gardiner. Although the big Boston-Gardiner steamboats managed to turn around in it for a hundred years, the river is scarcely a hundred yards wide at that point.

155

The usual hullabaloo and loud talk that smoked the air and divided towns against themselves while other Lilliputs were being conceived, was noticeable by its absence. It didn't attract much attention. The general public would be served and benefited only indirectly. The new Kennebec Central wasn't too widely known, either in its embryonic stages or in later years. The Soldiers' Home and the old soldiers would be the chief beneficiaries, along with the Federal Government which ran the Home. As far as the public-at-large went, it would have no reason to travel via the Kennebec Central Railroad. In other words, there simply wasn't anything on its line but Togus. If the public went to Togus it would go by the narrow gauge train. If it rode the train it necessarily had to go to Togus.

So, stock was issued—$50,000.00—and some bonds were sold to compensate for the stock certificates that failed to sell. The railroad was built. It was opened for traffic in the summer of 1890.

The tiny 25-pound steel followed the ups and downs of Mother Nature on the premise that steel was cheaper than grading. And it must have been; the new road cost only $10,000.00 a mile to build. The area was gently rolling terrain, and hairpin curves and breathtaking grades were conspicuous by their absence. The distance was only five miles from the Randolph waterfront to Togus, as the Lilliput hopped, and 150 yards less as the crow flew.

Bridges were hard to find between Randolph and the Home. The total trestling was only 165 feet, one 45-foot bridge being the longest one.

The Randolph yard was a model of brevity. The main line actually began under the long covered wagon bridge which spanned the Kennebec. It passed the station platform and continued on out of town. A runaround track guided the bantam engines from their trains, at the end of a run, and back onto the turntable. A neat 2-stall enginehouse faced the turntable. Another track paralleled the coal wharf where ocean barges unloaded their coal. Another track served pretty much as a storage space for cars not in use.

Leaving the station and the small yard, the main line quickly crossed Randolph's main street in a big curve combined with a sharp grade. That got it up from sea-level onto the rising ground. A hundred yards beyond there was a car shed where the much-varnished passenger cars were housed.

From here on to Togus there was only one place name—Chelsea. And Chelsea was nothing but a dirt-road crossing where trains would pick up or let off passengers, if passengers presented themselves for the privilege.

At Togus, or *The Home* as it was most often called, a colony of wood and brick buildings composed the general quarters of the semi-military post which was *home* to hundreds of aging veterans of America's wars—at this time, the 1890's, they were mostly from the Civil War. Here, a step from the Home's restaurant, was a station platform which served as the passenger depot. There was the usual runaround track. An ascending trestle carried another track high enough so the drop-side coal cars could dump coal down into the huge, thousand-ton pile which was used by The Home's big steam plant. Coal, as you may have guessed, was the principal commodity on the K.C.'s freight revenue list. These yards and tracks completed the new railroad's physical structure.

Equipmentwise, the little Lilliput began life with one engine. She was a Baldwin Forney built from patterns of the 1886 *S. W. Sargent* of the Franklin & Megantic Railroad. This one was named *Volunteer.* That was in honor of the old soldiers at The Home. The *Volunteer* boasted the weight of 16 tons. While she didn't stack up so well in comparison with the 1890 model Maine Central engines which labored up the main line across the river in Gardiner, she was quite capable of handling any trains the Kennebec Central might be called upon to run.

There were two handsome coaches, with odd, arched roofs. Their seats ran lengthwise of the car, setteewise. A similarly arranged combination baggage-passenger car made up the initial passenger carrying equipment. Half a dozen boxcars and as many flats, with three or four drop-side gondolas for coal, completed the freight rolling-stock. An undescribable contraption, half boxcar and half grader, was the snowplow.

To the casual observer, who didn't observe too closely, the Kennebec Central was an independent railroad. It had no visible connections with any of the other Lilliputs, or any *wide* gauge, either. However, when the more critical observer took squinting observations many names on the Kennebec Central staff of promoters and bosses were contemporaneously familiar on the Franklin County roads. It looked like the Sandy River and F.&M. owners had a finger in the Kennebec Central pie.

You'll remember that the Sandy River and the F.&M. were under the control of bankers Weston Lewis and Josiah Maxcey. The Maxcey and Lewis team were the big names on the new K.C. railroad. Most of the K.C.'s lesser lights were also lesser lights on the Franklin County roads. So, a relationship definitely existed, even if no physical connection or corporate tie-up was in effect.

After a year of operation, a second engine was added. Probably the tiny *Volunteer* was up for tubes, or down on the ties, or in some other way needed help. Maybe she was just lonesome. Anyway, the second engine was likewise a Forney, and likewise diminutive, but a product of the neighboring Portland Company. No. 2, which wasn't named, was similar in pattern and appearance to other engines of that famous builder of famous Lilliput Forney engines. You could spot her half a mile away as being a Portland engine.

Somewhere along this same time a second combination car was added.

Because the Kennebec Central was a relatively obscure Lilliput, and because it was abandoned and its records destroyed before railroad fans began preserving records, not much is known about its intimate details. Who built the passenger and freight cars, and such dramatics as mile-a-minute runs and blood-curdling wrecks, is information gone with those old records. In the case of chain-lightning runs and horrible wrecks, probably they never happened on the Kennebec Central, or the yarns would have survived.

Sometime in those early years an open excursion car appeared. It was similar to those on the Sandy River, and the Wiscasset's one-time open car. Some folks have come up with the logical guess that this K.C. car was transferred from the Sandy River. Maybe it was. That guess is as good as any. Anyway, the Kennebec Central had one, and a few years ago you could feast your eyes on what was left of it, beside the track at that dirt-road crossing called Chelsea. It had apparently been used as a passenger shelter when its be-wheeled usefulness was over.

Likewise in the early days the Kennebec Central had a brief, and pointless, desire to go places. Those five miles were too restricting. It wanted room to expand. It made an application to the Maine Railroad Commission for permission to build from Togus some 16 miles northeastward to South China. Why South China no one knows. It smells a little like a sardine sandwich left in the passenger car all night. From an intimate and lifelong familiarity with the country in question, there simply wouldn't have been any reason to build to South China. South China today is a tiny, dozen-house crossroads hamlet, and no spacious ruins or lengthy basement walls suggest forgotten industries which would have beckoned in the 1890's. But skepticism isn't the sire of explanation in this case, so we'll have to be content to merely know that the Kennebec Central once applied for and was granted permission to build and operate 16 miles of two-foot track from Togus up through Windsor to South China, Maine.

One wild hypothesis might be that, because the K.C. didn't own a spadeful of gravel along its entire 5-mile line, it wanted to go hunt for some. There wasn't any, between Randolph and The Home. That's unusual, too, in Maine where good gravel is dirt cheap. All the K.C.'s gravel had to be horse-carted to it from hills and hollows beyond its horizon. It cost money. Perhaps if a fine gravel deposit had been found up around South China the Lilliput could kill two legendary fowl with one spadeful of the precious stuff: it could procure a supply of ballast, as well as having some to sell, and its 16-mile railroad would open up new areas for passengers and freight. But, that's pure hypothesizing, and don't take it too seriously.

So, the little road made the best of it with what miles and what ballast it had. It was a paying proposition from the start, if old Maine Railroad Commission reports are any criterion. There's no reason to doubt its prosperity, remembering that owners Maxcey and Lewis were locally prominent bankers. Bankers are reputed to be cagey fellows, who know how to make railroads make money.

The K.C. paid interest on its stock. It paid interest on its bonds as well as paying those bonds off. By 1916, incidentally, the bonded indebtedness, or Funded Debt as they called it, was down to $19,500.00.

Freight to The Home, chiefly the coal, was a nice bit of revenue each year. Passenger fares was a sizable item, too. Mail and Express didn't go into boxcar numerals, but it was a refreshing dipperful in the bucket. Band concerts at The Home on Sundays and holidays, along with the popular ball games, kept the little trains running four trips a day, with many passenger extras on holidays and Sundays. Old soldiers, who weren't so old either, in the 1890's and early 1900's, were heavy riders back and forth to Gardiner, which added heavily to fares.

Those veterans, venerable and otherwise, who made their home at The Home included the inevitable few who had a lusty and shameless thirst. Maine was drier than a cork leg but even small cities like Gardiner were usually able and prepared to provide for the thirsty.

One of the few legends which grew around the mostly-routine Kennebec Central is of the warriors who took such shopping trips to town. They would ride over to Randolph on some of the day trains, with excellent intentions of returning on a late afternoon or one of the weekend evening trains. But, maybe you know how it is; "—the best laid plans of mice and drunks," or some such gag.

Usually the liquid resorts in backrooms of Gardiner buildings would see that a team ferried the old boys across the bridge to the narrow gauge depot. The understanding train boys did the rest—tiered the Grand Army up in the baggage end of the combination car for the trip to The Home. The legend is told in different ways, depending on who is telling it. Some will tell you The Home had a cast-iron rule forbidding family members to get plastered. This story has it that a point half a mile short of Togus, railroadingly known as *Drunkards' Roost,* served as an unadvertised flag stop for nocturnal trains, and the conductor and engine crew would unload those who couldn't possibly unload themselves—because they were hopelessly loaded. They'd sleep it off during the warm summer night, and make their weary way onto the reservation early next morning.

nebec Central No. 2, a tiny Portland Co. Forney which would almost fit in the engineer's
et. But if you'd been lucky enough to have ridden on her your impression wouldn't have been
small she was, but, "Why, she's a real engine!" The Randolph passenger depot is just behind
No. 2's tank, and the 2-stall enginehouse was just out of sight to the left.

Kennebec River sometimes goes on a Spring rampage, and in the Kennebec Central Railroad's
it usually had these consequences. Track at the Randolph yard seems in need of surfacing.
on is at right and the 2-stall enginehouse at left, under the old covered highway bridge
connecting Randolph with Gardiner.

An old print showing a Kennebec Central passenger train leaving Randolph bound for Soldiers' Home. The engine is No. 3 (later W.W.&F. No. 8, and ex-B.&S.R. No. 3), with of the odd-roofed combination cars. Note the old pump car, of a day long passed, setting on track right ahead of the engine.

Coach No. 4 on blocking after the 1936 freshet had raised Cain with the K.C. yard in Rando Another passenger car was carried away by the flood and washed down the raging Kenn River, never to be seen again. The K.C. cars had long bench seats, like the old trolley cars to have.

Other versions ignore Drunkards' Roost, but titter of rumpled heroes falling out of the baggage car door *en route*. Someone would get word to the head end, or the fireman would be watching backwards, and the train would be stopped to pick the Tiger of Bull Run from the brambles, sling him back aboard, and proceed.

How much of these legends are gospel and how much are told with a wink, is open to suspicion. But the fact does stand that in those days when Togus was a soldiers' home (it has more lately been rebuilt and now serves exclusively as a veterans' hospital) the visiting public was well aware that a high percent of its retired boys were unfamiliar with the splendid work of the W.C.T.U.

One of the old Kennebec Central firemen once told of another episode which was open to question. He told of the time a Randolph-bound train was dropping down around the curving grade into town, and the engine's bumper beam hit a town drunk in the posterior. The inebriate was a bulky fellow, the old fireman went on, weighing better'n two hundred pounds. The breezing little engine dealt him a wicked wallop, which sent the surprised man somersaulting down the bank. As soon as vacuum brakes could do so, the train stopped. The crew hustled back to hear the victim's last words, if any. Instead, they met him lurching up the bank to meet them.

"Listen, youse," he roared, "if I've hurt your little tin engine any I'll pay for it!"

By and large, however, the little Togus Road didn't kick up much dust. As it was conceived and built, without fanfare or shouting, so did it run its span. Nothing especially colorful or dramatic seems to have happened in those 39 years, unless the half-joking legends are considered. There must have been times when some baby engine splintered the ties or toppled over into the half-filled ditch. But the events were not recorded. For the most part the Lilliput seems to have made its routine runs from Alpha to Omega, served its limited patronage well, and fulfilled its purpose in the world. And, that's about all any railroad or any person can ask for.

When the Kennebec Central was about ten or a dozen years old the ugly head of competition rose snakily above the milkweed. A trolley line was built to Togus.

Togus was about equidistant from Gardiner or Augusta. Gardiner had the railroad and enjoyed the business trips and profits from Togus shoppers. The Gardiner bankers, Maxcey and Lewis, had probably planned on that. Augusta, however, was the State capital. It thought it should enjoy some of the rich pickings. Possibly too, although nothing is said about it in old newspaper clippings, the Togus gentry may have yearned for a change of liquid diet. So, a trolley line was built from Augusta to Togus.

Some folks argued that the trolleys didn't hurt the Lilliput railroad. They said the crowds which packed the old open cars were Augusta crowds, a new group which hadn't previously gone to Togus. Other folks wailed that the new electric line would shortly drive the narrow-gauge over the brink; there wasn't business enough for both.

The Lilliput was doing business, and still paying dividends, a quarter of a century later. And the Androscoggin & Kennebec Street Railway made plenty of shekels on its Togus branch.

No, from the looks of old balance sheets the Kennebec Central didn't suffer much from the big, open trolleys. In 1916, for example, it earned $8,577.66 for hauling 6,137 tons of freight. It raked in $2,992.65 for carrying 30,732 passengers. Another $212.31 came from Mail and Express paid it $457.50. That was a total, plus a few incidental revenues, of $12,243.00. Remember, again, the difference between 1916's dollar and today's. This gross earning in 1916 would be the equivalent of some $50,000.00 today. Today $50,000.00 wouldn't be peanuts for a five-mile, two-foot railroad.

The same year, 1916, the investment in road and equipment was shown as $81,267.65. There were two engines, four passenger cars, and 13 freight cars. Half of these were lowside coal cars. The hybrid snowplow wasn't mentioned. Maybe they were ashamed of it. There were nine employees, including the manager.

The operating ratio for 1916 was 89.00. Total expenses were $11,194.07, and interest on the funded debt and dividends on the stock were another $877.50. There was a tidy surplus in the treasury. Again, in terms of today's 30c dollar the Kennebec Central's showing for 1916 wasn't bad. It went to show, again, that old George

Mansfield knew his Lilliputs. Apparently the electric road from Augusta hadn't done much damage—unless it was to the morals of a few gay old soldiers.

A few years later, probably about 1922, No. 1 engine played out. Thirty-two years of work shouldn't have worn out an engine, unless someone let the water dry up. Anyway, the Kennebec Central successfully dickered with the Bridgton road for its Portland Forney No. 3.

No. 3, as she was also numbered on the Togus road, was four or five tons heavier than the K.C. engines had been. She weighed 18 tons. The load limit for axle weight on 25-pound rails, according to formula, is 12,000 pounds. That was almost exactly the driver axle weight of the 10-ton Portland Forney. She would be harder on track than numbers 1 and 2 had been but the little road couldn't afford another new engine right then, and those standard Portland Forneys were the only thing on the used-engine market. None of the K.C. legends include any gripes about the No. 3 being a track-smasher.

Three or four years later this bargain was done over again. The other old engine must have turned up her smutty little toes, so K.C. brass went shopping. This time, probably in 1925 or '26, they came home lugging S.R.&R.L. No. 6. This was probably a case of Brass Hat Maxcey of the K.C.R.R. instructing Brass Hat Maxcey of the S.R.&R.L. to send down one of the small engines.

No. 6 was identical to old B.&S.R. No. 3. So that made two 18 tonners which called Randolph enginehouse home. No. 6 was renumbered K.C.R.R. No. 4.

Timecards during the next few years were like the older ones had been. There were still four round trips, mixed, every weekday. Sundays and holidays they shuttled back and forth with the size of the crowd. The acres of automobiles which brought more baseball and concert fans to Togus after the War didn't compete with the trains and the trolleys so much, but brought in a still newer crowd. The railroad's figures for passengers carried and fares collected didn't vary much from the previous years.

However, time was running out on the Little Giant. Handwriting on the wall didn't show up and when the end suddenly came it was like a bolt of lightning. Unlike the demise of other two-footers, the Togus road's stroke wasn't the long expected result of an apparent situation. It was because the Government suddenly gave the coal haul to the trucks in the spring of 1929.

Without the thousands of tons of coal to haul the little Kennebec Central couldn't turn a wheel. While the passenger train revenues were holding up, and might well have stayed up until the present day due to the situation at Togus, they accounted for only one-third of the total. The other two-thirds was mostly coal. Deduct the coal earnings and 20,000 train-miles a year would have gone begging. Nine men on the payroll, 220 tons of engine coal a year, and the other small maintenance and general expenses still would have cost three times what the passenger trains would pay. The Kennebec Central was done.

Operations were suspended on short notice, in June 1929.

It was the first of the two-footers to die. That is, except for the almost stillborn demise of the Billerica & Bedford, half a century before. It was also one of the first abandonments of any kind in Maine, although plenty were destined to follow.

The Kennebec Central management didn't exactly say their road was abandoned. They called it *suspended.* The Kennebec Central was in suspenders, so to speak, for a number of years, tracks intact, engines and cars housed and cared for, ready to run again tomorrow, if that coal job could be recovered.

Vague rumors breezed around from time to time that strings were being pulled, and the people's hired men in Washington would be pressured to hand back the coal haul to the narrow gauge railroad.

During the years which followed the stout herdsgrass and clover grew lusciously over the rails. Bridge timbers and ties whitened with the seasons. Road crossings were covered as highway repairs were made, and there was no one to clean them out. The two clean, spic-and span Forney engines snoozed restlessly in their stalls under the Randolph-Gardiner bridge. In the car shed nearby, four passenger cars gathered cobwebs but lost none of their varnished sheen. Inside the neat turreted station, resplendent in its hardwood, varnished wainscoating, the ticket-case was still stocked with the multicolored card tickets which would be collectors' items if they had been saved. The little line was waiting and listening for the tramp of trainmen's feet.

They never came.

Trucks continued to haul the coal. The trolley line folded up and was dismantled. The concerts and ballgames ended. Togus ceased to be a National Soldiers' Home. It became a Veterans' Hospital. Its old buildings were wrecked and new, multistoried hospitals and administration buildings built. Times changed. Yet, the Kennebec Central Railroad was still intact.

Then came the mop-up.

It was in the early winter of 1933. The owner of the Wiscasset narrow-gauge, acting on the logical and lucky premise that buying second-hand engines was cheaper than repairing his own, made a dicker with the dormant Kennebec Central Railroad Company whereby he bought the whole shebang.

He worked quickly. Maybe he remembered the perennial rumors about the little road resuming operations, and feared it might come before he'd cleaned up. Or perhaps it was just that he was efficient and liked to keep unfinished business finished. Anyway, in a few days a big trailer truck was dragging the sleepy little engines out of their shadowy stalls, and onto the trailer. They were lurched and bumped over the highway to Wiscasset, 20 miles away. With hardly more than a coat of paint and the new numbers 8 and 9 respectively, they went to work again.

This man had no use for the cars. He had more passenger cars and freight cars of his own than business to put them to work. They were unceremoniously pushed into the weeds, their trucks salvaged for scrap. Neither did he have any use for the light 25-pound rail. His own 35-pound steel was small enough. It happened so quickly that few people who had lived within whistle sound knew about it—the Kennebec Central Railroad was no more. It went as quietly and with as little attention as it had come, forty-some years before.

In spite of its lifelong obscurity maybe the little Togus Road served an unappreciative world as well, within its five mile limits, as its more vaunted siblings did. It had never pretended to do more than it did do, excepting for that impulsive South China lark of its budding adolescence. It completely did all it was ever meant to do. It was faithful to those who brought it into the world, and to the old soldiers who depended on it for their shopping trips.

To the little Kennebec Central we may whisper a poignant, *"So long!"*

Wiscasset, Waterville and Farmington Railway

Complimentary Pass

Pass Bearer on Date Stamped.

AUG 21 1913　*S. J. Sewall*　Gen. Manager.

17

WISCASSET & QUEBEC RAILROAD

One of the great-grand-daddies of New England railroad charters was the Wiscasset & Quebec's. It was dated in 1854. That hundred-years-ago charter gave the embryo railroad the privilege of going pretty nearly anywhere it wished.

There was very little railroad in the State of Maine in 1854. Commerce depended more on coasting vessels and oxcarts. Maine's much indented coastline with deep water bays and miles-long rivers, and the 10 to 15 foot tides, made water transportation ideal. The oxcarts were likewise well-suited to the rocky roaded interior.

That was why Wiscasset was selected as a starting point. Although a dozen miles from the bounding ocean Wiscasset was on a deep, tidewater river, the Sheepscot. Any vessel which sailed the Seven Seas in 1854 could run up to Wiscasset without scrubbing her keel.

So, a railroad from such a seaport running into the hinterlands of Maine, or even to the Province of Quebec, could handle foreign traffic as well as commerce from Boston and New York. It looked good. The charter was granted along with a blessing or two.

However, that was as far as it went. For 40 years no railroad was built.

No gauge was definitely decided upon in 1854. In those forgotten times railroads were anywhere from six feet wide to ridiculous dimensions likewise forgotten. But the two-foot gauge was yet to be introduced on this side of the Western Ocean.

Some twenty years later the idea and the charter, were revived. By now Wiscasset was a way-station on the Knox & Lincoln Railroad, and this line could be used, as well as the still popular ocean routes. Perhaps the success of the 5½-foot Atlantic & St. Lawrence Railway, hitching Montreal to the ocean at Portland, Maine, had an influence on the revival.

Still, nothing was done.

It was in relatively recent 1890 that a third project gave it impetus. This time something was done.

As a result of hectic meetings and other promotional campaigns, plus the ever important money raising, the Wiscasset & Quebec Railroad emerged.

To say the Wiscasset & Quebec had grandiose dreams would be an understatement. To gullibly accept all the promises its promoters made would be an insult to our alleged intelligence. But the promoters mentioned distant and romantic termini beyond international borders. The wampam poured in, and construction began in 1894.

In order to have power to haul the work trains the company negotiated with the sixty-miles-away Sandy River Railroad, itself an adult of 26 summers, for one of its engines. The Sandy River wouldn't feel sorry to see the last of its No. 3 Forney. The fledging W. & Q. wasn't in a position to be choosey. No. 3 shortly moved to Wiscasset where a figure *1* was painted on her cab.

One day in late summer, 1894, Captain Doyle sailed his schooner up the deep-channeled Sheepscot River, decks awash from the heavy load of 35-pound steel rails in his hold.

Grade and bridges went up, and ties went down. Several contractors were involved. Ubiquitous if arrogant Mitchells from Quebec, who had lately built many miles of railroad in Maine, did the most of it.

Contemporaneously with grading and tracklaying they were building the deepwater docks along Wiscasset's river front. To get the narrow gauge track from its own yard across a bulge in the river to the Knox & Lincoln transfer yard (it had by this time become a part of the Maine Central) and to the wharves, a thousand feet of pile trestling was in order. Remains of it are plainly visible to this day.

tidal inlet separated the W.W.&F. yard from its transfer yard with the Maine Central. This long
trestle connected them. The Maine Central's depot shows to the left of this photo, while the
.W.&F.'s station is at the diamond crossing, at the far end of the trestle. The big, cream
ilding in the distance was the machine shop. At high tide these mud flats are under eight
feet of water.

hen the Wiscasset & Quebec was abuilding, this photo was made of its Engine No. 1 in the
ead Tide Gravel Pit. No. 1, a 14-ton Porter Forney, had recently been bought from the Sandy
ver Railroad which had bought her new in 1883, eleven years earlier. Probably this engine lived
t her life on the W. & Q. mostly as a yard and work engine, as no other photos of her in service
have come to light.

W.W. & F. No. 3, Portland Forney with a mixed train, at some forgotten station, some forgo
date. The Wiscasset road altered its closed-cab Forney engines by opening the back ends sim
to conventional cabs on tender-type engines—all but the last two which it bought from the K.C.F
and didn't have time to alter before the final wreck spelled *finis* to the W.W. & F.

At the turn of the century the W.&Q. Railroad changed its name to Wiscasset, Waterville
Farmington, and had the H. K. Porter Company build a 28-ton Forney engine, No. 4. This
print shows No. 4 with the extended cab which was supposed to keep coal and crew dry wl
blizzards rode the tail-wind. The extension shortly disappeared, and No. 4 finished her life w
coal and crew exposed to the weather, like other engines.

Progress northward from Wiscasset was satisfactorily rapid, and shortly a part of the new line was in regular operation whilst yet construction was clanging a few miles beyond. About a year and a half later, in 1895, the line was opened to Albion, 43½ miles from Wiscasset.

The new line followed the curvaceous Sheepscot river or some of its tributaries, for the first 20 miles, as far as Cooper's Mills. Five miles out of Wiscasset was the first station, Sheepscot. It was set in the woods. A wagon road ambled over the forested hills two or three miles to Sheepscot Village, and the neighboring village of Alna. Sheepscot station served these hamlets. From Sheepscot the new railroad began to climb. The top of the hill, which for years demanded a push from Wiscasset for heavy trains, was at Alna, a flag station. Then, dropping down a heavy, milelong grade called *The Mountain,* the track entered the village of Head Tide. Head Tide's two claims to fame are the big, white church perched on a knoll above the railroad track, and the fact that the village was the home of the poet Edwin Arlington Robinson. The stately church with its sky-reaching spire is still there.

A mile beyond Head Tide was the first roadside watertank. Beyond that the railroad's gravel pit. Following the tumbling Sheepscot, no longer an oily navigable river, the road came into Whitefield. Just short of Whitefield the track crossed the Sheepscot on a long iron truss-bridge which had once been a span in the Maine Central's old bridge across the Kennebec at Waterville.

Next came North Whitefield, another typical white house, red barn Maine village, 17½ miles above Wiscasset. Then Cooper's Mills, where the Sheepscot went one way and the railroad went another.

Cooper's Mills once had the only covered station on the W. & Q. These covered, or *through stations* as they were officially called, were popular once in Maine. By the time the W. & Q. finally got around to building depots the fad had succumbed to buildings of conventional design. The *through station* at Cooper's Mills burned one night and was replaced by a neat station of the later design. This replacement was the only one of the Wiscasset & Quebec stations to sport a bay window.

Above Cooper's Mills was more level terrain, and Windsor station. The nearby postoffice was called Windsorville, probably to distinguish it from postoffices in several other hamlets in the town of Windsor. Then came Weeks' Mills, destined presently to become an important, though shortlived, junction point in the two-footer's dreams of Quebec.

Beyond Weeks' Mills the country assumed more bosoms and gullies again, and there were numerous "puffing places" on the five-mile stretch to Palermo. If the Wiscasset & Quebec surveyors deliberately tried to avoid villages they deserve acclaim. More of the nine towns were a breath-taking walk from the railroad station than there were those where the track skirted the village. Palermo village, known as Branch Mills, was a mile from the rural depot.

A vigorous climb over The Horseback brought the winding track to China, also a goodly distance away from the village. From China the 5½ mile scoot to Albion was mostly across swampy ground where engineers were warned not to go off the track. In many places there was no bottom, as they speak of bogholes, and if an engine rolled off the firmer roadbed fill, she would go out of sight in the muck. Yet it was across that long bog that the little trains used to hang up their miniature speed records. Many a homeward bound passenger train dashed those 5½ miles in six minutes!

When the tiny construction trains reached Albion, in 1895, they went in to clear for a rest and a second wind, so to speak.

Maybe the Wiscasset & Quebec was the most impractical of all the two-footers. Perhaps visionary, or imprudent, venturesome, or harebrained. While the others knew pretty well what they were doing, and did it, this little line always had big ideas. Like a kid of whom it's said, "He's too big for his breeches." Those big ideas dogged it for years, and finally the grandiose extravaganza was its undoing.

Digging into old files and records which constitute the W. & Q.'s biography we could get a little cynical. There appear reasons to doubt its promotional sincerity. This Lilliput may have been a bit of a strumpet.

Along with the highfalutin Wiscasset-to-Quebec idea which persisted from 1854 to the late 1890's, there occurred periodic wayside ideas. One was to build a few branches of questionable necessity. One of these was a branch from Cooper's Mills to Togus, to tie up with the Kennebec Central. Another, which eventually was spiked to the Lilliput width, was to leave the main line at Weeks' Mills, 28 miles from Wiscasset, and meander northwesterly through the towns of China and Vassalboro to Winslow, which is directly across the Kennebec from Waterville. Still another, when the road to Togus had been forgotten, was to cut across to Augusta, the State capital.

Probably it was lucky these two westering branches weren't built. It would have been that much more track to abandon when shortly its impracticability had been proved.

As we mused a minute ago, this little Lilliput could easily be suspected of double talk and double-crossing. We may well wonder if its loquacious promoters ever intended to use the money so raised to build railroad track across the boundary into Quebec. We may likewise wrinkle our noses at their loose talk about Lilliput sleeping cars, diners, mammoth engines, and ocean liners connecting with international trains at Wiscasset. In the light of history their whole sales talk smells. If those founding fathers had called it a day when they spiked the last rail in front of Albion depot—half a mile from the village—the fate of stockholders' dollars might have been different. But no—*On to Quebec!*

Tracklaying soon was resumed from Albion. On into the north, through what is still, today, a pretty desolate region of swamps and woods and rabbit-country, the two-footer crept. On this stretch, sans hamlets or villages, one flag station shelter was built. We wouldn't know about that if mention thereof hadn't been contemporaneously made in an old report. Apparently it didn't get a name.

The grandiose plans at the time were to go north to the village of Burnham, bypassing it by about a mile, crossing the Maine Central's branch to Belfast, to eventually emerge in the middle of the town of Pittsfield. Pittsfield is on the Maine Central's main line,

Portland to Bangor. It was also, in the middle '90's, the southern terminus of the new Sebasticook & Moosehead Railroad. The S. & M. ran from Pittsfield north through Hartland to Harmony, 16 miles It was this same standard gauge line which the Monson Railroad had wooed, with the avowed intention of building south from .Monson Junction for a connection. There must have been some strong attraction about the Sebasticook & Moosehead, which appealed to its midget cousins.

The W. & Q. planned to confiscate the S. & M., narrow the gauge to two feet, and use those 16 miles to further its Quebecward thrust. By fair means or foul, so the investors were promised, the audacious midget would thither along through northwestern Maine and over the Canadian border into the mysterious and wealthy Province of Quebec.

Old records reveal things that made the proposed Quebec deal look like a humdinger. Just what P.Q. held in the way of transportable riches isn't explained. Valuable timberland, to be sure, but 1895 Maine was bristling with virgin forests. A hundred and fifty miles of railroad didn't have to be built into Canada to find trees. Quebec also had minerals, exploited and virgin. So did Maine. Some of the Province was agricultural, but the Grand Trunk, the C.P.R., and other established roads could handle the products easily. Whatever the potentials were supposed to be the promoters were confident that their Lilliput railroad, connecting the Promised Land with the Western Ocean, would shortly make the stockholders yelp with joy.

As things finally turned out the stockholders would have yelped with double joy if they could have got their money back.

And, freight wasn't the only thing the W. & Q. boys were gunning for. There would be passengers.

Where that passenger potential came from is another question. Quebec wasn't a savage wilderness in the 1890's, and its lush pastures and farming lands lacked nothing in fruitfulness. But the Province wasn't metropolitan. Its hardworking French people didn't need rail service to Maine. Ninety percent of them didn't *parlent l'Anglais,* and still don't. Passenger trains to Maine could have passed them a dozen times a day without stimulating them with wanderlust.

In the cruel light of hindsight it seems unlikely these French Canadians would have packed the midget sleeping cars nor gorged on *cuisine magnifique* in the speeding diners.

Sleeping cars and diners there were to be. They were on the drawing boards. *Les hommes et les mesdames* of French Quebec would ride in Victorian splendor as they journeyed to Maine and the sea. The hordes of unidentified folks who were to billow into Wiscasset by ship, *en route* to Quebec, would likewise enjoy their trip the more for the exquisite cuisine of Wiscasset & Quebec dining cars and the downy comfort of the elfin berths.

Best of all, however, would be the cornucopian dividends which lucky shareholders would clip by the bushel—all by being patient, and being generous in their investing.

As we've seen, after a breathing spell in Albion that 44 mile section was put into immediate operation. Workmen wiped their bearded lips, hitched-up their galluses, and hit the turf again.

In much less time than you'd expect the jaded graders and tie-layers had track down as far as Burnham town. That was in 1897.

Burnham village was side-stepped by a mile or so, true to this Lilliput's form. Steel gangs clanged down the last stick of 35-pound steel, which brought them up to the Maine Central's Belfast rails. Clawbars were poised to loosen Maine Central spikes, preparatory to installing the diamond crossing. But, they were stopped short in their tracks.

Shenannigans were afoot, 'twould seem. The big Maine Central wouldn't allow the Lilliput to cross.

From perusing old records and reports we can easily suspect that the promoters of the Wiscasset & Quebec didn't care a tinker's dam whether they crossed or not. We would think that a railroad company, which had lately spent hundreds of thousands of other people's dollars building 55 miles of railroad, would now fight like fiends to protect that investment. But no; they took it lying down.

To be sure, the promoters did squeak a feeble protest. They whimpered to the Maine Railroad Commissioners. But they did not, definitely, fight with tooth and toenail to get that diamond into the Belfast branch.

Just how long the construction crews idled around Burnham is uncertain. Maybe a few days. Maybe a month. Shortly the promoters of the W. & Q. and the defenders of the Maine Central met with the three Maine Railroad Commissioners.

There is no story about how deputy sheriffs and United States marshals had to hold the opponents from tearing each other—and the Commissioners—to shreds. Those reports blandly remark, with an ill-concealed yawn, that the Wiscasset & Quebecers wished to continue building their line (into and through the Maine Central's sacred domain) to Canada. And, that the aforesaid Maine Central preferred that no crossing of its Belfast branch be made.

But finally, perhaps with a merry twinkle in their honest eyes, the Commissioners did order that the Lilliput be permitted to cross the *wide* gauge track on an overhead bridge. And moreover, that while this overpass was being built the Wiscasset people might install a temporary diamond, *providing* the diamond could be installed without interrupting the passage of Maine Central trains.

The two jokers in the deal were, (1) that to cross the Belfast branch overhead would have been virtually impossible. The terrain at this point is as flat as a proverbial pancake. To have climbed high enough to gain overhead clearance would have meant going back half a mile on each side and building up the grade. The temporary installation of the diamond crossing was (2) the other joker.

The diamond crossing was hauled to the scene; so were plenty of workmen. The Lilliput knew it had to work fast so as not to interrupt Maine Central trains. There was a passenger or a freight every couple of hours, or so.

Maybe the boys with the clawbars and mauls were already to start, when *Bang!* The dream blew up.

Miser minutes behind the Maine Central train, a second section appeared. It passed. Just as the W. & Q.'s Italian boys were about to begin again, another train tooted menacingly. In a few minutes, another. According to local legend, either the Italians were slow to take advantage of between-trains opportunities, or the *wide* gauge was enjoying a sudden business boom. Anyway, the crews couldn't

& Q.'s 35-pound steel main-lining around the bay heading north out of Wiscasset. Heavy tides
pounding winter storms sometimes undermined these shore sections of track. Today very few
es survive along the tidewater edge. The black line to your right is the long trestle of the Maine
Central's Rockland Branch, crossing the bay eastbound.

W.&F. No. 5, the ex-B.&S.R. Hinckley No. 2. This photo appears to have taken at the
r of the Wiscasset enginehouse, and was probably made soon after the engine came to
scasset — in early 1907. Her boiler was serving for steam heat in the Wiscasset shop at the
time of abandonment, 1933.

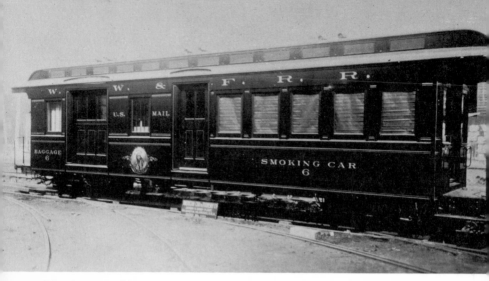

The elegant car *Taconnet* was a 3-way deal: express, Railway Post Office, and passenger. She [...] serviceable as long as the railroad ran but had been stripped to an express car except for a [...] passenger seats. The gilt emblem on her sides is the head of the Indian Chief Taconnet, a fr[...] of the white man three hundred years before.

In 1907 the W.W.&F. Railroad was sold lock, stock and barrel to Carson Peck, a chain-s[...] man. He forthwith changed its name to W.W.&F. Rail*way*, and ordered two new engines f[...] Baldwin. Prairie-type No. 6 was one. Still bright with the builder's paint stripes, she poses [...] Train 24 at Albion. The conductor's long buffalo coat looks comfortable, with winter coming [...]

install that diamond without "interrupting Maine Central train operations."

The joker was face-up on the table.

That is where, in the glow of hindsight, the whole deal had a funny smell. The Maine Central's action, it goes without saying, was clever. That company can be excused for protecting its territory and stockholders from invasion of possible competitors, and from that slant its action was commendable.

As for the Maine Railroad Commissioners it would seem that they weren't, perhaps, fulfilling their sacred trust to consider and protect *all* investors, along with the public good. The folks who had sunk their nest-eggs in W. & Q. stock should have been considered as much as those who owned stock in the Maine Central. At least, that would be one way of looking at it.

And why, with a fortune of stockholders' money in the bag, the Wiscasset & Quebec promoters so meekly tossed in the sponge is a mystery with several hypothetical answers. If their souls were free from rust and they had truly intended to build a railroad through to Quebec, why did they quit without even kicking the shins of those big boys who tripped them up?

Anyway, then and there the Quebecward scheme, as far as this route went, fizzled. The dream blew up.

For the nonce the Albion-Wiscasset segment settled down to regular operation. The eleven miles of narrow track between Albion and the almost-crossing of the Belfast branch was left intact for some time. Later it was dismantled. Today, from the mixed train of the Belfast & Moosehead Lake Railroad (the onetime Belfast branch of the Maine Central's) you can plainly see the old W. & Q. grade streaking south across an alder-grown marsh.

For a year or so a passenger train left Albion each morning for Wiscasset, connecting there with Maine Central trains of the Rockland Branch. It came back to Albion in the late afternoon. Some old timetables show it making this 43½ mile run in just over two hours including nine station stops. Forenoons a mixed train ran from Wiscasset to Albion, returning in the afternoon. A freight extra wasn't uncommon, too.

For a crowd of promoters who had been humiliated and thrashed on the bloody field of Burnham, these men recovered their poise quickly. That same year, 1897, they convened at a safe distance from the acrid smell of sweat and perfidy and organized a new company, promoting a new route. They either really were sincere in their Quebec-or-Bust obsession, or the idea was a good stock seller. The new company was named the Franklin, Somerset & Kennebec Railroad.

The choice of a cognomen was maybe the only logical aspect of this new plan. Those were the three counties through which the Wiscasset boys were to drive location-stakes.

They were already in Kennebec County from Windsor to Albion. The new route would skirt the southern edge of Somerset and run ten or a dozen miles into Franklin, to tie up with the Sandy River Railroad at Farmington.

The new line would connect with the Wiscasset & Quebec at Weeks' Mills. Through rolling hills and fragrant woods it would pass through the villages of South China, East Vassalboro, and North Vassalboro to Winslow, which is on the east bank of the Kennebec River. A bridge crossing the Maine Central's main line and the river would put its rails into the city of Waterville. From there it would dodge Oakland village, duck into southern Somerset County, duck out again, and dash across the few miles of Franklin County to Farmington. The entire distance, from Weeks' Mills, would be some forty miles.

That wasn't all. To further complicate the scheme, and maybe to pad its pants against another boot from conscientious objectors, the promoters formed still another company to build the 14 miles from Weeks' Mills to Winslow—the Waterville & Wiscasset Railroad. The F.S.&K. would build those miles from yer to yon, ending with the marriage at Farmington.

During 1898 and '99 nearly all the work was done. Bridges were installed, excepting for the sizable structure spanning the Maine Central and the Kennebec River at Waterville. That was two-thirds complete. Miles of rail were laid. Today you can follow most of this old grade. Parts of it now are covered by the main, hard-topped highway.

Solid granite abutments peep through the trees here and there, where there were bridges for Lilliput trains to scoot across.

No steam engines were used in building the F.S.&K. The work was done by horses hauling dumpcars. The Waterville & Wiscasset segment, from Weeks' Mills to the east bank of the Kennebec, where the Winslow station and yard was built, took shape quickly. In fact, before this bubble broke the W.&W. was pretty well completed.

Oh yes, the unlucky Lilliput's luck stayed with it, and this bubble exploded, too.

The Maine Central seems to have had a foot in this pie. When the Lilliput bride was about to hop-skip-and-jump into Farmington and the blessed embrace of her mate, the Sandy River, the Maine Central again protected its stockholders, and our Lilliput went sprawling again.

In order to make the connection with the Sandy River the F.S.&K. had to cross a small parcel of land adjoining the joint Maine Central-Sandy River terminal, which was owned by the big road. The big road said, "No! Nothing doing."

We can't guess what the long-suffering W. & Q. stockholders said.

No it was. Again, without a struggle, without even biting the giant's ear, the Wiscasset boys quit.

Once more that Burnham aroma whiffs up our nose. The question again arises, why didn't the narrow gauge crowd shift their survey a few hundred yards, or even a mile or so if necessary, so as to hit the Sandy River beyond the Maine Central's reach? There was room enough, God knows, in Franklin County.

There's a chance that the Sandy River-Phillips & Rangeley Railroads weren't overly enthused about being a link in the Wiscasset to Quebec chain. These roads appear to have lent not a hand to the W. & Q.'s cause. About this time, we must remember, those Lilliputs of Franklin County were, themselves, toying with notions of expansion. Perhaps they didn't relish this intrusion of the hussy from the Coast. She might reduce the Sandy River and its brother roads to the status of captive bridge-carriers. She could confound all their own pet plans for extensions. So, the Sandy River could have been in cahoots with the Maine Central when that worthy knocked the dancing two-footer for a loop.

It's all beside the point; water over the dam; smoke behind us.

The Wiscasset & Quebec failed twice to poke its tiny rails across the border into Quebec. Both times the Maine Central got the blame. Both times the Lilliput's stockholders took a painful licking. And now, their extravagant dreams were done. The Wiscasset & Quebec Railroad was broke.

A receiver was appointed in 1900. If the catastrophe had happened 25 years later, probably total abandonment would have been the result. In 1900 the railroad industry hadn't got abandonment-conscious. They were more determined to stay in business than railroads are today. They had more show then, perhaps. So, a new company was formed. The following year, 1901, the assets (if there were any) of the Wiscasset & Quebec Railroad were taken over by the new Wiscasset, Waterville & Farmington Railroad.

All the two-footers which went through reorganizations seemed to follow a pattern of changing their name to something which shortly they wouldn't be doing. Like the Bridgton & Saco River changing its name to Bridgton & Harrison, then forthwith abandoning the line to Harrison.

The new company took the name Wiscasset, Waterville & Farmington, and promptly erased any semblance of connections toward Farmington. It never set foot in Waterville, either, for that matter.

The new W.W.&F. Railroad acquired the operating 44 miles from Wiscasset to Albion. Probably it also got the 11 miles from Albion to Burnham, although we don't know exactly when that rail was picked up. It got the nearly completed lines of the Waterville & Wiscasset R.R. and the F.S.&K.

It inherited engines numbers 1, 2 and 3, and 50 or 60 freight cars. There were probably a couple of coaches, a mail-express car, and probably an old combination baggage-passenger car which has historians baffled today.

The new owners began by following in the foot tracks of predecessors. Another company was formed, called the Franklin Construc-

...ursion car No. 7 gave 56 people a drafty ride, in the days when open cars were in style. She later boarded in and became a combination express-RPO-passenger car, with the distinction ...being finally the very last 2-foot gauge Railway Post Office car to operate in the United States. She was the widest of the Lilliput cars, measuring eight feet over her matched sheathing.

...r the Wiscasset, Waterville & Farmington was abandoned in June, 1933, its engines were ...lessly stored at the Wiscasset machine shop. Here is No. 3, and directly behind her the highly ...eled No. 9, ex-Kennebec Central No. 4, ex-ex-S.R.&R.L. No. 6, and ex-ex-ex-Sandy River R.R. 5! Identical to the 2 and 3, she was later bought by a railroad fan, and in 1958 still reposed on the farm of Mr. Ramsdell near Putnam, Connecticut.

W.W.&F. No. 6, the "big" Prairie type, before the outside valve-gear was installed. She was northbound at North Whitefield, about 1912 or 1914. See the engineer hauling back on the whistle-rope!

tion Company. It was to complete the Weeks' Mills-Winslow line, ready it for operation, and under terms of its contract equip it with one new engine, two passenger cars, and a few new freight cars. This deal was probably to protect the Wiscasset-Albion road and its equipment from possible lawsuits, in case the Waterville & Wiscasset job was also a flop.

A year later, in 1902, the Weeks' Mills to Winslow road was ready. It was laid with big, 45-pound steel. The H. K. Porter Company had delivered a brand spanking new Forney engine to the Franklin Construction Company. The coach *Vassalboro* No. 5 and the R.P.O. Express-Passenger combination *Taconnet* No. 6 had been built by the Jackson & Sharp Car Company of Wilmington, Delaware. The Franklin Construction Company turned the new line over to the W.W. & F. fully equipped.

When the No. 4 engine was delivered they thought she was a regular whale, her 28 tons was so much bulkier than the midgets 1, 2 and 3. They were scared of her. On a Sunday morning they ran her to Weeks' Mills, barely creeping, using three hours for the 28 mile trip.

About this time, or shortly after, the Jackson & Sharp works also built an open excursion car, No. 7. She was practically identical to a 14-bench open streetcar. For what specific purpose it was built, or how much service it ever saw as an open excursion car isn't on record. Shortly afterward it was pushed into the shop and boarded up, emerging as a combination mail-express-passenger combination. Although it was the widest of all the Lilliput cars (being eight feet wide over the sheathing) it was thereafter called the *Little Combination.*

To go with this rebirth and splurge in additional equipment the company had a rash of correspondence with the H. K. Porter Company about building some sizable Consolidation engines. The Porter Company replied with recommendations for Moguls instead. Which was which didn't matter, because none was ever built. But Porter did supply the W.W.&F. with a set of blueprints of the Consolidation —Blueprint No. 9816, Dec. 5, 1901, Class D-2-T-8 Code Word Hatijo. These engines were to have cylinders 13x16 inches, drivers 33 inches, 48,000 pounds on drivers, 55,000 pounds total engine, and a tank weighing 29,500 pounds. We missed something when these engines were turned down! Another of the lamentable failures of the Wiscasset Lilliput.

During the following five years the W.W.&F. didn't do so bad, trafficwise. The annual reports didn't gladden the new owners' hearts because bonded indebtedness and other sins of youth cast a reddish glow. Otherwise, the little road would have made an excellent showing.

In its early days the W.W.&F. was so poor it couldn't buy paint for the engines. Earl Keefe tells of firing the No. 3 in 1905 with a grate broken and bricks stacked in the ashpan to hold it up! The new company had to fork over the cash before anyone would sell 'em anything. When Carson Peck bought the road in December, 1906 the crews hadn't seen a paycheck for several weeks.

The territory it served was heavily agricultural, and thousands of acres of standing timber added to the traffic potential. Potatoes and lumber went out in volume. Milk cars were part of the daily consist. Quantities of cattle, grain and general merchandise, as well as such farm machinery as existed in those years, was hauled north to the towns along the line.

In the early 1900's the timetables showed a galaxy of trains. The main line was now Wiscasset to Winslow. Albion was on a branch. Sometimes the Albion trains shuttled back and forth, connecting at Weeks' Mills with the main line jobs. Other seasons saw them run down to Weeks' Mills, connect, then run around the wye to continue up to Winslow, performing a sort of commuter service between those towns and Waterville.

In those days the town of North Vassalboro boasted a big textile mill which swelled the village's population. Apparently frequent train service into Waterville (just over the bridge from the Winslow station) appealed to the distaff side of this population.

The textile mills also gave heavy tonnage to the Lilliput. Cloth goods outbound and coal and raw materials inbound filled the little freight trains out to enviable tonnage.

The same electric line, the Androscoggin & Kennebec, which once threatened ruin to the Kennebec Central, built its Augusta-to-

Waterville road out around North Vassalboro, in order to capture some of this lush business. It grabbed plenty of it, both in its big semi-interurban cars and its freight trains.

Because of the line's heavy indebtedness the new owners weren't too happy. It couldn't seem to make money, no matter how many trains it ran or how many passengers and how much freight it hauled. After a few years of financial misery there appeared a chance for them to get out from under. A prospective purchaser was in sight.

In December 1906 the W.W.&F. Railroad was sold to Carson Peck, a department store baron in Maine. If Carson Peck had made money in the store business he lost it in the field of transportation.

Owner Peck began this union as most men do, by bedecking his fading hussy with things he thought would improve her. Among these trinkets were two baby Baldwins, and a name change from *Railroad* to *Railway*.

In 1907 the Baldwin Locomotive Works delivered to him a heavy freight engine, No. 6, and a fast-stepping passenger engine, No. 7. The No. 6 was a 26-ton Prairie type, similar to those on the Sandy River. No. 7 was a 28-ton 2-4-4RT Forney much like the Sandy River's No. 9. Nos. 6 and 7 were fine engines. The multi-drivered 6 could haul long freight trains over the relatively easy grades of the W.W.&F., and the quick-gaited 7 could cuff the wind with anyone's passenger train. She often was clocked whizzing through a mile in 60 seconds.

Shortly after Peck's purchase of the road the W.W.&F. bought from the Bridgton & Saco River its old No. 2 Hinckley Forney. She became W.W.&F. No. 5. The legend is that the W.W.&F. couldn't pay for it. So, one day a group of Bridgtonites rode to the hounds, and came home that night with one of the Wiscasset's prized passenger coaches in the bag. Whether the legend is the sober truth or diluted with a little tittle-tattle is open to question. The fact is, however, one of the W.W.&F.'s nice coaches did go to the B.&S.R., and after doing years of service there, is today frolicking through the green, cranberried acres on the Edaville Railroad.

Carson Peck's adventure in the broad field of transportation never rolled him on the red carpet of wealth. It may not have sent him to an early grave, but within a few years that was where he landed. It wouldn't be unreasonable to lay some of the blame to the Strumpet Lilliput's door.

Those years, however, weren't devoid of tonnage and earnings. In 1912, for instance, the W.W.&F. hauled nearly 200,000 bushels of potatoes. The lucrative Railway Post Office car was a sizable item in the gross revenues. Passengers added up, too, in those days. Excursions were popular and in keeping with the era. The various county fairs and the Fourth of July celebrations were occasions for special train operations. The flanges on No. 1's head drivers were worn so thin they ran her backwards all the time. New tires cost money.

Around 1912 things weren't doing so well on the old Waterville & Wiscasset line, from Winslow down to Weeks' Mills. The A.&K. trolley line was siphoning off some North Vassalboro tonnage. Whether the American Woolen Company's big mill was shipping by trolley, or what the story was, is beside the point. The Peck management saw fit to take action which was fifty years ahead of its time.

The line was cut back, from Winslow to North Vassalboro. The surviving ten miles to Weeks' Mills became freight only. Once more the road to Albion became the main line. Except for the fiasco of the F.S.&K. connection with Farmington, this abandonment of the Winslow line was the first actual break in the established trackage which once was part of that vast and courageous scheme of tying the Atlantic Ocean with the French province of Quebec. The episode must have created a dazed amazement, too, in Central Maine. It was an age when railroads were necessary to the life, liberty and pursuit of taxes in their communities. It was an age when railroads were still being built, instead of dismantled. That early demise of a stretch of busy, main line railroad, even if it was a narrow gauge, probably set the mustached townsmen back on their heels, so to speak.

Whether or not the Wiscasset road's typical response to its problems—running away from them—was any help this time, would be pretty hard to say, today. The fact remains the little road kept running, on what track it pleased to retain. Earnings kept abreast of expenses, and sometimes a little better.

The year 1916 seems to make itself noticed in old records. Nothing really spectacular nor alarming happened, but rather a number of little things.

Automatic couplers were installed on two engines, two passenger cars, and six freight cars. A new flag station was built at Preble's Crossing. On the unhappy side was the reported abandonment of the 9.9 miles of track from North Vassalboro down to Weeks' Mills. The rails were immediately sold for scrap.

On the somewhat sunnier side was a gross revenue of $65,500.00. Freight accounted for $53,623.00 of it. $6,194.00 was from passengers. In those days mail was only $2,318.12 and express $2,570.00. The investment was quoted as being $308,956.00 with no funded debt. Capital stock was $300,000.00.

Total expenses matched up with $64,689.00. The operating ratio was 99.00. At least, the Lilliput with the long trail of hard luck was breaking even.

There were 81 employees that year. Six engines, four passenger cars and one baggage car, and 92 freight cars were on the roster. At the year's end the Little Failure had carried 16,018 passengers and 27,052 tons of freight.

A gross earning of $65,000.00 sounds like peanuts now. Actually it wasn't to be snorted at forty-odd years ago. We've had two major wars since then, inflation following them both. In today's watered dollars that $65,000.00 would have been easily the equivalent of $300,000.00. A 44 mile shortline today, grossing $300,000.00 would stack up pretty well.

In view of this comparison it is hard for us to see why the W.W.&F. didn't prosper. Men were paid $2.50 and $3.00 a day— one-fifth of today's average railroad rates. There were no pension taxes, no 40-hour week, no overtime. Coal was only $4 or $5 a ton and a ton would keep a passenger engine hot from Albion to Wiscasset and return, plus banking its fire for the night. No union wages and schedules and terrible fringe benefits gave the management cause to wail.

Electric headlights didn't come to the W.W.&F. for a number of years, and then only when the law caught up with it. Airbrakes never did come. The not-too-reliable vacuum brakes pinched the trains to the end, although by then they worked only on the engines. The brake equipment on the freight cars wasn't kept in repair. Butterfly air-doors on the fireboxes were installed when I.C.C. regulations flatly demanded it, and not before.

All the two-foot gauge cars had wonderful hand brakes. Whether this was because their light weight improved the leverage of brake rods, or some other reason, is for mechanical folks to guess. It was rare that a narrow gauge freight or passenger car couldn't be stopped almost in its length, with the old hand binder.

In the final years of operation, when the vacuum equipment didn't work any more, the conductor and brakeman clubbed the trains with those hand brakes. Vacuum functioned after a fashion on the engines, but with ten or a dozen cars rock-and-rolling down The Mountain the engineer needed some help.

Everything considered, the W.W.&F. was remarkably lucky in the matter of wrecks. The Sandy River was the bantam which specialized in pile-ups. But with its 120 miles of road, fifteen to twenty crews, and a hundred train-miles to the Wiscasset's one, the Sandy River's record was in keeping with the other two-footers. Spills on the W.W.&F. or the Kennebec Central were pretty much in proportion to the train-miles.

The W.W.&F. had one grand, rip-roaring wreck. It is proved by those made-in-Germany colored postcards, still to be found in crossroad stores. It happened at the foot of The Mountain, just south of Head Tide. According to local recollections it was a Fourth of July excursion train, although the fly-specked postcards don't say. The engine went off just before it ran onto the short wooden bridge alongside the highway. The bridge collapsed. The askew coaches had more or less skun the engine's shins and buttocks when the photograph was made. No one was seriously hurt, and it was a beautiful wreck—for postcard purposes.

There were a few incidents when an engine toppled over. She would shortly be toppled back up again, her smokestack pushed back, and away they'd go! Lilliput engines didn't brood over these episodes. As soon as the ballast was cleaned out of their driving-boxes,

and wrongs had been made right, they'd roll their little drivers
through the curves without a backward peep.

Not counting minor derailments, which are routine on anyone's
railroad, one of the last spills on the W.W.&F. was about 1930. Two
or three boxcars jumped the track while curving along the riverbank.
It was winter. The river was frozen solid. The cars careened away
from the track, down the bank, and skidded out onto the glassy ice.
It took the clean-up crew several days to skate them ashore again, and
up the embankment to the track.

About that time another train was bounding down The Mountain
one afternoon when a boxcar suddenly set up a galloping gait. She
seemed to be leaping along like a lame rabbit. The train stopped. The
boys converged on the crazy boxcar from their respective ends of the
train, and found a washtub-size boulder under one of its trucks. Probably sliding down the side of the mountain just as the train went by,
it had lodged itself under the boxcar truck, and acting like a ball-
bearing it had rolled over and over, staying inside the rails and keeping the boxcar in line with the rest of the train. Ties were badly
mauled for half a mile back, but as soon as the boulder was removed,
with the help of a jack and a crowbar, everything was ready to go.

The winter before the W.W.&F. turned up her toes, two or three
flatcars were derailed near Head Tide, in about the same place as the
Fourth of July wreck. Time was running out, and there were more
flatcars than would ever be used again. So why lug heavy rerailing-
frogs back from the engine and waste half a day getting three flatcars back on the rails? They didn't. They cut a stout white birch, used
it as a pry, and toppled the flatcars over into the river. The train was
re-coupled and made it into Wiscasset with only a few minutes delay.
Unless some wartime patriots cleaned them up in a Save-America
scrap drive the little flatcars are still down there in the brambles.

But, back to better days.

1916 had been a somewhat eventful year. The decade which followed didn't bring about any changes worth mentioning. Earnings
and expenses still got along fairly well. Some years a few hundred
dollars would be banked. But the heirs of Carson Peck were pretty
well glutted with running a railroad. Buying it twenty years before

hadn't been their idea, anyway. Even when Peck was alive he had left the management to his able General Manager, Sam Sewell. Now, with Mr. Peck gone and Mrs. Peck not too interested in his hobby, it was arranged with Manager Sewell to sell the road.

That was in 1926. Excitement followed the announcement. Even in times as recent and modern as 1926 the folks along the line didn't want to lose the hardluck girl whose railroadish escapades had endeared her to them. With flutterings and streetcorner discussions reminiscent of the fifty-years ago organizations of new railroad companies, the local farmers and businessmen raised the sum which the Pecks had set; $60,000.00. They bought it.

Sam Sewell stayed as Manager. He was as much a part of the railroad as the five engines and the hundred cars.

But railroading, narrow gauge at least, had gone off the gold standard. Red was nearer the current color scheme. The farmers didn't retire on dividends from their $60,000.00. The fact was, they lost their long-tailed shirts.

During the four years following the farmers' purchase Sewell kept the little railroad clattering along pretty much as it had been doing. The books for 1930 showed a gross earnings of $43,700.00. That would equal at least $120,000.00 today. The investment in road and equipment had increased only $3,000.00 since 1916. It was $311,136.00. Capital stock was shown as $53,090.00, with no debt. Freight had paid $30,329.00 and passengers $1,659.00. Mail and express amounted to $11,712.00. On the other side expenses were $48,974.00. That was an operating ratio of an unhealthy 112.07.

Whether Sam Sewell was actually taking $5,000.00 out of the treasury to make up a deficit, or if he was using such empty items as depreciation of equipment which couldn't depreciate, interest the stock should have paid, and such, which was $5,000.00 worth of the $48,974.00 expenses, we can only guess. It seems unlikely an actual loss of $5,000.00 existed.

One of the curtailments Sewell made, under the farmers' ownership, was to cut out the mixed train which left Wiscasset in the forenoon, three times a week, for Albion and return. The regular mixed

job, tying up in Albion, had to handle the total business now. One
of the little Portland engines, usually the No. 2, still acted as switcher
between the main yard and the transfer, as well as frequently pushing
the regular train to the top of The Mountain. The other engines
reposed in the enginehouse and in the big yellow shop.

Instead of the chain lightning two hour trips of yesteryear, the
train now took three hours, and sometimes more, making the 43½
mile run. This wasn't as bad as it sounds, however. The nine station
stops, with mail and express to handle and the switching to be done,
took from 45 minutes to an hour of this time. Even in its latter
days the W.W.&F. train made running time as fast as many neglected
wide gauge trains. The narrowness of the track didn't matter.

But the situation wasn't getting better fast. It was getting worse.
Track was wobbly here and there, track crews were cut down. When
cars needed repairs they were poked into an empty siding, to wait.
Still business slumped. This was the period when its onetime nick-
name, *Weak, Weary & Feeble Railway* was finally appropriate.

The depression, which was just landing, didn't pep business up,
either. The line's proximity to the Maine Central didn't help. Its
first few miles out of Wiscasset made it easier for shippers to truck
direct to the Rockland branch, where the old promoters had bypassed
every town by half a mile or more. From Whitefield up through to
Weeks' Mills the waystation towns were a scant eight or ten miles
from the Maine Central's main line at Gardiner or Augusta. Farther
up, and Waterville was only a few minutes drive. In the early 1930's
folks thought it was progressive and even patriotic to help the poor,
struggling truckmen. Verily, the W.W.&F. was heading up the well
known creek.

Railroads' own attitudes and their poor public relations fostered
this help-the-trucks notion. All these factors contributed generously
to the Lilliput's anemic condition.

But there was a cat in the grass watching the poor little mouse
creeping its way along. A lumber baron from another part of the
state, who owned several million feet of standing timber up in
Palermo, didn't see any profit in losing the railroad before his trees

were cut and hauled. He had been watching the deteriorating situation. He moved in at the crucial moment.

The farmers in 1930 were not only willing to throw in the proverbial sponge, but they were begging someone to jump up and catch it. This lumberman was the catcher. He not only owned timberlands in Palermo but he owned wood-working mills over around his home town. He had plenty of outlets for lumber. He needed the W.W.&F. And folks thought that maybe the W.W.&F. needed him.

The man's business activities took him through the railroad's communities frequently, and he began killing several birds with one stone. He acquired a few shares of stock from this farmer, and from that one. Sometimes he paid them a little. Other farmers generously gave their stock to him, if he would keep the railroad running. In this way he quickly scooped up controlling stock for something like $6,000.00.

The joker was that the railroad had some $5,000.00 in its treasury, so actually he acquired the Lilliput for about a thousand dollars!

The next two and a half years weren't happy ones for W.W.&F. folks. With the encroaching depression business continued to slide. The W.W.&F.'s new owner used the proverbial axe with skill. Track crews were cut to six men for the 44 miles. Train crews withered to three men, the engineer, fireman, and conductor. One shopman stayed on, and was kept comfortably busy doing machine work for Winter's new sawmill, lately set up in the Wiscasset yard. The transfer engine and most of the transfer crew were abolished. This new management functioned in a manner which must have made many a government-union controlled railroad boss turn a brilliant, envious green.

Equipment repairs were next to nothing. Engines were kept in running order, and so were a few cars. The lumberman needed flatcars for his logs, and he needed that Railway Post Office car, which paid him $9,200.00 a year.

The nearby Kennebec Central, which had been abandoned a few years before, presented an inviting source of whatever equipment the W.W.&F. might need. That meant power. There were more cars scattered along the 43½ miles than would ever be needed again, both passenger, freight, and work equipment. But motive-power was posing a problem right now.

The engines which the lumberman acquired with the W.W.&F. Railway were old Portland Forneys Number 2 and Number 3; the Franklin Construction Company Porter Number 4, and the new Baldwins 6 and 7. All of them needed this and that done to them in way of repairs. Repairs cost money. The two excellent Kennebec Central Forneys, in mothballs these many years, were ready to run. So, a deal was made whereby the entire Kennebec Central plant changed hands.

Its passenger and freight cars, and the hybrid snowplow car, were disposed of by untrucking them, cutting up the metal, and perching the car bodies on blocks for someone to buy for chicken houses.

A big semi-trailer outfit, one of the few such rigs in Maine in 1932, was spotted. The two little engines were pinched aboard and trundled over the wintry road to Wiscasset. A paint job was applied, with the bright, white letters *W.W.&F.* No. 8 and No. 9.

The No. 9 was a little boomer engine. Lately K.C. 4, previous to 1925 or '26 S.R.&R.L. No. 6, and before that Sandy River R.R. No. 5. She was destined to have at least one more owner before her end.

No. 9 made a few trips on the W.W.&F., then broke an iron in her tender frame. That laid her up. No. 8 took over.

The little railroad, youngest of its breed, had soaked up about all the tough luck that 69 miles of onetime line could absorb. These last days were bitter. Track had gone down to a point where derailments were becoming frequent, and the six men—mostly old-timers —couldn't hope to give it even cursory attention. Business had gone down with it, and except for the mail car and the lumberman's logs from Palermo to Wiscasset, the tiny engine and the three-man crew were hauling more memories than revenue tons. Everyone knew the last trip wasn't far away.

On a clear, sunny morning, the 15th of June, 1933, it came.

Engineer Earl Keefe, with Fireman Glidden on the opposite side of No. 8's vest-pocket cab, had just left Whitefield, on the run to

Wiscasset. The elfin train was puffing and weaving through the curves along the Sheepscot River bank. No. 8's lead drivers were squealing and singing as the 35-pound rails crowded her around the curves. Conductor Baker and Mail Clerk Bonney were back in the lurching combination, preparing for the station stop at Head Tide three or four miles ahead. Out of Albion since 5:30 that morning, this promised to be another uneventful run.

No. 8 screamed and squealed around another curve, at the end of which she would nose into the Whitefield Iron Bridge, rumble across the river, and scoot along the west bank of the river the remaining 12 miles into Wiscasset. They were on time out of Whitefield, 7:28 a.m. Five minutes later, almost around the curve to the bridge, it happened. No. 8 broke the outside rail.

The rail snapped. Keefe big-holed the vacuum brake lever. The lead drivers lurched off the iron and onto the ties. The few-car train, devoid of brakes, slammed up against the engine tank and gave her a further shove. She slewed around sideways, wallowed in the gravel ballast, and nosed down the steep bank toward the tumbling river.

That was it. Keefe had no choice other than to ride her down. As it happened he wasn't even shaken up. Before he untangled himself from the tiny cab seat, he flipped out his watch. 7:33 a.m.

Two or three cars were derailed. It was a minor wreck which a few years before would have been cleaned up during the day. But this wreck wasn't cleaned up.

The saga of the W.W.&F. could end here. But let's glance at the days, and years, which followed.

It was a week or so before the W.W.&F.'s owner would say whether he would continue operation, or not. He hired a stake-body truck to haul the mail and the mail clerk. Shortly, the Post Office department cancelled the mail route. That was the very last R.P.O. to operate on two-foot tracks.

A year later the wreck was still there. Vandals, and maybe a few otherwise respectable railroad fans had scratched the surface in places. No. 8's windows were broken. Her big, cleartoned bronze bell was gone. So was her chime whistle. Kids had wrecked the Little

here are three W.W. & F. stations left—and this one, at Palermo, has been rebuilt into a house.
s the milepost in the foreground says, it was 33 miles from Palermo down to Wiscasset. The
llage of Branch Mills is a mile east of the depot, on Route 3 from Augusta to Belfast, Maine.

he end of track, at Albion, shortly after abandonment. The 2-story depot is still there, used as
two-family dwelling. The other buildings have gone. In the photo one of the snowplows and
e of the flangers sit by the station. Only one engine was housed at Albion. The main track, in the
nter, once went another eleven miles, on to Burnham, as part of the abandoned to-Quebec survey.

perations on the W.W. & F. were abandoned suddenly, at 7:15 in the morning of June 15, 1933, hen the early morning train hit a broken rail south of Whitefield. The crew walked home and ft the foundered Forney to its fate—as the pictures on these pages illustrate. The photo at p was taken exactly one year after the wreck, and, while vandalism had made its mark, no serious amage had been done. The lower shot, seven years later and after the rails had been torn up, nows the No. 8 still keeping her lonely vigil. Then, when scrap for war became important, some-he sneaked across the Whitefield Bridge one night, cut up the little engine, and on the way back cut up the iron bridge too!

A year or two before abandonment, the enginehouse at Wiscasset burned. Nos. 6 and 7 were insid
While not seriously damaged, they were never repaired. A few years after being built the big No.
was equipped with Southern valve gear, the only Lilliput engine to have it. For years No. 7 w
the mainline passenger engine and No. 6 was usually on freights.

For several years following the wreck which finished the W.W. & F. the train sat on a siding a
Head Tide, Maine. In this photo you see, for the last time, the car which began as an open excursio
car, and finished its career as the last R.P.O. on 2-foot gauge track. A pre-war scrap drive saw al
the wayside rolling-stock burned and the metal salvaged.

obably the only surviving W.W. & F. freight car is this No. 312. Today, sheathed in fireproof
ingles, she serves as a tool house on a Cooper's Mills, Maine farm close to the abandoned railroad
ade. This photo was made shortly after abandonment. Side and end ladders on W.W. & F. boxcars
were on the opposite side to the usual railroad practice.

Weeks' Mills, onetime busy junction between the main line and the branch to Palermo and Albion.
his station is the only W.W. & F. building which is still untouched and unaltered since the days
railroad operation. Perhaps not exactly untouched, because the heavy hand of time has recently
caved in the station roof, and caused the freight house to lean Pisa-ly.

The W.W.&F. was the only one of the lamented Lilliputs to be dismantled by a horse and wago. Maybe old Dobbin chortled satanically as he helped do the job. After all, a century earlier th encroaching railroads had helped put him on the shelf. Here Jack and Jerry haul a regular flatca loaded with rail as the end of track creeps nearer and nearer Wiscasset—and the deep blue se

Finis. Taps. Or whatever kind of benediction you wish. The end of a railroad, anyway. This eternal empty W.&Q. grade broods beside the tinkling Sheepscot River, a short distance upstream fro. the old wreck, and half a mile south of Whitefield Depot. It symbolizes not only the end of an e. and the end of a railroad, but the end of the rollicking Lilliputs!

Combination, smashing windows, slashing upholstery, and littering the floor with cigarette butts—some of them tinged with lipstick.

The waystations were similarly vandalized. Otherwise everything was intact, and ready to go again, if the wreck could be cleared. Overtures were made to Owner Winter but no one could seem to make a deal to buy the property.

During the final year or so of operation, so the local story was, the railroad had bought materials and supplies, some of which hadn't been paid for. One of these purchases was a quantity of paint. Now, a year-and-a-half after the wreck, in the fall of 1934, the paint company decided to collect. It attached the main line rails.

This is phraseology to remember, *the main line rails.*

Some local men were hired to do the job. With a span of horses hitched to a flatcar, they followed the phrasing of the attachment to the letter: they dismantled the main line rails. Not a spike, nor a fishplate, nor a frog was touched. Neither were any rails on the sidetracks removed. It was just the main line rails.

When the job was finished, in December 1934, every switch and frog and siding and all the cars were in place. That is, excepting the cars at the wreck. The span of horses had hauled these cars down to Head Tide siding, one at a time, and dropped them in. The track was hauled two or three feet to one side, to allow them to jog out around No. 8's tank, which had stopped, fouling the track.

More years came, and went. Stations fell in. Some were burned. At Wiscasset the general office, down by the diamond crossing, was ransacked, and later burned. The big yellow shops stood for years, slowly collapsing, and finally burned one night. The depot at Head Tide fell down. The one at Whitefield burned. The station at North Whitefield survived for years, complete even to the ticket case and office records. It too disappeared in 1956 or '57. Cooper's Mills burned in the late 1930's. In the fall of 1958 the station at Windsor was being, at long last, remodeled into a dwelling. At Weeks' Mills, in late 1958, the station and freight house were unchanged from the days when a dozen trains a day—from Wiscasset, from Winslow and from Albion—paused at their door. Except, the roof was caving in, and the windows had fallen apart. Trees six inches in diameter grew up through the platforms and on the old grade. The watertank still stood just across the highway crossing, its galvanized spout still creaking gently as breezes swayed it back and forth.

The Palermo station had been remodeled into a house years before, by the widow of Agent Coombs, a longtime W.W.&F. man. At China the station had been moved away. The big, two-story depot at Albion had likewise been made into a dwelling, sans any outside alterations.

Here and there, along the 43½ miles, timber trestles can be seen sagging into the gullies or brooks which they crossed. On Nigger Meadow, between Whitefield and North Whitefield, you may still see the boiler of old Porter No. 1, installed many years ago as a culvert. The old grade still streaks across fields and curves and around hills, but for the most part bushgrown, bleached, and old.

During the war the remaining iron finally went for junk. Boxcars in the Wiscasset yard and scattered on sidings at waystations, were toppled over and the metal in the trucks salvaged. All but Boxcar 302 at Cooper's Mills. A trackside farmer bought her, and she stands there today, on a foundation, serving as one of his farm buildings—the last W.W.&F. boxcar.

The engines were scrapped, all except boomer No. 9. She was bought by a railroad fan, William Monypeny, along with a flatcar and a few lengths of rail, and trailered down to a Connecticut farm where he hoped someday to build a small, garden railroad. No. 9, ex-K.C. 4, ex-ex-S.R.&R.L. 6, and ex-ex-ex-Sandy River 5, was still there in 1958, on the farm of the late Frank Ramsdell.

Today that is all that's left of the old Wiscasset & Quebec Railroad, which scant yesterdays ago boasted that she would crack the north woods wide open, lay track through the forest aisle, and haul the riches of Quebec to Wiscasset, and the ships of the Seven Seas.

Rest In Peace, Little Lilliput. . . .

APPENDIX

In the last 80 or 90 years there have been plenty of industrial tramways spiked to two-foot gauge. Most of them were powered with *dinky* engines of the saddletank specie with the coal supply carried where the fireman would normally sit. Most of them were known no farther than the confining fence of the parent industry. However, a few of these got out of bounds, and for a short time came under common-carrier status.

The Peekskill Valley Railroad was one, which served a mine in eastern New York State, in the early 1870's. It had five or six miles of road and a locomotive which weighed 4½ tons. That much, and no more, appears in an ancient Poor's Manual of Railroads.

Another was the Gilpin County Tramway, built in the late 1880's in Colorado. Its total trackage added up to some 20 miles of spurs and sidetracks serving mines and mills around Central City. It had, during its life, five Shay geared engines ranging from 12 to 18 tons in weight. The road was discontinued around the time of the first World War.

Another of these was built in New Mexico in the early 1900's and was 15 or 16 miles long. The name was almost as long—Silver City, Pinos Altos & Mogollon. It also served mines, and its habitat was at some 7,000 feet altitude along the Continental Divide. Its engines were Shays, two allegedly being former Gilpin engines and two more said to have been new for the company. It is supposed to have been abandoned in 1907.

Along in the late 1880's the Cornwall & Lebanon Railroad in Pennsylvania sponsored a two-foot passenger line four miles long from Mount Gretna to a park called Governor Dick, with a short spur to a rifle range. It operated seasonally until about 1915. Its chief claim to fame was the three 4-4-0 engines which hauled its open, streetcar-type cars.

A few lumbering roads have been built to two-foot gauge. A number of roads of this gauge were projected but never built.

Mexico had at least three such railroads, the last one reportedly abandoned in the middle 1950's.

South America has or had a few as did also South Africa, India, and other foreign countries. These were usually 60-centimeter actually three-eighths of an inch narrower than our two-foot. The French call them *deceauville* railways.

The British Isles, of course, sported two or three of these midgets which varied from 23½ inches to an even two feet in width. The great granddaddy of them all, the hundred-year-old Festiniog Railway still survives, something like the Edaville Railroad in South Carver, Massachusetts, as an operating railroad museum.

The surviving remnants of the two-foot gauge railroads, and the Edaville Railroad on which these few engines and cars still operate, should be mentioned. The Edaville Railroad, however, is known to many people who didn't even know about its predecessors in Maine and elsewhere. The fact that the little private, passenger-carrying, scenic line in South Carver, Massachusetts does represent all that's materially left of the two-footers is, as far as we're presently concerned, its emphatic talking-point.

As we've already seen, the Edaville Railroad, named for its proprietor's initials—Ellis D. Atwood—is a 5½ mile loop of two-foot track circling the 1,800 acre cranberry farm, just off Route 58 between Whitman, Massachusetts and South Middleboro, where it merges with Route 28 to The Cape.

Ellis Atwood built it at tremendous cost in 1945 and '46, originally for his own pleasure. Other people were so interested, and streamed into his three-square-mile estate to see it, that he began giving them rides. Those rides led to bigger crowds, and more rides. The first thing Ellis Atwood and his wife knew, they were running the most popular recreation center in New England. That was when and why he decided to go along with the crowd, and try to make the project self supporting.

WINTER SCHEDULE, DECEMBER 14, 1947

EDAVILLE RAILROAD

Narrow (2-foot) Gauge. The Cranberry Belt Route

Winter at Edaville

MAIN OFFICES AND SHOPS

EDAVILLE

SOUTH CARVER, MASS.

Telephone Carver 54–4

ELLIS D. ATWOOD, Owner

MAP OF THE
EDAVILLE RAILROAD
Scale: one-half
mile to the inch
SEPTEMBER 1947

EASTERN STANDARD TIME

EDAVILLE TO BALL PARK VIA EAST SIDE

TABLE I

		1 Edaville Screech Owl	25 The Bankers	27 Early Black Local	29 Berry Pickers Local	31 Ocean Spray Local	33 The Governor Bradford	35 Edaville Express	37 Pride of the Bogs	39 Carver Special	47 The Atwood Special	51 St. Nicholas Express	55 Star of the East
Miles		Thursday Runs Jan. 1 only	Sun & Hol	Sun & Hol	Sun & Hol	Sun & Hol	Sat, Sun & Hol	Sat, Sun & Hol	Sun & Hol	Sun & Hol	Dec. 14-Jan. 1 only Sun & Hol	Dec. 14-Jan. 1 only Daily	Dec. 14-Jan. 1 only Daily
		A.M.	P.M.	P.M.	P.M.	P.M.	P.M.	P.M.	P.M.	P.M.	P.M.	P.M.	P.M.
0.0	Edaville Lv.	12:01	1 00	1 30	2 00	2 30	3 00	3 30	4 00	4 30	6 30	7 30	8 30
0.6	Cranberry Valley Due		See Note	1f32	2f02	2f32			4f02				
1.0	Reservoir			1f34	2f04	2f34			4f04				
1.6	Sunset Vista			1f36	2f06	2f36			4f06				
2.6	Ball Park Due	12:11	1 10	1 40	2 10	2 40	3 10	3 40	4 10	4 40	6 40	7 40	8 40

BALL PARK TO EDAVILLE VIA WEST SIDE

TABLE II

		2 Edaville Screech Owl	26 The Bankers	28 Early Black Local	30 Berry Pickers Local	32 Ocean Spray Local	34 The Governor Bradford	36 Edaville Express	38 Pride of the Bogs	40 Carver Special	48 The Atwood Special	52 St. Nicholas Express	56 Star of the East
Miles		Thursday Runs Jan. 1 only	Sun & Hol	Sun & Hol	Sun & Hol	Sun & Hol	Sat, Sun & Hol	Sat, Sun & Hol	Sun & Hol	Sun & Hol	Dec. 14-Jan. 1 only Sun & Hol	Dec. 14-Jan. 1 only Daily	Dec. 14-Jan. 1 only Daily
		A.M.	P.M.	P.M.	P.M.	P.M.	P.M.	P.M.	P.M.	P.M.	P.M.	P.M.	P.M.
0.0	Ball Park Lv.	12:14	1 12	1 42	2 12	2 42	3 12	3 42	4 12	4 42	6 42	7 42	8 42
0.3	Mount Urann Due		See Note	1f44	2f14	2f44			4f14				
1.4	Plantation Center			1f48	2f18	2f48			4f18				
2.3	Eda Avenue			1f52	2f22	2f52			4f22				
2.9	Edaville Due	12:29	1 25	1 53	2 23	2 55	3 25	3 55	4 25	4 55	6 55	7 55	8 55

NOTES

f Stops on Signal or Notice to Conductor.

Trains will run as required by traffic during the Holiday period, December 15 to January 1 inclusive.

EQUIPMENT

Parlor and Observation Cars for Special Occasions.
Heated Coaches on all trains.

EDAVILLE IS THE ONLY TWO-FOOT GAUGE RAILROAD IN AMERICA

During the rest of Mr. Atwood's life the midget railroad, which carried some quarter of a million folks every year, remained fairly static. He built a station-restaurant-casino, arranged for Burton Logan to use part of the big brick screenhouse for a railroad museum, as a concession, and supplied other attractions and entertainment for the crowds which made Edaville a nine-months-a-year attraction.

In November 1950 Mr. Atwood died as a result of an explosion of the screenhouse's heating boiler. The malfunctioning oil gun in the firebox exploded, blowing off the firedoor at the moment he was stooping down to examine it.

Mrs. Atwood and her nephew, Dave Eldredge, ran the show for the next five or six years. Then they sold the railroad and leased right-of-way privileges to Nelson Blount and Fred Richardson, of Rhode Island.

The Blount-Richardson boys will be remembered, in railroad fandom, as the kids of 1936 who authored about the first genuine railroad book, *Along the Iron Trail*. It was an astounding accomplishment for two 18-year-old boys, especially in a day when railroad books just weren't salable. *Along the Iron Trail* was.

With the passing of the years Nelson Blount became quite an industrialist. He owned some packing enterprises, canning factories, fishing boats, and other profitable affairs. Fred Richardson was always his righthand man. They thought of the possibility of buying the Lilliput railroad at South Carver, and found the Atwoods willing to sell. That was when the Blount-Richardson team entered the picture.

Today, two or three years later, they have added much to Edaville. A new "station", or casino-like building has been built. New boilers have been added to the two Bridgton & Saco River engines. Such attractions have been brought in as an antique auto collection, an old fire engine display, Blount's own personal collection of ancient guns, and a number of standard gauge engines and cars for display and atmosphere. Rumor has it that still further expansion of this kind is in the cards.

Edaville continues being as popular as ever, a dozen years after its conception. In a small book published in 1947 by Ellis Atwood, entitled *Edaville Railroad,* I said, "—when . . . the last two-footer had whistled off, leaving only memory trains to scoot through the mid-regions of the past. . . . That's why the Edaville Railroad stands out; why it's a splendid anti-climax to an era of colorful midget railroading. Not so much because it's the last survivor . . . as a resurrection—an ideal risen from the ashes of Yesterday. . . . Not a synthetical reproduction but those very same engines and cars which made railroad history . . . alive and puffing again. . . ."

That benediction is as appropriate today, in this book, as it was when it was written in 1947.

B.&S.R. No. 7 streaks along the Edaville cranberry bog with a faked freight train. Boxcar No is an Edaville number, the original B.&S.R. number being lost in the haze of years. The cab is S.R.&R.L. No. 557. The dikes separating the bogs served Mr. Atwood admirably as pre-fabric railroad grades.

LOCOMOTIVES OF THE SANDY RIVER RAILROAD—1879 to 1908

NO.	1	2	3	2nd 2	2nd 3	4	5	8	16
TYPE	0-4-4RT	0-4-4RT	0-4-4RT	2-6-0	2-6-0	0-4-4RT	0-4-4RT	2-6-2	2-4-4RT
BUILDER	Hinckley	Hinckley	Porter	Baldwin	Baldwin	Portland	Portland	Baldwin	Baldwin
DATE	1877	1877	4/1883	9/1893	10/1892	10/1890	6/1891	3/1904	9/1907
NUMBER			565*	13733	12964	616*	622*	23874	31826
CYL	8x12	8x12	9x14	12x16	12x16	10½x14	10½x14	12x16	11½x14
DRIVER	30	30	33	33	33	33	33	33	35
TOTAL WGT	23,750	23,750	28,000	39,360	39,360	36,000	36,000	50,000	55,650
DRIV WGT	14,350*	14,350*	18,000*	33,960	33,960	22,000*	22,000*	37,500	30,150
BP	120*	120*	120*	140	140	140	140	180	180
TF	2636*	2636*	3540*	8305	8305	5363	5363	10,680	8094
FORMER #	Ariel	Puck			(Note)				
FORMER OWNER	B. & B.	B. & B.			(Note)				
DISPOSAL	To SR&RL	To P. & R. Bo-peep	To W&Q 1893	To SR&RL 18	To SR&RL 16	To SR&RL 5	To SR&RL 6	To SR&RL 19	To SR&RL 8
SCRAPPED	1915-20*	1915-20*	1914-15	9/1936	10/1935	1915-20*		9/1935	(Note)
TANK				1500 Gal.	1500 Gal.	600 Gal.	600 Gal.	1500 Gal.	800 Gal.
COAL				2 Tons	2 Tons	1500-lbs.	1500-lbs.	2 Tons	1½ Tons

*Not Certain—Approximate.
(Note) 2nd #3 ex-Laurel River & Hot Springs R.R. *James Wyman*, North Carolina.
(Note) Retired Feb. 1923; Cut up Dec. 1935.

LOCOMOTIVES OF THE FRANKLIN & MEGANTIC R.R. 1884-1908   LOCOMOTIVES OF THE EUSTIS RAILROAD 1903-1911

NAME	B. V. Meade	S. W. Sargent			
NO.	1	2	7	8	9
TYPE	0-4-4RT	0-4-4RT	0-4-4RT	0-4-4RT	0-4-4RT
BUILDER	Hinckley	Baldwin	Baldwin	Baldwin	Baldwin
DATE	1884	1886	5/1903	2/1904	2/1904
NUMBER			23245	23754	23755
CYL		9x14	12x16	12x16	12x16
DRIVER		30	33	33	33
TOTAL WGT		32,000	57,950(1)	57,950(1)	57,950(1)
DRIV WGT		20,000	41,150	41,150	41,150
BP		130	140	140	140
TF		4158	8305	8305	8305
DISPOSAL	SR&RL 1908	SR&RL 1908	SR&RL 20 1911	SR&RL 21 1911	SR&RL 22 1911
SCRAPPED			12/1935	11/1935	8/1935
WATER	1915-20*	1915-20*	800 Gal.	800 Gal.	800 Gal.
COAL			1 Ton	1 Ton	1 Ton

*Not Certain—Approximate.
(Note) Builder's certified weight was without airbrake equipment. When Straight-air and Train-brake was added after 1911 this weight would probably have increased by 2,000-lbs. Eustis engines generally spoken of as 30-ton engines.

LOCOMOTIVES OF THE MONSON RAILROAD 1883 to 1943

NO.	1	2	3	4
TYPE	0-4-4RT	0-4-4RT	0-4-4RT	0-4-4RT
BUILDER	Hinckley	Hinckley	Vulcan	Vulcan
DATE	1883*	1883*	1912	1918
NUMBER				
CYL			10x14*	10x14*
DRIVER			32*	32*
TOTAL WGT			36,000*	36,000*
DISPOSAL			Note 1	Note 1
SCRAPPED	About 1912	About 1918		

*Not Certain—Approximate.
Note 1—Sold to Ellis Atwood by junkmen, 1945.

LOCOMOTIVES OF THE KENNEBEC CENTRAL RAILROAD
1890 to 1929

NO.	1	2	3	4
TYPE	0-4-4RT	0-4-4RT	0-4-4RT	0-4-4RT
BUILDER	Baldwin	Portland	Portland	·Portland
DATE	1890	12/1890	4/1892	6/1891
NUMBER		621	624*	622
CYL	9x14		9⅞x14	10½14
DRIVER	30		33	33
TOT WGT	32,000		38,000	36,000
DRV WGT	20,000		23,000	22,000
BP	130		140	140
TF	4158		5240	5363
FORMER #			3	6
FORMER OWNER			B.&S.R.	S.R.&R.L.
DISPOSAL			to WW&F 1933	to WW&F 1933
SCRAPPED	About 1922	About 1926	1941/42	(1)Note

*Not Certain—Approximate.
(1) Note: Sold to William Monypeny about 1937, and moved to Connecticut. Still there. Not used. Engine No. 1 named "Volunteer."

LOCOMOTIVES OF THE PHILLIPS & RANGELEY RAILROAD
1890 to 1908

NAME	Calvin Putnam	Isaac Walton	Geo. M. Goodwin	Bo-peep
NO.	1	2	3	4
TYPE	0-4-4RT	0-4-4RT	2-6-0	0-4-4RT
BUILDER	Portland Co.	Baldwin	Baldwin	Hinckley
DATE	10/1890	3/1893	3/1891	1877
NUMBER	615*	13276	11706	
CYL	10½x14	12x16	13x16	8x12
DRIVER	33	35	33	30
TOTAL WGT	36,000	56,000	47,000	23,750
DRIV WGT	22,000	39,000*	42,000	14,350*
BP	140		130	120
TF	5363		9,000	2636
FORMER #				2
FORMER OWNER				S.R.R.R.
DISPOSAL	To SR&RL #7	To SR&RL 17	To SR&RL 15	To SR&RL
SCRAPPED	1915-25	8/1936	12/1935 Retired 2/1923	1915-20

*Approximate—Not Certain.
Nos. 2 and 3 equipped with new boilers 1915-16.
No. 3 also rebuilt into 2-6-2 Type, and other changes. See SR&RL.
As built, these engines equipped with vacuum brakes.
Nos. 2 and 3 equipped with air at time of rebuilding.

LOCOMOTIVES OF THE BRIDGTON & SACO RIVER R.R.—1883 to 1941

NO.	1	2	3	4	5	6	7	8
TYPE	0-4-4RT	0-4-4RT	0-4-4RT	0-4-4RT	2-4-4RT	2-4-4RT	2-4-4RT	2-4-4RT
BUILDER	Hinckley	Hinckley	Portland	Porter	Portland	Baldwin	Baldwin	Baldwin
DATE	1882	1882	4/1892	8/1901	11/1906	9/1907	12/1913	3/1924
NUMBER			624*[1]	2360*[1]	628*[1]	31827	40864	57659
CYL			9⅞x14[1]	11x16[1]	11x14[1]	11½x14[1]	12x16	12x16
DRIVER			33	33	33	35	35	35
TOTAL WGT			38,000[1]	47,000[1]	54,580[1]	55,650	69,700	75,000*
DRIV WGT			23,000[1]	31,500[1]	30,180[1]	30,150	38,800	45,000*
BP			140	150[1]	160[1]	180	180	180
TF			5240	7480	7854	8094	10,072	10,072
DISPOSAL		to WW&F #5 1907	To KCRR #3 about 1922				To Edaville 1941	To Edaville 1945
			To WW&F #8					
SCRAPPED	Early 1900s	About 1912		About 1930	About 1930	About 1936		
TANK, WATER			573 Gal.[1]	800 Gal.[1]	800 Gal.[1]	850 Gal.[1]	1000 Gal.	1000 Gal.
TANK, COAL			1500-lbs.[1]	1540-lbs.[1]	2150-lbs.[1]	3000-lbs.[1]	3000-lbs.	3000-lbs.

*Not Certain—Approximate.

[1] From Company Data; Not Always Correct.

LOCOMOTIVES OF THE WISCASSET, WATERVILLE & FARMINGTON RWY.—1893 to 1933

NO.	1	2	3	4	5	6	7	8	9
TYPE	0-4-4RT	0-4-4RT	0-4-4RT	0-4-4RT	0-4-4RT	2-6-2	2-4-4RT	0-4-4RT	0-4-4RT
BUILDER	Porter	Portland	Portland	Porter	Hinckley	Baldwin	Baldwin	Portland	Portland
DATE	4/1883	11/1894*	11/1894	3/1902	1882	9/1907	9/1907	4/1892	6/1891
NUMBER	565*	626*	627*	2497		31691	31692	624*	622
CYL	9x14*	10½x14	10½x14	11x16*		12x16	11½x14	9⅞x14*	10½x14
DRIVER	33*	33	33	33		33	33	33	33
TOTAL WGT	28,000*	36,000	36,000	47,000*		51,500	56,000	38,000*	36,000
DRIV WGT		22,000*	22,000*	31,500*		40,000	28,300	23,000*	22,000
BP	120*	140	140	160		180	180	140	140
TF	3540*	5363	5363	7978		10,680	8300	5240	5363
FORMER #	3				2			3	6
FORMER OWNER	S.R.R.R.			**	B.&S.R.			K.C.R.R. B.&S.R.	S.R.&R.L.
SCRAPPED	About 1914-6	About 1937	About 1937	About 1937	About 1912	About 1937	About 1937	About 1941-2	
TANK, WATER		600 Gal.	600 Gal.	800 Gal.*				600 Gal.	600 Gal.
COAL		1500-lbs.	1500-lbs.	1500-lbs.*				1500-lbs.	1500-lbs.

*Not Certain—Approximate.

No. 9 Engine, ex-K.C.R.R. 4, ex-ex-S.R.&R.L. 6, ex-ex-ex-S.R. R.R. 5. Sold about 1937 to William Monypeny, taken to Connecticut, and still there, although never operated there.

**Built for the Franklin Construction Co. of Wiscasset, Maine.

While builder's dates shown are from records of these builders,

W. W. & F. engine men insist that Nos. 2 and 3 were delivered in 1893 in spite of the Portland Company record that the engines were built in 1894. The H. K. Porter records show Engine No. 4 was being built in March, 1902, but engine men state that she was delivered in 1901. This discrepancy may be explained by the fact that builder's construction dates sometimes differ from the dates of actual delivery.

LOCOMOTIVES OF THE SANDY RIVER & RANGELEY LAKES R.R.
1908 to 1935

TYPE	0-4-4RT	0-4-4RT	0-4-4RT	2-4-4RT	2-4-4RT	2-4-4RT	2-6-2	2-6-2
NO.	5	6	7	8	9	10	15	16[5]
FORMER #	4	5	1	16			3	2nd 3
FORMER OWNER	S.R.R.R.	S.R.R.R.	Calvin Putnam P.&R.	S.R.R.R.			Geo. M. Goodwin P.&R.	Old Star S.R.R.R.
BUILDER	Portland	Portland	Portland	Baldwin	Baldwin	Baldwin	Baldwin	Baldwin
DATE	10/1890*	6/1891	1890	9/1907	7/1909	5/1916	3/1891	10/1892
NUMBER	616[1]	622	615[1]	31816[8]	33550	44231	11706	12964
CYL	10½x14	10½x14	10½x14	11½x14	11½x14	12x16	12½x16[2]	12x16
DRIVER	33	33	33	35	35	36	33	33
TOTAL WGT	36,000	36,000	36,000	55650	56750[3]	75750	49500[2]	47500[2]
DRIV WGT	22,000[1]	22,000[1]	22,000[1]	30150	30950	45000	37000	34000
BP	140	140	140	180	180	180	180	160
TF	5363[1]	5363[1]	5363[1]	8094	8094	9793	11250[1]	9495[1]
DISPOSAL		[4]	Ret. 1920-22	Ret. 2/1923			Ret. 2/1923	
SCRAPPED	1915-20*		12/1935	12/1935	9/1936	8/1936	12/1935	10/1935
TANK CAP'Y	600 Gal.[1]	600 Gal.[1]	600 Gal.[1]	800 Gal.	800 Gal.	1000 Gal.	1400 Gal.[1]	1500 Gal.[1]
COAL	1500-lbs.[1]	1500-lbs.[1]	1500-lbs.[1]	3000-lbs.	3000-lbs.	3000-lbs.	4000-lbs.[1]	4000-lbs.[1]
TENDER WGT							37000-lbs.[1]	25000-lbs.[1]

LOCOMOTIVES OF THE SANDY RIVER & RANGELEY LAKES R.R.—1908 to 1935 (continued)

TYPE	0-4-4RT	2-6-2	2-6-2	0-4-4RT	0-4-4RT	0-4-4RT	2-6-2	2-6-2
NO.	17	18	19	20	21	22	23	24
FORMER #	2	2nd 2	8	7	8	9		
FORMER OWNER	Isaac Walton P.&R.	S.R.R.R.	S.R.R.R.	Eustis R.R.	Eustis R.R.	Eustis R.R.		
BUILDER	Baldwin	Baldwin	Baldwin	Baldwin	Baldwin	Baldwin	Baldwin	Baldwin
DATE	3/1893	9/1893	3/1904	5/1903	2/1904	2/1904	10/1913	5/1919
NUMBER	13276	13733	23874	23245	23754	23755	40733	51803
CYL	12x16	12x16	12x16	12x16	12x16	12x16	13x16	12x16
DRIVER	35	33	33	33	33	33	33	33
TOTAL WGT	56,000²	47500²	50,000	57950⁶	57950⁶	57950⁶	63,000	54,000
DRIV WGT	40000	34000	37,500	41150	41150	41150	50,000	42,000
BP	160	160	180	140	140	140	180	170
TF	8952	9495¹	10,682	8307	8307	8307	12,536	10085
DISPOSAL				Ret. 1920-22				Note⁷
SCRAPPED	8/1936	9/1936	9/1935	12/1935	11/1935	8/1935	8/1936	10/1937
TANK CAP'Y	800 Gal.¹	1500 Gal.¹	1500 Gal.¹	800 Gal.¹	800 Gal.¹	800 Gal.¹	2000 Gal.¹	2000 Gal.¹
COAL	2200-lbs.¹	4000-lbs.¹	4000-lbs.¹	2200-lbs.¹	2200-lbs.¹	2200-lbs.¹	6000-lbs.¹	6000-lbs.¹
TENDER WGT		25000-lbs.¹	37000-lbs.¹				43000-lbs.¹	37000-lbs.¹

*Approximate—Uncertain. ¹SR&RL-Me. C Mech. Dept. Records; not always correct. ²Mech. Dept. Figures after Rebuilding. ³Wgts. after Airbrake installed, Co. Mech. Dept. records. ⁴Engine 6 sold about 1926 to K.C.R.R. as No. 4. ⁵Engine 16 built as Laurel River & Hot Spring R.R. James Wyman, North Carolina. Sold about 1893-4 to W. & Q. which didn't take delivery. Sold to S.R.R.R. about the same year, as 2nd No. 2. ⁶Original weights before air brakes installed. ⁷Sold 6/1936 to RR fan for $250.00. ⁸Discrepancy between official Baldwin builder's number and number apparent on photo of engine's number plate. Baldwin's record and S.R.&L.R. record shows number as 31826.

When The Consolidation came in 1908 all existing power was renumbered into the new S.R.&R.L. engine roster; the numbers 1, 2, 3 and 4 were drawn by F. & M. 1, F. & M. 2, S. R. 1, and P. & R. 4, but no record exists which states which engine became which number. We know only that the four first numbers were those four engines.

Tractive force for the little "Portland engine" actually amounts, according to formula, to 5566-lbs., but Company mechanical data gives it as 5363-lbs. Likewise, the formula gives Nos. 16 and 18 as 9435-lbs., while Company data says 9495-lbs.

Kennebec Central Railroad Co.

Pay Roll No. ....

For the Month of The Last Half of January, *19*10.

	NAME.	OCCUPATION.	NO. DAYS.	RATE.	AMOUNT.		Paid by Check No
1	A. B. Thompson,	Superintendent,			41.66	1	3590
2	Fred C. Moore,	Station Agent,			20.00	2	3592
3	Fred A. White,	Station Agent,			20.00	3	3591
4	W. P. Conner,	Engineer,	16	2.25	36.00	4	3593
5	W. L. Moody,	Engineer,	3 1/2	2.00	7.00	5	3594
6	W. L. Moody,	Fireman,	14	1.50	21.00	6	"
7	E. J. Harriman,	Fireman,	2	1.50	3.00	7	3595
8	Geo. Kersey,	Firemen,	1 1/2	1.50	2.25	8	3597
9	E. J. Harriman,	Watchman,	16	1.25	20.00	9	3595
10	F. A. Sanborn,	Brakeman,	17 1/2	1.65	28.88	10	3596
11	Geo. Kersey,	Brakeman,	1	1.65	1.65	11	3597
12	W. H. Goldsmith,	Section Foreman,	13	2.00	26.00	12	3598
13	W. A. French,	" Man,	13	1.50	19.50	13	3599
14						14	
15						15	
					$240.94		

We, the undersigned, hereby acknowledge to have received of the KENNEBEC CENTRAL RAILROAD COMPANY the sum set opposite our respective names, in full for services rendered during the month of .... January, 31st. .... *19*0.

Approved,

.... *Supt.*

WISCASSET, WATERVILLE AND FARMINGTON RAILWAY CO.

EXCURSION

—TO—

WISCASSET

Sunday, Aug. 15

1915

This train arrives in Wiscasset in season to connect with Maine Central Trains for Portland and Old Orchard, giving excursionists an opportunity of visiting either of these famous resorts. See Maine Central posters for fares and train schedule.

FARES TO WISCASSET AND RETURN

Albion,	$1.00	Coopers Mills,	$ .50
China,	1.00	North Whitefield,	.50
Palermo,	1.00	Whitefield,	.50
Weeks Mills,	.75	Head Tide,	.35
Windsor,	.75	Sheepscot,	.20

TRAIN SCHEDULE

LEAVE	A. M.	LEAVE	A. M.
Albion,	6.00	North Whithfield,	7.23
China,	6.15	Whitefield,	7.35
Palermo,	6.30	Head Tide,	7.50
Weeks Mills,	6.45	Sheepscot,	8.05
Windsor,	6.58	Wiscasset, arrive,	8.20
Coopers Mills,	7.10		

RETURNING, leave Wiscasset after the arrival of Maine Central Train from Old Orchard.

S. J. SEWALL, General Manager.

Wiscasset, Waterville and Farmington Railroad Co.

THE NEW AND MOST DIRECT ROUTE

TO THE SEA

- " - AND - " -

CHINA LAKE.

G. P. FARLEY. Gen Mgr. & C. E.

A. H. DURGIN, Asst. Superintendent.

WISCASSET, WATERVILLE & FARMINGTON RAILROAD COMPANY.

REFERENCES.

Unavoidable delays excepted and subject to change without notice.

(f) Stops when signaled or on notice to Conductor.

American Express Company transacts business at all points on this line.

NOTE.—Trains No. 3 and No. 06 will be run as special between Wiscasset and Weeks' Mills without regard to time or connection.

CONNECTIONS.

At Wiscasset and Winslow with Maine Central Railroad. At Wiscasset with stage for Boothbay Harbor, a. m. and p. m.

Transfer carriage will leave City Hall Square, Waterville, DAILY (except Sunday) at 6 a. m., 11 a. m., and 4.05 p. m., and will meet trains at Winslow at 8.30 a. m., 1.12 p. m., and 6.30 p. m.

SUNDAYS.

Sundays will leave City Hall Sq are at 9.35 a. m. and meet train at Winslow at 5.20 p. m.

W. D. PATTERSON,   G. P. FARLEY.
O. P. & T A.   Gen'l Mgr.

WISCASSET, WATERVILLE & FARMINGTON RAILROAD COMPANY.

GOING NORTH.

		3	17	11	31 (SUNDAYS ONLY)
Numbers of Trains.		A. M.	A. M.	P. M.	P. M.
Mls.	STATIONS.				
0 0	Wiscasset, lv.			3.40	
4 8	Sheepscot,			4.00	
6 4	Alna Centre,			f4.07	
9 1	Head Tide,			4.15	
13 3	Whitefield,			4.30	
15 7	Prebles,			f4.36	
17 4	North Whitefield,			4.45	
20 4	Cooper's Mills,			5.00	
23	Maxcy's,			f5.11	
24	Windsor,			5.15	
28 2	Weeks' Mills Jct. {ar./lv.}	12.15	7.35	5.30	4.30
31 5	South China,	12.28	7.47	5.40	4.42
32 7	China Lake,	f12.32	f7.50	f5.52	f4.45
33 7	Clark's,	f12.37	f7.55	f5.55	f4.50
36 5	East Vassalboro,	12.50	8.05	6.00	4.59
39 1	North Vassalboro,	1.00	8.15	6.09	5.07
42 7	Winslow, ar.	1.12	8.30	6.30	5.20
		A. M.	A. M.	P. M.	P. M.

GOING NORTH.
Weeks' Mills Junction to Albion.

		21
Numbers of Trains.		P. M.
Mls.	STATIONS.	
0 0	Weeks' Mills Jct., lv.	5.35
2 8	Newell's,	f5.42
4 7	Palermo,	5.53
8 3	Cole's,	f6.04
9 8	China,	6.10
11 8	South Albion,	f6.17
15 3	Albion, ar.	6.30
		P. M.

WISCASSET, WATERVILLE & FARMINGTON RAILROAD COMPANY.

GOING SOUTH.

		8	16	6	30 (SUNDAYS ONLY)
Numbers of Trains.		A. M.	A. M.	P. M.	A. M.
Mls.	STATIONS.				
0 0	Winslow, lv.	6.20	11.20	4.25	10.00
3 6	North Vassalboro,	6.35	11.35	4.40	10.12
6 2	East Vassalboro,	6.43	11.43	4.49	10.20
9 0	Clark's,	f6.51	f11.51	f4.58	10.28
10 2	China Lake,	f6.55	f11.55	f5.00	f10.32
11 2	South China,	7.10	11.59	5.05	10.36
14 5	Weeks' Mills Jct {ar./lv.}	7.20	12.10	5.17	10.50
18 7	Windsor,	7.35			
19 7	Maxcy's,	f7.38			
22 3	Cooper's Mills,	7.56			
25 3	North Whitefield,	8.05			
27	Prebles,	f8.11			
29 4	Whitefield,	8.20			
33 6	Head Tide,	8.35			
36 3	Alna Centre,	f8.47			
37 9	Sheepscot,	8.52			
42 7	Wiscasset, ar.	9.10			
		A. M.	P. M.	P. M.	A. M.

GOING SOUTH.
Albion to Weeks' Mills Junction.

		20
Numbers of Trains.		A. M.
Mls.	STATIONS.	
0 0	Albion, lv.	6.20
3 5	South Albion,	f6.32
5 5	China,	6.40
7	Cole's,	f6.45
10 6	Palermo,	6.48
12 5	Newell's,	f7.0
15 3	Weeks' Mills Jct. ar.	7.15
		A. M.

Bridgton & Saco River Railroad

EMPLOYEES'

Schedule of Trains

No. 85

IN EFFECT   SEPT. 17, 1906

Harrison to Bridgton Junction.

Miles		No. 1	No. 3	No. 5	No. 7
		A. M.	A. M.	A. M.	P. M.
	Harrison, leave,	5.05	9.30	11.56	5.10
1	North Bridgton,	5.10	9.35		5.15
5	Bridgton, arrive,	5.25	9.50	12.15	5.30
	Bridgton, leave,	5.40	10.00	—	5.40
7	Sandy Creek,	5.48	10.07		5.47
9	*So. Bridgton,	5.58	10.12		5.52
11	*Ingalls Road,	5.58	10.17		5.57
12	*Perley's Mills,	6.03	10.22		6.02
13	*West Sebago,	6.08	10.27		6.07
15	†Gravel Pit,	6.14	10.33		6.13
18	†Mullen Siding,	6.25	10.44		6.24
19	*Rankins Mill,	6.28	10.47		6.27
21	Bridgton Jct. ar.	6.35	10.53		6.33
	Bridgton Jct. lv.				
	MCRR.,	6.46	11.00		6.42
	Portland, arrive,	8.05	12.10		7.55

*Stops on Signal or Notice to Conductor.
†Does Not Stop.

STAGE CONNECTIONS

At Harrison for Waterford 11.51 a. m., 4.03 p. m.

Harrison for Norway, 4.53 a. m.

At Harrison for Sweden, 11.51 a. m.

At South Bridgton for South Bridgton Village, 11.14 a. m. and 3.28 p. m.

At Perley's Mills for Hillside, 3.14 p. m.

No train or engine must be run across Portland street, Mill street or Main street, at a speed greater than five (5) miles an hour. The bell must be sounded continuously while passing through the mill yard of the Bridgton Lumber Co.

Bridgton Junction to Harrison.

		A. M.	P. M.	P. M.
	Portland, lv, MCRR.,	9.05	1.25	6.05
	Bridgton Jct, arrive,	10.20	2.43	7.32

Miles		No. 2	No. 4	No. 6	No. 10
	Bridgton Jct lv.,	10.22		2.45	7.34
2	*Rankins Mill,	10.29		2.52	7.41
3	Mullen Siding, ar.,	10.34			
	Mullen Siding, lv.,	10.44		†2.55	†7.46
6	†Gravel Pit,	10.53		3.03	7.55
8	*West Sebago,	10.59		3.09	8.01
9	*Perley's Mills,	11.04		3.14	8.08
10	*Ingalls Road,	11.09		3.19	8.11
12	*South Bridgton,	11.14		3.24	8.16
14	Sandy Creek,	11.19		3.29	8.21
16	Bridgton, ar.	A. M. 11.26		3.35	8.29
	Bridgton, lv.	4.25	11.31	3.40	8.33
20	No. Bridgton	•——	11.46	3.55	8.46
21	Harrison, ar.	4.53	11.51	4.00	8.53

Train No. 4 will take siding to cross No. 3.

Trains No. 3 and No. 4 will cross at Mullen Siding when on time. If No. 4 train is not on the siding when No. 3 arrives, No. 3 will wait until five (5) minutes past card time and then proceed, keeping five (5) minutes behind card time until Rankin's Mill is passed.

Train No. 4 will not go north of Mullen Siding until after No. 3 has passed.

If train No. 4 cannot leave Bridgton Junction by 10.34 a. m., crossing will be made at Bridgton Junction.

J. A. BENNETT, Manager

his Lima two-foot Shay was built a generation or so ago for the Central Cambalache Co., wherever at may have been. The little *San Daniel* No. 11 weighed 13 tons, had 22-inch wheels, 6x10-inch linders and had 6050-pounds tractive force. Wherever it was that she ran, it's safe to say she's now in a better world.

> **The photos on this and following pages are examples of 2-foot equipment found elsewhere in the world.**

his photo of Shay No. 4 is supposed to have been taken on the Silver City, Pinos Altos & Mogol- n R.R. in New Mexico. But wherever it was taken, it was a two-foot Shay, and the four-man crew look well fed and capable.

A Baldwin builders' photo of the two-foot Pacific engine built for a road in Africa. Her cylinders were 13½x18, drivers 36 inches, driver weight 45,000 and total weight of engine 66,000. The tender weighed another 47,000. Boiler pressure 160, boiler diameter 43 inches, her tank held 2040 gallons of water and five tons of coal.

German built 2-6-0 on the Mexican sugar road Ingenio Tilapa, which branches off the Mexican Southern's road at Aldama, in the State of Oaxaca (pronounced Wah-hah-ka). This engine is typical of the Mexican sugar plantations—no data. Only a roving railroad fan with a keen scent for such things will find them.

About all the information on the "Susana" is that she was 60 centimeters (23⅝ inches) gauge and built for service in Mexico. The photo is interesting as an example of a 4-4-0 engine of two-foot gauge.

This 60-centimeter road ran (and perhaps still does) in the Brazilian jungle, and owned a number of these tiny Baldwin engines. 10x14-inch cylinders, 28-inch drivers, weight on drivers 30,000, total weight 34,000, pressure 175, boiler diameter 30 inches. This engine *America* was built in 1920. Just how much good this little Consolidation would have been on the Sandy River or the W.W. & F. is an interesting speculation.

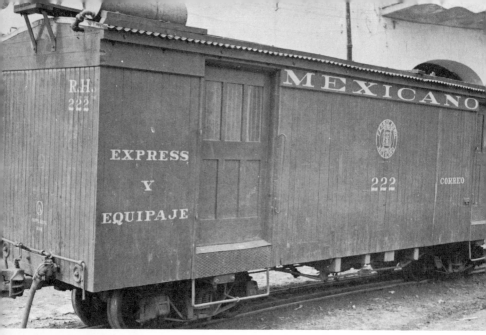

A two-foot mail-baggage car, Mexican style. This was the only one they had, so was appropriate
numbered 222. The word *Equipaje* is Spanish for *baggage,* and *Correo* on the other end of t
car means *mail*. This was snapped at Cordoba in March 1948.

Mogul No. 1 of the old Ferrocarril Cordoba a Huatusco, later the Mexican Railway's two-foot bran
out of Cordoba. This two-footer was discontinued in 1951 and torn up in 1952. This photo taken
Cordoba in March 1948.

Baldwin Mogul built for the La Torre y Tepetong in 1897, and a close runner-up of the Maine two-foot Moguls of that same period.

his Baldwin 2-6-2 side tanker was built for the La Torre & Tepetong, later the Cazadero & Tepeng, a two-footer which once branched off the National of Mexico's Mexico City-Acambaro road at Tepetong.

Public Library of Brookline

MAIN LIBRARY
361 Washington Street
Brookline, Mass. 02146

IMPORTANT

Leave cards in Pocket